The Father
of Forensics

The Father of Forensics

The Groundbreaking Cases of Sir Bernard Spilsbury, and the Beginnings of Modern CSI

Colin Evans

Foreword by Jarrett Hallcox and Amy Welch

BERKLEY BOOKS, NEW YORK

THE BERKLEY PUBLISHING GROUP
Published by the Penguin Group
Penguin Group (USA) Inc.
375 Hudson Street, New York, New York 10014, USA
Penguin Group (Canada), 90 Eglinton Avenue East, Suite 700, Toronto, Ontario M4P 2Y3, Canada
(a division of Pearson Penguin Canada Inc.)
Penguin Books Ltd., 80 Strand, London WC2R 0RL, England
Penguin Group Ireland, 25 St. Stephen's Green, Dublin 2, Ireland (a division of Penguin Books Ltd.)
Penguin Group (Australia), 250 Camberwell Road, Camberwell, Victoria 3124, Australia
(a division of Pearson Australia Group Pty. Ltd.)
Penguin Books India Pvt. Ltd., 11 Community Centre, Panchsheel Park, New Delhi—110 017, India
Penguin Group (NZ), Cnr. Airborne and Rosedale Roads, Albany, Auckland 1310, New Zealand
(a division of Pearson New Zealand Ltd.)
Penguin Books (South Africa) (Pty.) Ltd., 24 Sturdee Avenue, Rosebank, Johannesburg 2196,
South Africa

Penguin Books Ltd., Registered Offices: 80 Strand, London WC2R 0RL, England

This book is an original publication of The Berkley Publishing Group.

FIRST EDITION: August 2006

Library of Congress Cataloging-in-Publication Data

Evans, Colin, 1948–
    The father of forensics : the groundbreaking cases of Sir Bernard Spilsbury, and the
beginnings of modern CSI / Colin Evans.—1st ed.
        p. cm.
    ISBN 0-425-21007-3
    1. Spilsbury, Bernard Henry, Sir, 1877–1947. 2. Medical examiners (Law)—Great
Britain—Biography. 3. Forensic pathology—Case studies. 4. Homicide investigations—
Great Britain—Case studies. I. Title.

    RA1025.S6E93 2006
    614'.1—dc22

                                                                    2006009530

PRINTED IN THE UNITED STATES OF AMERICA

10   9   8   7   6   5   4   3   2

ACKNOWLEDGMENTS

My thanks to Kim McCann of the U.K. Passport Office; Ray Seal, Curator of Archives at Scotland Yard; Greg Manning; David Anderson; staff at the British Library, the British Newspaper Library, and the Public Records Office. A special thank-you to my agent, Ed Knappman, and everyone at NEPA. Samantha Mandor's fine editorial hand guided this book through from inception to completion, and I am also indebted to Jarrett Hallcox and Amy Welch of the National Forensic Science Institute who graciously agreed to provide the foreword. Thanks to Sandy Su for an excellent job copyediting this book. Needless to say, while all of those mentioned contributed so much to the book, any errors or omissions are the author's alone.

Finally, I would like to express my heartfelt gratitude to those tireless and largely anonymous "special correspondents" who, working under almost impossible deadlines, daily delivered beautifully crafted accounts of the cases that form the backbone of this book. How they did it I'll never know, but without their efforts, our knowledge of this fascinating era would be infinitely poorer.

Contents

Foreword

Like no other time in history, we are bombarded with the advances of forensic science and the new high-tech world of crime scene investigation. Today's society is so consumed with advanced technologies that people forget a time when those technologies did not exist. For us, two people who have been thrown into this setting by the seat of our pants, we too fall prey in taking our humble forensic beginnings for granted. Where would we be without the true pioneers of modern-day forensic science?

Since Cain decided to end the life of his brother Abel, society has had to deal with murders, and turn-of-the-century England was no exception. Heinous acts of violence occurred regularly, and many went unsolved unless those in law enforcement just happened to stumble upon the perp in the act. Back then, crime scene investigation was no more than a crude photo of the body displayed on a morgue hook or a very cursory walk through where the crime was committed. But, fortunately for us, all of that began to change with one man's ambition to answer the question why. That man was Sir Bernard Spilsbury.

In the book *The Father of Forensics*, the author tells the in-depth and fascinating story of the first true forensic pathologist, Sir Bernard Spilsbury. The author takes the reader on a wonderful journey back in time, chronicling Spilsbury's life and some of his most famous cases, from his first buried body to his very last courtroom trial. The story itself is a woven tapestry between actual cases and stories from Spilsbury's life, and, at times, it reads like an old-fashioned murder mystery set in a time when forensic science was in its embryonic stage.

Modern-day CSIs are fortunate to have places like the National Forensic Academy to educate themselves in the science beyond the art of investigation. Spilsbury had no such luxury and was left to his own devices, ushering in the revolutionary concept of scientific research with regard to crime scene investigation. In doing so, he laid the groundwork for future generations of crime scene investigators and left an inestimable legacy to the world of forensic science.

The Father of Forensics is a must read for CSIs and wannabes alike.

Jarrett Hallcox and Amy Welch
National Forensic Science Institute

Introduction

As the twentieth century dawned, forensic science in Europe was finally coming of age. Decades of distrust—public as well as judicial—were crumbling in the face of some truly astonishing medico-legal advances. The charge had been spearheaded in France, where two giants of criminology, Auguste Ambroise Tardieu in Paris and the even more celebrated Professor Alexandre Lacassagne at the University of Lyons, had dealt a succession of hammer blows to a startled French underworld. Preaching a mutual doctrine of laboratory-driven detection, they kept the prisons full, the guillotines well-greased, and the criminals wary. Shortly thereafter, in 1879, a Parisian police statistics clerk named Alphonse Bertillon added a powerful new weapon to the armory. Study over several years had convinced him that no two humans—not even identical twins—looked exactly alike, a belief he distilled into the world's first codified system of human identification. Based on hundreds of meticulously accurate bodily measurements, anthropometry, or *bertillonage* as it came to be known, proved to be remarkably successful in catching criminals, and for a while its inventor achieved a strutting prominence that only dimmed with his catastrophic intervention in the Dreyfus Affair of 1894.*

Dreadful as Bertillon's blunder was, it registered only as a minor blip on the graph of French progress in forensic science, and where France led, other countries followed. To the east, German scientist Karl Landsteiner was close to unlocking the secret of the ABO blood grouping system that would ultimately lead to a Nobel Prize; while his compatriot Paul Uhlenhuth's precipitin test, based on rabbit serum, had at last provided a definitive means of distinguishing between human and other animal blood. Considering the part played by blood and bloodstains in violent crime, these were hugely significant developments that would have a global impact on crime fighting. Elsewhere in Germany, scientists were using microphotography to detect the minute marks and striations left on expended bullets, thus laying the groundwork for what would become modern ballistics analysis.

Across the border in Austria, Professor Eduard von Hofmann in Vienna had, since 1875, waged a one-man campaign to restore the reputation of forensic science in his homeland after some early setbacks. Welcome assistance came in 1893, when his countryman Hans Gross, a magistrate with some bloodcurdling ideas on social engineering but a brilliant analytical brain, published his revolutionary *System der Kriminalistik* (translated into English as *Criminal Investigation*), the world's first treatise on what nowadays would be called criminalistics. In this fascinating volume, Gross laid out a template for proper evidence processing that exists to the present day.

All across Europe, it seemed, the laboratory was sealing off ever more avenues of escape for the criminal. But there was still one country where the message had yet to sink in.

---

* Stepping well outside his area of expertise, Bertillon testified that French army captain Alfred Dreyfus was the author of a handwritten treasonable letter that had been passed to the German military. Despite plenty of expert-witness testimony to the contrary, Bertillon carried the day, and Dreyfus spent twelve years on Devil's Island until the real traitor, Ferdinand Walsin Esterhazy, was finally exposed.

Britain was trapped in a fit of forensic schizophrenia. Scotland, with its independent legal code, had long enjoyed a fine tradition of university-based forensic excellence—led by such family dynasties as the Duncans and the Littlejohns—that was the rival of anything found on the Continent. England, by contrast, was still mired in the Dark Ages. Somewhere deep within the John Bull psyche lurked a visceral distaste for the laboratory as a crime-fighting tool. Apathy only accounted for a fraction of this heel dragging; mostly it was the product of intense skepticism, inspired by a string of high-profile criminal cases in which medical men had, for one reason or another, emerged with egg on their faces. The most grotesque example came during the 1859 trial of Dr. Thomas Smethurst. Charged with poisoning his bigamous "wife" Isabella Banks, Smethurst insisted that she had died from gastric complications, only for the greatest toxicologist of the age, Professor Arthur Swaine Taylor, to proclaim that he had detected arsenic in a sample from Miss Banks's body. Once on the witness stand, Taylor's certainty began to totter. He flapped, he blustered, he prevaricated, he conceded flaws in his methodology, yet unbelievably the sheer weight of his illustrious name was enough for the jury, and Smethurst was condemned to death.

Pandemonium broke out. The loudest and most bellicose voices in the clamor came from the medical profession, where opinion polarized. One esteemed journal felt sufficiently exercised to bark, "We must now look upon Professor Taylor as having ended his career, and hope he will immediately withdraw into the obscurity of private life, not forgetting to carry with him his favorite arsenical copper."[1] (It was a vain hope. In 1865, *Taylor's Principles and Practice of Medical Jurisprudence* was published to great success and, under various editors, continued in print for over a century.) But the uproar reached such decibel levels that the Home Office was forced to act. Leading surgeon Sir Benjamin Collins Brodie investigated the matter and, on his recommendation, Smethurst was pardoned and set free (though he was later convicted of bigamy and served twelve months in prison). In the eyes of the general public—from whom all juries were drawn—forensic science was now a seriously flawed product.

And the embarrassments didn't stop there. The outcome of murder trials involving two foreign-born women, Adelaide Bartlett from France and Florence Maybrick, an American, also soured the public palate. Both stood accused of poisoning their respective husbands. In the first trial, no one doubted that Edwin Bartlett had died from swallowing chloroform—his stomach was awash with the stuff—but experts bickered over how it was possible for so much of the searing fluid to have been administered without the victim howling the house down (other members of the household had heard nothing). Mrs. Bartlett benefited from the confusion and walked free. Three years later, in 1889, Mrs. Maybrick was not so fortunate. Despite a glut of equally contradictory expert testimony—it was never actually clear whether the alleged victim, James Maybrick, had died from ingesting arsenic or simply gave up the ghost naturally—Florence came within days of being hanged before she was reprieved and her sentence commuted to life imprisonment.

Such inconsistencies only hardened prejudice against the physician and the test tube. Yet, oddly enough, in the midst of all this medical tomfoolery, it was England that could lay claim to the most momentous forensic development of the nineteenth century: the discovery that no two humans have the same fingerprint. Even here, what should have been national triumph disintegrated into mind-numbing confusion. While police forces as far away as Argentina had gained murder convictions as early as 1892 through the use of fingerprinting, turn-of-the-century England, the country that had pioneered its use as far back as 1858, was still agonizing over the new technology. For years an undignified "fingerprint war" had been waged in the medical journals—or rather two wars. The first was fought between William Herschell and Henry Faulds over bragging rights to the title "Father of Fingerprinting." (Neither side emerged victorious; it was more of a dishonorable draw.) The second less rancorous but far more important battle hinged on whether fingerprinting was sufficiently advanced and accurate enough to usurp *bertillonage* as the primary means of criminal identification. Die-hard anthropometrists still clung to the hope that they would carry the day, but the steam was slowly hissing out of their campaign. Too many big guns were lined up in the other corner. And the biggest gun of all, Sir Francis Galton, the eccentric gentleman scientist who first attempted the monumental task of classifying fingerprints into a useable system, had turned his back on *bertillonage*. "There was," he wrote, ". . . a want of fullness in the published accounts of it, while the principle upon which extraordinarily large statistical claims to its quasi-certainty had been founded were manifestly incorrect."[2] Understandably, English juries were confused. After all, if the so-called experts couldn't make up their collective mind over scientific matters, what chance did the layperson have?

But all that was about to change. On October 2, 1899, a twenty-two-year-old student, newly graduated from Oxford, presented himself to the admissions officer at St. Mary's Hospital Medical School in Paddington, London. Physically, he cut an impressive figure—an inch or two over six feet, conspicuously well-dressed, and endowed with a haughty, aristocratic bearing that many found intimidating—but there was nothing in his frankly lackluster academic background to hint at the greatness to come. Certainly his Oxford acquaintances would have laughed off any suggestion that in little more than a decade this introverted young man would acquire the heroic status of a real-life Sherlock Holmes, someone credited with possessing almost supernatural deductive gifts, able to solve the kind of fiendish crimes that defied ordinary mortals.

He was not only the first great CSI (crime scene investigator), the forerunner of all those ghostly, white-suited figures that we nowadays take for granted on our TV screens, but he also invented the role of the expert witness. All the modern luminaries—such as Michael Baden, Herbert MacDonell, Henry Lee, and Cyril Wecht—can trace their lineage back to this remarkable man. Single-handedly he transported forensic medicine from the mortuary to the front page with a series of stunning, real-world successes that dwarfed those of his European predecessors. Where they preferred the comfort of the predictable laboratory, he clambered across muddy fields, stood knee-deep in icy water, bent his back into howling blizzards, wrinkled his nose over foul-smelling corpses, prepared to travel to any destination and endure any hardship in order to study the fractured detritus of death. For his efforts, a grateful nation responded by elevating him into a national icon, the most famous and powerful medico-legal expert who has ever lived. His name was Bernard Henry Spilsbury.

---

1 *Crimes and Punishment*, vol. 14 (Paulton, England: Phoebus, 1974), 130.
2 Francis Galton, *Memories of My Life* (London: Methuen, 1908), 251.

CHAPTER ONE

A Conspicuous Beginning

On a chilly July morning in 1910, two men shouldered their way through the crowds that thronged London's New Oxford Street until they reached a lofty building called Albion House. In size and bearing, both men exhibited that slightly menacing air of authority that accrues from long service in the police force. Nobody could have mistaken them for anything else except coppers. All business, they double-checked the address, then marched inside. A wall directory steered them to the offices of the Yale Tooth Specialists, a dental practice run by two Americans. Once inside, the older and taller of the visitors introduced himself as Chief Inspector Walter Dew of Scotland Yard, and demanded to speak to one of the partners, Hawley Harvey Crippen.

When Crippen appeared, neither Dew nor his sergeant, Arthur Mitchell, showed any flicker of emotion, though both must have wondered if they had the right man. The scandalous allegations had suggested some dashing Casanova type; instead, the forty-eight-year-old from Michigan who confronted them was short, balding, with a ridiculous walrus mustache and bulging, watery eyes that peered myopically through gold-rimmed spectacles. A second look did knock the edge off this first impression. Whatever physical attributes Crippen may have lacked were more than made up for in affectation. He was foppishly dressed, a popinjay almost, with his frock coat, canary yellow tie, navy blue shirt, and patent leather shoes, and he topped it all off with an easygoing transatlantic affability that was as disarming as it was rare in stuffy Edwardian England.

Instinct told Dew to keep up his guard. From background checks, he already knew that Crippen was fond of styling himself "doctor," when, in truth, he had only ever dabbled on the fringes of medicine, and that since moving to London in 1897, he had earned a precarious living by peddling mail-order quack remedies. It was rumored that Crippen had always sailed close to the financial wind; from all accounts, he was now in danger of being swamped by a tidal wave of debt.

Dew explained his business. Anxious friends of Crippen's wife—a blowsy and spectacularly unsuccessful vaudeville chanteuse who luxuriated in the stage name of Belle Elmore—had recently contacted Scotland Yard because they were disturbed by her inexplicable disappearance. No one had seen her for five months, not since the last day of January. Crippen had originally soothed concerns with stories of Belle returning to her native America. Then, in March, teary-eyed and with a voice choked with emotion, he had revealed awful news from California: Belle had succumbed to double pleuropneumonia. Numb incredulity among Belle's friends speedily turned first to spluttering outrage and then to gimlet-eyed suspicion when the newly bereaved widower imported a woman some twenty years his junior into the marital home. In those less forgiving times, Ethel LeNeve was judged to have made the transition from Crippen's typist to live-in mistress with jarring haste, an elevation made worse by her habit of brazenly flaunting herself in the missing woman's jewelry and furs.

Crippen shifted uncomfortably as Dew reeled off this litany. For a few moments he remained silent, obviously weighing his options; then he sighed, "I suppose I had better tell you the truth." Dew nodded sagely, and Crippen continued, "The stories I have told about my wife's death are untrue. As far as I know she is still alive."[1] It had all been a subterfuge, he confessed, a smoke screen thrown up to mask his own embarrassment; in reality, his wife, an alcoholic serial adulteress throughout most of their troubled marriage, had run off to Chicago with her latest lover, an ex-prizefighter.

Dew listened thoughtfully as the whole tawdry saga unfolded. Crippen, the long-suffering cuckold, too craven to admit the truth: it all sounded so plausible. By his own subsequent admission, Dew felt nothing but sympathy for the shamefaced little fellow who shuffled nervously before him. Even Belle's closest friends admitted that when she was drunk, which was pretty much all the time, her venomous tongue could sting like a box jellyfish. It was a viciousness born out of professional frustration—a thousand failed auditions can do that to a soul—and mostly it was directed toward her miserable shrimp of a husband, especially when, after years of silent suffering, the worm had turned and struck up an extramarital dalliance of his own.

Sympathetic, maybe, but Dew was still a hardheaded copper, and he sternly cautioned Crippen against any further repetition of such foolishness. Crippen, hangdog and contrite, humbly acknowledged his folly. After the two men lunched together at a nearby restaurant—it was a very relaxed interview and apparently Crippen tucked into his steak with enormous gusto—Dew accompanied Crippen to the latter's house at 39 Hilldrop Crescent, a featureless villa in Camden, poked his nose around a couple of doors, looked in a few closets, found nothing untoward, and left. Saying his good-byes on the front doorstep, Dew warned Crippen that Belle's whereabouts would need to be established before this matter could be cleared up, but privately he didn't hold out much hope. Nor was he greatly concerned. This bore all the hallmarks of a domestic storm in a teacup, tragic for those concerned but hardly a police matter. Mentally relegating this affair to the "waste of time" filing cabinet, Dew made his way back to Scotland Yard.

The Suspects Flee

Two days later, on July 10, the chief inspector received the shock of his professional life. He had called back at 39 Hilldrop Crescent to clarify a few points with Crippen, only to find the house deserted except for an agitated French maid who'd only been hired recently. In her halting English, she explained that the master had left hurriedly just the day before. And he'd taken Ethel with him.

Dew bristled with indignation. He had been duped, no doubt about it. Crippen's flight could only have been inspired by fear. But fear of what? Dew stalked from room to room. The abandoned packing cases, half-full with clothes and belongings, only emphasized the sense of panicky haste. Gut instinct cried out that the secret to Belle's disappearance lay somewhere in this three-storey house, with its hideous pink décor and garish drapes, more bordello than family home. Rolling up his sleeves, Dew grabbed a spade and began digging up the backyard. At the same time he gave orders for the house to be ransacked, brick by brick if necessary.

For two long, hot days the searchers sweated and strained in the sticky summer heat. All to no avail. They found nothing suspicious, nothing to indicate why Crippen had abruptly fled.

Then, on the third day, worn out and close to quitting, Dew returned for one final look at a coal cellar that ran under the front steps. Suddenly his eyes narrowed. One of the flagstones appeared to be loose. Taking a poker, he levered the flagstone upward. As he did so a foul, unmistakable stench began seeping out. Dew barked orders for digging to commence. Eight inches down the spade slid into something soft and greasy, this time uncorking a cloud of vile-smelling gas that caused a stampede for the exits. Outside in the yard, the officers gasped for breath. Several minutes would elapse before Dew, suitably fortified by a brandy flask that he kept for occasions such as this, plucked up the courage to return to the cellar and peer down into that dreadful pit.

The next day, July 14, a team of forensic experts descended on

39 Hilldrop Crescent, soon to be the most infamous address in the world. At their head was sixty-one-year-old Augustus J. Pepper, the Home Office pathologist. He was by any criterion—experience, academic, practical, or judicial—the premier medico-legal expert in the land, someone whose evidence had featured in countless murder trials. Until recently he'd held the post of chief resident pathologist at St. Mary's Hospital in Paddington, the top medical teaching school in England, but advancing years and an increasing criminal caseload had prompted his reluctant retirement from the faculty. Alongside Pepper today were two other faculty members from St. Mary's: a chemist named Arthur Pearson Luff, who acted as senior analyst for the Home Office, and William Willcox, youngest of the three and arguably the most versatile, equally at home with either dissecting knife or test tube, though by instinct he preferred the laboratory to the morgue. Between them, Pepper, Luff, and Willcox formed the pinnacle of early twentieth-century English forensic science. Fraternal links forged with both the Home Office and Scotland Yard meant that whenever a complex murder needed investigation, it was the St. Mary's trio that got the call.

Today, though, veteran reporters watching the experts troop into 39 Hilldrop Crescent noticed that a fourth member had been added to the team. He was a tall, studious-looking fellow, square-jawed and huskily built, and, from a journalistic point of view, irritatingly anonymous. Prolonged head scratching produced no answers. Some might have had dim recollections of the stranger giving testimony in various draughty coroners' courts around London, but it's doubtful if any could put a name to the face. Certainly the newcomer wasn't inclined to ease their burden. He ducked past the clamoring reporters without saying a word, gray eyes fixed resolutely ahead, ears deaf to their frantic pleas. Although it would have been inaccurate to brand him a rookie—he had already spent more than a decade at St. Mary's as Pepper's acknowledged protégé and, on the latter's retirement, had assumed the post of chief resident pathologist—today did mark something in the nature of a graduation for the young doctor. Dr. Bernard Henry Spilsbury was about to take his first excursion into the pressure-filled world of high-profile homicide.

The Early Years

He had been born thirty-three years earlier in the Midlands town of
Leamington Spa, the son of a wholesale chemist, and the eldest of four
children. It was a comfortable upbringing. There was enough money to
keep the family firmly ensconced in the Victorian middle class and
provide the financial wherewithal for the young Bernard to be edu-
cated at home until age ten. Only a psychologist could decide if this
early isolation from the company of other children was responsible
for all those later accusations of aloofness that plagued Spilsbury's career, but certainly he was a loner from infancy, an introverted lad who
sparkled only when helping out in his father's research laboratory. Science fascinated him. Where other children had lead soldiers or dolls to
play with, this pragmatic youngster fashioned a down-to-earth world
populated with slides, test tubes, Bunsen burners, and pipettes.

When he did begin to attend school, the results were disappointing.
Lessons seemed to bore him, and his grades were worryingly low for a
father whose heart was set on seeing his son become a doctor. James
Spilsbury's own ambitions for a medical career had been thwarted by
parental bullying, and he was determined that Bernard should not suffer a similar fate. His relentless cajoling seemed to do the trick, and in
1896, having just about scraped together the necessary grades, the
nineteen-year-old went up to Magdalen College, Oxford.

It was the fieriest of baptisms. Being thrown in amongst the bright-
est of the bright only brought Spilsbury's academic limitations into
horrible relief. There could be no coasting here, just hour after hour of
remorseless study if he was to keep pace with all that effortless brilliance on display around him. Almost every waking hour was given
over to either textbooks or tutorials. It was a punishing schedule that
turned an already shy youth into an acutely withdrawn adult.

But he did gain that all-important degree, and in October 1899 he
journeyed to London to take up the place he'd won at St. Mary's Hos-

pital Medical School. There, he fell under the mesmeric spell of Pepper, Willcox, and Luff. Their combined nurturing removed from the young man's mind any thoughts of a career in general medical practice; henceforth, it was pathology all the way, with particular emphasis on the medico-legal side. Spilsbury made the most of his opportunities. His workaholic attitude, ruthless self-reliance, and utter loyalty were traits highly prized by Pepper, who set about grooming the youngster as his successor. Pepper's patronage paid off in October 1905 when, just after gaining his full medical degree, Spilsbury was appointed resident assistant pathologist at St. Mary's. Three years later Pepper again pushed Spilsbury's career in the right direction, sponsoring him for membership of the Medico-Legal Society. Here, in a convivial clublike setting, everyone who mattered in the forensic world would gather to exchange views, discuss cases, and argue over the latest medical papers. There was also ample opportunity to bemoan the lackluster state of expert testimony in the contemporary courtroom. For almost half a century, ever since accused murderer Dr. Thomas Smethurst had been controversially convicted and then pardoned in 1859, English courts had adopted an ambivalent attitude to medical testimony, with most juries yawning their way through such evidence. It was all so different in France and Germany, say, where science was changing forever the face of criminal investigation and judicial procedure. What England needed, Pepper grumbled through the cigar smoke, was one of those once-in-a-decade cases, a real headline maker, something guaranteed to shake the judicial system out of its self-induced torpor and awaken everyone to the exciting possibilities offered by the criminological laboratory.

Now, in July 1910, if the press was right—and their instincts rarely failed them in such situations—what had already been dubbed "The North London Cellar Murder" might just be that case. Already some newspapers were proclaiming it the crime of the still-young century.

As Spilsbury edged his way into the crowded basement, he paused, his nose adjusting to the stench of death, which clung to the walls like mildew. This would become a habit of his, sniffing the air for clues, and woe betide anyone foolhardy enough to smoke cigarettes or pipes in his professional presence. Much later, one officer recalled being on the rough end of Spilsbury's tongue. "He sniffed twice, looked round the room, and said 'You mustn't smoke, please, Johnson. I can't smell the smells I want to smell.' He then bent down over the corpse and sniffed away like it was a rose-garden."[2] But all that lay in the future. Today Spilsbury was very much the observant acolyte, just finding his feet.

Cellar's Grisly Secret

The coal cellar measured only about six feet by nine feet, and most of its floor had been dug over. Against the far wall, at the head of a rectangular pit, a wooden-handled spade protruded from the overturned earth. It had been left in situ to provide a scale reference for the police photographer, but only the stoniest heart could fail to notice its haunting similarity to a gravestone.

Spilsbury watched intently as Pepper went about his work. A sparrow of a man with gold pince-nez, Pepper perched himself on the edge of the shallow grave to better study its foul contents. Only a trained eye would have guessed that the several pounds of greasy, gray pulp spread over the floor of the pit had once been a human body. Male or female, it was impossible to tell. The head, the arms, the legs, all were missing, as were whole segments of skin and muscle, the genitalia, anything that could aid identification. Even the nonhuman items were confusing: a man's pajama jacket and trousers, and a woman's hair curler. As Pepper poked and prodded the mess, one conclusion was abundantly clear: whoever disposed of this body had done so with grisly efficiency. The corpse had been filleted like a piece of oven-ready meat, every single bone scooped out and discarded, never to be seen again. A similar fate would await the rest of the missing body parts—lost forever.

Even though this was Spilsbury's first major case, Willcox and Luff had no hesitation in taking a backseat to the younger man. Luff, of course, was an analyst, and Willcox, too, by this stage of his career, had both feet firmly in the analytical camp; their time would come later. For now the pathologists held sway. Pepper and Spilsbury, mentor and pupil, put their heads together. They agreed that the level of dissection suggested a killer with an above-average knowledge of human anatomy. Crippen's medical background—no matter how spurious—placed him squarely in this category. That much was clear. Far more vexatious was the answer to Dew's question: Are these the mortal remains of the missing Belle Elmore? Logic came down heavily on the side of a positive response, but was there any scientific basis for this conclusion?

Never before had forensic science attempted to identify a human being from just a few handfuls of flesh and tufts of hair. Even today, with the modern miracle of DNA typing, such a task would be far from straightforward as Belle's only surviving relatives were a clutch of half brothers and half sisters scattered across America. In 1910, it was a colossal undertaking. Despite this, Pepper retained a grain of hope. He'd already spotted a potential clue. First, though, he needed to examine the remains in more appropriate surroundings, not this hellhole. After supervising the removal of the corpse to Islington mortuary, he reassured Dew that he and Spilsbury would be able to provide more answers within the week. Off the record, he had little doubt that Belle Elmore had been found.

Which is more than could be said for her will-o'-the-wisp husband.

Crippen's disappearing act, with his young lover, had caused a sensation. Sightings of the "demon doctor" came in from all across England: Liverpool, Southampton, Ramsgate, even as far afield as Barcelona and Sardinia, every place, or so it seemed, where a ship could slip its moorings. Such excitement was sparked mainly by the relative scarcity of murder at this time. Edwardian London might have been the largest city on earth, with a population of seven million, but its citizens were remarkably law abiding, killing each other at a rate some ten times lower than their New York counterparts. As a consequence, any homicide, no matter how mundane, received acres of press coverage, and on this occasion Fleet Street pulled out all the stops.

The police, too, adopted an unusually aggressive approach. Handbills, posted in prominent public places, giving descriptions of the missing couple and declaring them to be "WANTED FOR MURDER AND MUTILATION," produced a flood of leads, all of which had to be investigated. A ratcheting-up of public interest—if that were possible—greeted the revelation that on the day of his disappearance, Crippen had purchased a young boy's outfit. Newspaper editors tantalized their readers with imaginative representations of how the sensual Ethel might look disguised as a postpubescent male. Each day brought new and ever more fanciful speculation, but still no clue as to the whereabouts of Crippen and LeNeve.

As the hullabaloo mounted, so did the pressure on Pepper and Spilsbury. Long hours at the Islington mortuary poring over the mass of flesh in minute detail convinced them that, judging from the degree of decomposition, the remains had lain under the cellar floor for no more than eight months. This was significant on two counts: (a) Crippen had lived in the house since September 1905, and was therefore resident at the time of the interment; (b) Belle had last been seen alive on January 31, well within the eight-month time frame.

Unsurprisingly, given the skimpiness of the remains, there was no obvious cause of death. Strangulation, stabbing, gunshot, bludgeoning, anything was possible. As the recognizable internal organs—heart, lungs, esophagus, stomach, liver, kidneys, and pancreas—showed no visible signs of organic disease, Pepper turned them over to Willcox for further analysis.

All these procedures and findings were recorded by Spilsbury on white three-by-four-inch cards. Over the course of his long career, these cards, all written in Spilsbury's own spiky hand—apart from a brief period in the 1920s, he never bothered with a secretary—would become the deadliest weapon in British justice. Filed away in his laboratory for his eyes only, they formed an unrivaled and lethal reference source. "According to my records . . ." was a verbal dagger that Spilsbury could deliver to the heart of any troublesome courtroom inquisitor, secure in the knowledge that informed contradiction of his stated opinion was unlikely, and rebuttal all but impossible.

Spilsbury's index files would eventually contain three cards relating to the Crippen case, but preliminary findings revealed that the investigators had enjoyed at least one stroke of good fortune. In his desperation to destroy every body fiber, the killer had mistakenly and foolishly doused the remains with slaked lime. Unlike quicklime, which destroys human residue, slaked lime actually tends to preserve or mummify flesh. Without this blunder, the remains, after months in the ground, would have been an unidentifiable goo; as it was, Pepper and Spilsbury had been handed a forensic lifeline, one that they grasped with both hands.

In the meantime, newspaper frenzy about Crippen's whereabouts had reached volcanic proportions. And not just in Britain. As details of the little doctor's colorful background emerged, savvy editors in his homeland climbed on the Crippen bandwagon and cooed in appreciation as their circulations soared. But as every investigative avenue meandered into yet another cul-de-sac, Fleet Street sharpened its fangs and rounded ferociously on Dew, especially when, after more than a week, he had still not apprehended the suspects.

Pepper took advantage of this uneasy hiatus to prepare his report. Among the remains he had isolated a patch of skin about $5\frac{1}{2} \times 7$ inches, fringed with what appeared to be pubic hair. Across its surface, and about four inches in length, was a strange horseshoe-shaped welt. Conceivably the mark might have been caused by postmortem wrinkling of the skin, but Pepper, drawing on his decades of surgical experience, was confident that he was looking at an operation scar. This scrap of skin, he felt certain, held the secret to identifying the victim, particularly in light of comments from Belle's friends, who recalled that, while still a teenager in New York City, the missing woman had undergone a hysterectomy.

As Pepper discussed this flap of skin with Spilsbury, he could be excused a mild sense of self-satisfaction. Just two years earlier he had floated an idea past his young apprentice: Why not conduct a special study of scars and scar tissue formation? Spilsbury, aware of the identification possibilities that such a study might provide, had jumped at the opportunity. The experiments he conducted and the published reports he had devoured meant that by the time of the North London Cellar Murder, Spilsbury knew as much as anyone alive about the scarring of human skin. For this reason, Pepper handed the flap of skin over to the young man for microscopic examination.

The other items recovered from the pit provided a mixed blessing for investigators. First there were the man's pajamas. For some inexplicable reason the police ignored these, despite the fact that a brand name—Jones Bros., Holloway—was marked on the fabric. Not until the very eve of the trial itself, in mid-October, did this lapse come to the attention of the Crown prosecutor. His fury over this unforgivable oversight reddened faces down at Scotland Yard* and may have done something to hasten Dew's subsequent retirement, but its most immediate benefit was a quick scurrying round that yielded crucial evidence. According to the manufacturer's records, this particular type of material had not been woven until 1908, and in January 1909, no fewer than three pairs of these pajamas had been sold to Hawley Harvey Crippen.

With these revelations still buried deep in the mists of yet-to-come, the hank of peroxided hair proved more immediately useful. It was entangled around a Hinde's hair curler. First made fashionable in the 1890s, Hinde's curlers were popular with well-coifed ladies on both sides of the Atlantic. Belle was known to use them. The hair, dark brown at the root, graduated to a bleached strawberry blonde at the tip, was exactly like Belle's; while its length—six inches—made it almost cer-

---

* On November 5, 1910, following the conclusion of Crippen's trial, Dew abruptly resigned from the police force after twenty-nine years' service. After pursuing several lucrative libel actions against various newspapers, he became a private investigator and occasional columnist.

tainly female in origin, since very few Edwardian men grew their hair to such an extravagant length. Everything, therefore, pointed to these being the mortal remains of Belle Elmore. But what had killed her?

Willcox thought he knew the answer.

He had discovered hyoscine in the bodily organs. Hyoscine, or scopolamine, is a vegetable alkaloid found in the leaves and seeds of henbane, a botanical relative of the deadly nightshade. The drug acts as a depressant on the central nervous system and is used medically in minute doses to treat travel sickness and for preoperative examination of the eye. A quarter of a grain may prove fatal, producing convulsions, hallucinations, unconsciousness, and death through respiratory failure. Willcox had found twice the lethal amount in the remains.

This was a toxicology first. As far as anyone knew—and Willcox had spent days scouring the medical literature—never before had anyone used hyoscine as a murder weapon. More significant still, just two weeks prior to Belle's disappearance, Crippen had purchased no fewer than *five* grains of hyoscine from a London pharmacy.

A disappearance, a sudden flight, the discovery of human remains in the suspect's cellar, and a receipt for the purchase of poison found in those remains—the circumstantial evidence was piling up at Crippen's door like a snowdrift. Now all the authorities needed was to find the elusive little "doctor." After what seemed like an age but in reality scarcely amounted to more than a week, investigators got their breakthrough.

Transatlantic Chase

On July 22, Captain Henry Kendall, master of the cargo vessel *Montrose*, in the Atlantic en route from Antwerp to Montreal, radioed a telegram to England, conveying his strong suspicion that a couple on board, a Mr. Robinson and his "son," were the "Cellar Murder" fugitives. Kendall's squinting observation was that as the couple walked around the ship hand in hand, the young lad's pants seemed patently ill designed to accommodate the womanly curves within.

Dew set off at once in pursuit. He rushed to Liverpool and boarded a faster ship, making sure that the press was kept fully abreast of his every move. For millions around the world the chase became the greatest cliff-hanger in newspaper history. Would Crippen, the master murderer, dodge justice and make his escape? Or would the indefatigable Dew nab his man? In America the excitement was especially acute. Even the *New York Times* got in on the act. "Never were two ships more eagerly looked for,"[3] it salivated on page one.

The whole episode was entirely manufactured, of course, as phony as any Hollywood car chase. A simple telegram to Canadian police would have done the job just as well, with a lot less fuss, but that wouldn't have created anywhere near as much fun over the breakfast table. As a result of all the publicity hordes of tourists gathered at Father Point, Quebec, to glimpse "a real Scotland Yard detective"[4] when the *Laurentic* berthed on July 29. Dew seemed bemused by the cheers and the popping flashbulbs that greeted his arrival. Over the next forty-eight hours the already nail-biting suspense was further heightened when a storm blew up in the Saint Lawrence River, slowing the *Montrose* to a crawl. The climax was reached on July 31, when Dew took the pilot's boat and leapt aboard the *Montrose* even before it reached Father Point and personally arrested the astonished runaways.

Crippen immediately threw a protective cloak around his young lover, insisting that she was entirely blameless in the whole affair. By comparison, his own protestations of innocence were decidedly lukewarm. Such selflessness has prompted a certain sympathy for Crippen in some quarters. Many view him as a tragic figure, henpecked and taunted beyond endurance, until he finally snapped and slaughtered his tormentor. When trapped, his only thought was for Ethel, the woman he called "wifie." Certainly Crippen displayed a nobility rare in killers, who are usually keen to spread the blame as far and as wide as possible. However, no rose-tinted revisionism can explain away the squalid mess he left buried in the basement or the fact that within forty-eight hours of Belle's disappearance he was hocking her jewelry in a London pawnbroker, desperate to get his hands on the money to stay financially afloat. After all, it had been Belle's refusal to keep bankrolling her husband's harebrained business ventures, not unfulfilled romance, that had brought this crisis to a head. Crippen and Ethel had been lovers for years. Had they wanted to elope together at any time, they could have done so. Instead, Crippen preferred to stay and sponge off Belle, only resorting to murder when the money threatened to run out.

With the extradition formalities complete, Dew returned with his charges to Britain. On August 10, milling crowds thronged the Liverpool dockside to jeer the handcuffed couple as Dew paraded them down the gangway. Possibly somewhere in the back of Crippen's imagination, as he surveyed the baying mob, flickered a glimmer of hope. Would any jury dare condemn someone to the gallows without a positive identification of the murder victim? And who could possibly put a name to that shambles in the cellar?

If Crippen did entertain any such hopes, they were gravely misplaced; Spilsbury was close to cracking the mystery.

For weeks he had studied every square millimeter of that vital flap of skin with just two questions in mind: Did it come from the abdomen? Was the mark typical of scars resulting from hysterectomies of the kind Belle had undergone?

Spilsbury knew that, in isolation, a few pubic hairs were insufficient to identify the flap of skin as definitely abdominal in origin. A positive identification would only come if he found muscle or sinew tissue characteristic of the abdominal region between pubis and navel. And find them he did: Part of the rectus muscle of the abdominal wall, several broad ribbon-shaped tendons or aponeuroses, and some of the smaller muscles attached to the rectus muscle. From there it was a matter of preparing slides, comparing tissues, matching his specimens against known sections of abdominal walls. The results were indisputable, at least to Spilsbury: This patch of skin had been excised from the middle abdomen.

He now turned his attention to the horseshoe-shaped welt. The notion of using scars as a means of identification was not a recent phenomenon. As far back as 1820, French dermatologist Marie-Guillaume-Alphonse

Devergie had devised ways of rubbing or beating the skin so that any scars present would show up as areas of paleness on the reddened surface. This had inspired him to study the physiological differences between scars from diseases and scars caused by injuries, but since his death in 1879, Devergie's pioneering work had been largely neglected.

Thirty years on, Spilsbury took up the baton. His microscopic inspection of cross-sections of tissue taken from the welt revealed some illuminating anomalies. Operation scars are characterized by hard, hairless, and glandless tissue, yet one spur of the horseshoe mark showed hair roots and sebaceous glands, obviously the result of the skin wrinkling while it lay buried in the cellar. At the other end of the horseshoe it was an entirely different story. Here, the mark consisted of a firm, light-colored stripe widening somewhat toward the bottom. Pepper confirmed this widening as a common feature of operation scars that ran down from the navel, and was caused by downward pressure from the intestines.

Every cross-section from this region showed normal hair follicles and sebaceous glands to either side of the mark, but not on the line of the scar itself. This was typical of a surgical incision and subsequent formation of scar tissue. Only at one spot did Spilsbury discover microscopic remains of sebaceous glands and small particles of fat in the actual scar. Again Pepper stepped forward with an explanation. When operation wounds are sutured, the upper layer of skin is frequently turned inwards, so that parts of this upper layer with remnants of glands grow into the scar. Usually, the suturing needle marks disappear completely in the course of time or leave only faint traces. Such was the case in this instance. Spilsbury found only minuscule traces of the needle.

For the most part, Spilsbury carried out his research in austere and uninterrupted isolation. It would be his chosen style throughout his career. Never gregarious by nature, he found no one in the laboratory whose company he preferred to his own. Each day he would run his experiments, and each night he would gather up his thoughts and his paperwork and join the thousands of other commuters flocking out of town on the newly electrified Metropolitan Railway. Settling into his seat, he could watch with a tinge of pride as his journey carried him through a metropolis whose city limits seemed to bulge outward every few days. In 1910 London was at the peak of its prosperity and power. Commerce was king, and London was the undoubted hub of the commercial universe. Any clouds on the European horizon seemed distant indeed. For Spilsbury and millions like him, the future stretched out limitless and golden. The affluence could be seen in the suburbs flashing by through his window, out to leafy Harrow-on-the-Hill and the neat bijou house where Spilsbury lived in the shadow of the famous school with his wife, Edith, and their baby daughter, Evelyn.

In the two years since they had been married, Edith had come to realize that theirs would be no conventional union. Spilsbury's driving ambition played havoc with his domestic life, and the Crippen case provided an early taste of what was to come. As his celebrity grew and the demands on his time increased, so the cracks between them would widen. But for the time being, Edith found it impossible not to get caught up in the excitement.

After a brief snack—food was fuel, not pleasure—Spilsbury would retire to his makeshift laboratory and resume his studies, often long into the night, always checking and rechecking his data. Anyone knowing him from his school days would have marveled at the transformation. The youthful diffidence had vanished entirely, replaced by a steely resolve and intense powers of concentration.

Early the next morning, the journey was reversed as Spilsbury caught the train back to Paddington station, followed by the short walk to St. Mary's. He was consumed by the Crippen murder, aware that if he and his colleagues were to realize Pepper's dream and rewrite forensic history, there could be no margin for error.

At this distance of time it is sometimes easy to lose sight of the difficulties faced by the great medico-legal pioneers of the nineteenth and early twentieth centuries. In the main, they had no literature to consult, no comforting peer review to fall back on; basically, they were flying by the seat of their forensic pants. Experiments were conducted in the dark, and often—too often in some cases—conclusions were drawn under the same circumstances. If ever forensic science was to gain a meaningful foothold in the English courtroom, then it was imperative that the new wave of practitioners, people like Spilsbury, got it right. On this occasion he subjected his data to the closest scrutiny then available. Finally, after eight weeks of exhaustive and exhausting labor, he was convinced: The piece of skin *did* come from the abdomen, and the scar *did* correspond in position and type to the kind of incision made for a hysterectomy.

Pepper digested these findings. Given that the remains had been interred since the time of Belle's disappearance, that Spilsbury's analysis pointed overwhelmingly to the existence of a hysterectomy scar on the flap of skin, that Belle's medical records showed just such an operation, and that the strand of hair wrapped around the curler was congruent in color and length with Belle's strawberry blonde locks, then the inference was obvious and damning: Belle Elmore—or what was left of her—had been found.

Although Pepper felt confident in this conclusion, he still couldn't shake off a feeling of deep unease. Following a long string of medico-legal debacles, caused by squabbling doctors who placed ego some way ahead of facts, English juries had become notoriously reluctant to convict on the evidence of medical experts alone. Just eighteen months previously, Pepper had suffered firsthand from this Luddite mulishness when a Wiltshire laundress named Flora Haskell, accused of slashing her own son's throat, walked laughing from court, despite powerful testimony from Pepper that blood spatter evidence clearly damned her as the killer. Pepper was left shaking his head in disbelief as the jury swallowed defense protestations that such a heinous crime was morally incompatible with motherhood and returned a not guilty verdict. (Coincidentally, Dew had been the chief investigating officer on that case as well.)

This time around, Pepper was taking no chances. In long discussions with the prosecuting team, he argued that Spilsbury ought to take the stand; no man in England was better qualified or more thoroughly prepared to deliver such groundbreaking identification testimony.

So it was that Hawley Harvey Crippen, who'd already made history as the first murder suspect captured through the use of wireless telegraphy, now earned a second distinction in the crime annals: principal player in the first capital murder trial of Dr. Bernard Spilsbury's career.

The proceedings opened at the Old Bailey on October 18. (It was decided to try Ethel LeNeve separately on a charge of accessory after the fact.) The chief defense counsel, Alfred Tobin, KC (King's Counsel), argued from the outset that it was absurd, even downright dangerous, for the Crown to claim that these scraps of human flesh were the identifiable remains of Belle Elmore. There was no precedent for such an assertion, and no substantive evidence. It fell to the prosecutor, Richard Muir, KC, to convince the jury otherwise.

Muir's role in this case had been crucial. His disgust at police sloppiness and Dew's grandstanding for the press had driven him to take the extraordinary step of assuming direct control of the Crippen inquiry, and it had been Muir who'd realized the critical significance of the pajamas purchase. At a stroke this robbed the defense of its strongest card: The claim that the remains could have been buried in the cellar years before Crippen took over residency of the house. Such meticulous attention to detail had earned Muir his reputation as the toughest prosecutor in the British courtroom. In an era when murder trials were reported at huge length in the press, high-profile attorneys received the kind of celebrity treatment nowadays lavished on movie stars or rock idols. And Crippen was obviously someone who'd studied his newspapers. Reputedly, on hearing that Muir was to lead for the Crown, he had muttered darkly, "I wish it had been anyone else . . . I fear the worst."[5]

Muir marshaled his case like a field general in battle. First, he wheeled out the heavy artillery, his expert witnesses. He guided Pepper skillfully through the medical evidence, and the wily old campaigner began well enough. The remains were those of an adult, he said, though he conceded there was no anatomical indication of sex. The evisceration of the body bore the hallmarks of someone skilled in dissection, and burial of the remains had taken place shortly after death. Necks craned during Pepper's testimony as a formalin-filled dish containing the seven-inch strip of skin was twice passed around the court for inspection. Crippen, in particular, seemed fascinated by the exhibit and strained for a closer look.

Thus far, Pepper's effectiveness was unquestioned. His problems began when the long cross-examination switched to the effects of lime and clay on putrefaction. In framing his answers he became bogged down in technical jargon, a common complaint against expert witnesses then and now. As jury box eyes glazed over, the defense seized its chance. There was nothing, sniffed Tobin, to prove categorically that these were the remains of Belle Elmore, was there? Pepper grudgingly conceded the point. And this so-called scar, wasn't it really just a fold caused after death? Here, Pepper stuck to his guns, insisting that the blemish was a scar from an abdominal operation. When Tobin asked, "How many times did you examine the skin before you came to the conclusion that there was a scar?" Pepper rapped back, "I came to the conclusion immediately." Then, bizarrely, he proceeded to pull the rug from under his own feet by adding meekly, ". . . after about ten or fifteen minutes."[6]

Spilsbury Center Stage

Such lame qualifiers had no place in the Spilsbury lexicon, as became evident the next morning. Long regarded as the pivotal moment in his career—which indeed it was—his performance in the Crippen trial highlights the fact that in the courtroom, as elsewhere, style matters. Despite occupying the stand for a mere fraction of the time taken up by Pepper, it was the charismatic newcomer who captured all the plaudits. Hard-bitten reporters perked up when Spilsbury strode purposefully to the stand. Still only in his early thirties, he was toweringly handsome, immaculately turned out, with a fresh red carnation in his buttonhole, not at all the stereotypical mortuary habitué. Spilsbury oozed star quality even before he opened his mouth. But it was his testimony, or rather the manner of its delivery, that really set him apart from the crowd. Clear, resonant, without any trace of uncertainty, it cast an instant and hypnotic spell over court number one. Not all experts make expert witnesses, but in Spilsbury the Crown had unearthed a gem of quite remarkable quality.

In crisp sentences he briskly outlined the results of his microscopic examination of the skin, reinforcing what Pepper had said; the skin had come from the lower abdomen, and the mark was a scar. At one point the judge, Lord Chief Justice Alverstone, interjected, "You have spoken of the position and arrangement of certain muscles. Would you say that was more or less consistent with the flesh of any other part of the body?"

"No, it is not,"[7] Spilsbury retorted.

This brevity—almost to the point of terseness—was a foretaste of decades to come. Spilsbury never used three words when two would do. He formed his opinion; expressed it in the clearest, most succinct manner possible; then stuck to it come hell or high water. It was a refreshingly straightforward approach, one that would endear him to generations of juries and judges and infuriate just as many advocates.

An early example of his self-confidence came with his scything dismissal of defense accusations that he was merely a "yes-man," thrown in to rubber-stamp his superior's testimony. "The fact that I have acted with Mr. Pepper has absolutely no influence on the opinion that I have expressed here."[8] When the judge added his own misgivings, Spilsbury's firmness became more apparent. "I have an independent position of my own, and I am responsible for my own opinion, which has been formed on my own scientific knowledge, and not in any way influenced by any supposed connection with Mr. Pepper."[9] Still unconvinced, Mr. Justice Alverstone pushed, asking Spilsbury if he had any doubt regarding the scar. "Absolutely none at all,"[10] came the implacable reply.

Members of the press box exchanged knowing looks, and their pencils scribbled that little bit faster. They'd found their strapline for tomorrow's editions!

Then Spilsbury played his ace in the hole. Turning to the judge, he said, "I have my microscopic slides here, and I shall send for a microscope in case it should be wanted."[11]

An audible frisson of expectation rippled through the public gallery and into the well of the court itself. Spilsbury had calculated that his offer would cause a sensation, and he wasn't disappointed. The microscope duly appeared, and—Pied Piper–like—he led the delighted jury into an adjacent room, where he explained each cross-section of the scar tissue. He showed them the distribution of the hair follicles and sebaceous glands and pointed out how remnants of these glands could be incorporated in the wound in the process of surgical suture.

As a coup de théâtre it was magnificent; never before had an expert witness deigned to share his knowledge with the jury in so intimate a manner, and they were marvelously flattered. As a legal stratagem its usefulness was debatable. Junior prosecuting counsel Ingleby Oddie, who would come to know and admire Spilsbury enormously, found the gesture "as futile as it was unusual."[12] No matter, the popular press seized on this dazzling innovation, and henceforth Spilsbury would forever be the "People's Pathologist."

And he wasn't finished yet. In the febrile, fiendishly cutthroat world of medical jurisprudence, there had always been a red-toothed animosity between St. Mary's and its great crosstown rival, the Pathological Institute at the Royal London Hospital. The latter bitterly resented St. Mary's proprietary attitude toward forensic medicine, particularly the way it had insinuated itself into the Scotland Yard/ Home Office nexus. St. Mary's, deeply protective of its exalte position, had been wearily enduring its rival's complaints for decades. Now it had the chance to lower the boom on its petulant adversary. To Spilsbury fell the task of silencing the dissenters, once and for all.

The opportunity had arrived courtesy of Crippen's solicitor,* a flashily dressed rogue by the name of Arthur Newton. Nobody doubted Newton's cleverness, just his honesty. A copper-bottomed publicity hound with the ethics of an alley cat, he had first sprung to notoriety in the sensational Cleveland Street homosexual scandal of 1888, which led to him being jailed for six weeks for having "conspired to defeat the ends of justice."[13] Seven years later he figured prominently in the trials of Oscar Wilde. His most recent headline grabber had been the Camden Town Murder of 1907, when, against all odds, Robert Wood was acquitted of killing a prostitute named Phyllis Dimmock.

Even before Crippen was extradited from Canada, Newton was pounding the telegraph, pleading to be appointed as his solicitor. This promised to be the biggest trial in decades, and the crafty old fox had no intention of languishing on the sidelines. Not once did Crippen's impecunity crop up during the telegraphic correspondence as, behind his back, Newton had already begun negotiations with various newspapers, selling "exclusives" to all comers.†

When it came time to muster a defense, being Newton, he took the sly route. By chance—or maybe not—he was attending a bridge party when he happened to fall into conversation with Dr. Hubert Maitland Turnbull, director of the Pathological Institute. Newton's finely tuned antennae began to twitch. Like most in London's close-knit legal community, he knew of the deep-rooted jealousy that the Royal London Hospital harbored toward its more illustrious rivals at St. Mary's. Here, he sensed, was an opening. Casually he asked Turnbull if he would mind examining the all-important flap of skin, just out of curiosity. Turnbull did so and raised no objection when Newton suggested that

---

* In England, a solicitor is the first point of legal contact for most litigants. If the case proceeds to upper court, the solicitor usually instructs a barrister to act for his or her client.

† Newton's conduct in the Crippen case led to a twelve-month suspension from duty. He was later jailed for three years for an unrelated fraud.

he sign a report—nothing binding, of course—to the effect that the skin came from the thigh, not the abdomen, and that the supposed scar was a fold in the skin. A colleague of Turnbull's, Dr. Reginald Wall, was similarly cajoled into signing a form to that effect.

To their horror, within days both men received subpoenas ordering them to give evidence for the defense at Crippen's trial. Turnbull panicked and contacted Spilsbury, whom he knew slightly, complaining bitterly about Newton's duplicity. Spilsbury thought the solution was obvious: withdraw the report. Inexplicably, Turnbull refused. The price for this hubris was a courtroom massacre.

On October 21 Turnbull walked to the witness stand with the air of someone approaching the gallows. Stubbornly he repeated his earlier unwitting deposition: there was no scar, and the skin had not originated from the abdomen but the thigh. Then he waited for his career to collapse about him.

Muir, never one to waste time with the rapier when a bludgeon was at hand, immediately requested permission to recall Spilsbury, in order that he might point out to Turnbull the existence of a tendon that the witness claimed not to have seen. Spilsbury performed his role with icy theatricality, plucking at the specimen with a pair of forceps, raising what was indubitably a sliver of tendon so the jury might see. Again and again, Turnbull refused to admit that he had blundered. The impasse only concluded when an exasperated judge finally leant forward and demanded, "Please answer this one way or the other; it is most important. Do you find that tendon there or not?"

Finally backed into a corner from which there was no escape, Turnbull could only croak, "Yes."[14]

Still, though, Turnbull refused to go quietly. In a furious and quite astonishing outburst, he lashed out at neophytes "unaccustomed to the microscope" being allowed to testify in court. Muir silenced him with an imperious wave of the hand. "We are not talking about people unaccustomed to the microscope. We are talking about people like Mr. Spilsbury."[15]

The deification of Bernard Spilsbury had begun.

In due course, Dr. Reginald Wall was similarly humiliated, and the trial then pursued its inevitable path. Crippen, despite standing up defiantly to a withering cross-examination from Muir "with wonderful composure and calmness,"[16] could provide no answer to what was an overwhelming barrage of circumstantial evidence. He was found guilty and sentenced to death. Following the rejection of an appeal, his life now lay in the hands of the home secretary, Winston Churchill. Only a reprieve from Churchill stood between Crippen and the hangman's noose. Despite a surprisingly vigorous public campaign to commute the death sentence—one elderly soldier even offered to be executed in Crippen's stead—Churchill refused to interfere with the process of law, and on November 23 the little man from Michigan was hanged.*

Pepper was both relieved and jubilant. The Crippen case had been a remarkable achievement, no doubt about it, one without precedent in international medical jurisprudence. He and Spilsbury had taken a handful of human remains and convinced a jury that these were the mortal remains of Belle Elmore. Of course there had been plenty of circumstantial evidence to support the prosecution's claim that Crippen was a pitiless and calculating killer, but it was the science that people remembered; that was what gripped the public imagination. As the famed pathologist Dr. Michael Baden put it, the Crippen case was when "things came together"[17] for forensic medicine.

Spilsbury wore his triumph well. In early July he had been an anonymous hospital pathologist; now, in the parlance of the times, he was "a coming man," someone earmarked for greatness. Even when others had doubted him, the young Midlander had never lost his focus or self-belief. Deep down he must have realized that his success had been more a triumph of style over substance. After all, it had been Pepper

---

* Ethel LeNeve was later acquitted of all charges and freed. She subsequently moved to Canada.

who identified the hysterectomy scar, Willcox who isolated the hyoscine; Spilsbury's contribution could be likened to that of a closing pitcher in baseball, coming off the bench to nail down a victory gained earlier.

And yet it was the protégé who caught the public fancy. Although his great solo medico-legal tours de force still lay in the future, what this case provided was early evidence of his towering courtroom presence. Most people who trade in the business of law do so gingerly at first, as it can be a minefield for the rash or the unprepared. Spilsbury was neither. The Crippen case might have been his first capital trial, but the ability to steamroller the opposition, to swat conflicting arguments as if they were irritating flies, was already fully developed. It was an awesome beginning. The newcomer, after a slow start, had placed himself at the very heart of the forensic science fraternity, and he was there to stay.

1 Tom Cullen, *Crippen: The Mild Murderer* (London: Penguin, 1977), 121.

2 Hamilton M. Graham, *Light and Shade at Scotland Yard* (London: Murray, 1947), 122.

3 *New York Times*, July 28, 1910, 1.

4 *Ibid.*, July 30, 1910, 1.

5 Cullen, *Crippen: The Mild Murderer*, 157.

6 *Times* (London), October 20, 1910, 4.

7 *Ibid.*

8 Jurgen Thorwald, *Dead Men Tell Tales* (London: Pan, 1968), 91.

9 *Times* (London), October 21, 1910, 6.

10 *Ibid.*

11 D. G. Browne and E. V. Tullett, *Bernard Spilsbury: His Life and Cases* (London: Harrap, 1951), 156.

12 Cullen, *Crippen: The Mild Murderer*, 156.

13 *Ibid.*, 146.

14 Thorwald, *Dead Men Tell Tales*, 91.

15 *Ibid.*, 92.

16 Cullen, *Crippen: The Mild Murderer*, 159.

17 Michael Baden and Judith Adler Hennessee, *Unnatural Death* (New York: Ballantine, 1989), 51.

CHAPTER TWO

The Pathologist at War

In the early years, serendipity never strayed far from Spilsbury's shoulder. When Pepper loosened his connection with St. Mary's in 1909 and renounced the position of chief resident pathologist, it had been the newly qualified intern whom he unhesitatingly recommended as his successor. Now the Fates shone on Spilsbury again. Still basking in the afterglow of the Crippen triumph, Pepper decided, at the relatively early age of sixty-one, that now was the moment to step aside as Home Office pathologist, although he would remain a consultant. Whitehall protocol dictated that Willcox should have stepped into Pepper's shoes, but Willcox, his heart firmly fixed in the chemistry lab, had little stomach for the mortuary. In 1908 he had become the H.O. senior analyst, and he now retained that role, while Spilsbury, barely able to credit the bewildering pace of events, suddenly found himself catapulted into the headline role of H.O. pathologist. It was the beginning of an association that would survive two world wars and last almost four decades.

In assuming the rank of senior analyst, Willcox had leapfrogged over yet another St. Mary's faculty member, John Webster, who though not medically qualified was an exceptional analytical chemist. When the dust from all this interdepartmental turmoil finally settled, one fact was manifestly clear: St. Mary's stranglehold on the English medico-legal system was stronger than ever.

Spilsbury plunged headlong into a hectic caseload. One of the most curious autopsies he performed in his first year of office was that on "Lord" George Sanger, a flamboyant eighty-three-year-old circus show-man who had died under mysterious circumstances in his winter quar-ters at Finchley, London. An ex-employee, Herbert Cooper, who had recently been fired for stealing £50, had returned to the Sanger house-hold on the evening of November 28, 1911, to retrieve some property. A fight had broken out between the razor-wielding Cooper and vari-ous members of the Sanger household. Despite his advancing years, Lord George sprang from his chair, determined to join the fray. The next anyone knew, he was prostrate on the floor, blood gushing from a head wound, a large broken ornament on the floor beside him. Every-one stood aghast, especially Cooper, who, after a moment's hesitation, spun round and fled into the darkness. That night Sanger died in his bed. Utterly distraught, Cooper returned to his lodgings, wrote two notes of remorse, then disappeared into the fog. Two days later, on the railroad tracks between Highgate and Crouch End, workmen found his decapitated body.

When Spilsbury examined Sanger's body, he said that "death was due to hemorrhage following fracture of the skull."[1] Jointly held in-quests recorded that Cooper had murdered Sanger and then had com-mitted suicide while being of unsound mind. Family members, though, believed the courts got it wrong. They maintained that Sanger had ac-cidentally killed himself. In the act of springing from his chair and grabbing the ornament as a weapon, they claimed, Sanger had stum-bled and hit himself over the head. This was one mystery that not even Spilsbury could solve.

Whatever the true circumstances of Sanger's death, just two weeks before Spilsbury conducted that autopsy at Islington mortuary, he had been summoned to the same venue to examine the remains of a woman who had died some two months earlier. And this time there wasn't a shadow of doubt that he was dealing with a case of murder.

The subsequent trial of insurance agent Frederick Seddon for poisoning his lodger Eliza Mary Barrow in order to get his hands on her money, provided the first great showcase for the new Home Office troika of Spilsbury, Willcox, and Webster, and this time it was Willcox who garnered most of the praise. Spilsbury had no doubt that the marvelously preserved body lying on his mortuary slab was stuffed full of arsenic, but it was Willcox who showed how Barrow had died from acute and not chronic arsenical poisoning, as the defense had claimed. Even so, many in court doubted that Seddon would be convicted. Until he took the stand. Like so many murderers-for-profit, he was utterly incapable of gauging his audience. What passed for sound business practice in Seddon's warped universe left horrified listeners sick to their stomachs. It was a very public form of suicide. On April 12, 1912, unrepentant and furious because the sale of his property had realized so little, Seddon stamped off to the gallows. Two days later, the hullabaloo that attended his execution fell quiet, silenced by other more momentous news—the *Titanic* had sunk on her maiden voyage to New York.

This year also marked a period of great upheaval in Spilsbury's private life. Toward the end of 1912, with Edith expecting their second child, suddenly the house in Harrow seemed to shrink about him. Also, the pressures of work were relentless; he was on call day and night. The solution to this dual problem was a large house in the fashionable district of St. John's Wood, 31 Marlborough Hill, within easy commuting distance of St. Mary's.

No sooner had the Spilsburys moved in than calamity struck. In early February 1913, Edith was laid low by an inflamed appendix. Despite being seven months' pregnant, she had no alternative but to undergo life-threatening surgery. Fortunately, the operation was successful, and she made a complete recovery; but the strain showed in the third week of March, when the Spilsburys' first son, Alan, was born prematurely. Delicate from birth, he would be a source of constant worry to both parents.

Spilsbury masked his concerns with a feverish pace of work, all the while keeping one anxious eye on the dark political clouds gathering over Europe. The storm finally broke in August 1914 when, almost by accident—or so it now seems—the world found itself at war. As a great surge of patriotic fervor swept through Britain, the enlistment offices were overrun with volunteers (conscription wasn't introduced until 1916). Although Spilsbury and Willcox immediately offered their services in any capacity, both were considered more valuable in a civilian capacity. And judging from a particularly unsettling aeronautical development, both men could expect to be kept busy—Zeppelin airships had been sighted off the east coast of England.

Although they were merely on reconnaissance flights—the bombs came later—the panic that these hovering monsters generated throughout East Anglia soon spread to the capital. With Edith pregnant once again and London under imminent threat of air attack, Spilsbury arranged for his family to see out hostilities in the rural safety of Malvern in the West Midlands, close to Edith's birthplace. As a result, 31 Marlborough Hill became a virtual ghost house, more hotel than home, somewhere Spilsbury returned to late at night to grab a quick snack and a few hours' sleep before rushing back to St. Mary's. It was an exhausting schedule.

Not everyone was so discomfited by the war. John Lloyd, for instance, a middle-aged self-styled land agent based in the west of England, took the emergency in his leisurely stride. While the armies of Europe floundered in the mud-filled trenches of Flanders, this flashily dressed businessman could be seen sauntering through the genteel shops and arcades of Bath, twirling his cane and his mustaches, seemingly without a care in the world, every inch the man about town. Glued adoringly to his arm was a thirty-eight-year-old spinster named Margaret Lofty.

She could be forgiven for looking so ecstatic. At long last her fortunes seemed to be on the upswing, and if anyone deserved a stroke of good luck, it was this slightly built clergyman's daughter. The previous year had been desperate. First came the humiliating discovery that her fiancé was already married; then, in July, she'd been fired from her job as a companion to a wealthy woman. Out of work, heartbroken, and penniless, she was forced to return to her mother and two sisters in Bristol.

And then she'd met Lloyd. He was charismatic, a few years older than herself, impossibly elegant in his frock coat and high silk hat, and he had the silkiest line in flattering conversation, larded with quotes from Shakespeare and the classics. Even someone so scarred and battered by life's vicissitudes as Margaret Lofty was helpless in the face of such blandishments. Within days she fell helplessly in love. Even when Lloyd suddenly announced that business pressures required his prolonged absence from Bath on yet another property deal, Margaret kept a beacon shining in her heart.

Sure enough, as 1914 neared its close, her gallant knight returned. The anxiety that had gripped Margaret for so many weeks burnt off like mist in the sun. Giddy with excitement, on December 15 she told her family in Bristol that she was going out for a meal, and she never went back. Two days later she and Lloyd were married at the Bath registry office and that night journeyed to London, where they found accommodation at 14 Bismarck Road* in Highgate.

Before agreeing to the rental terms, Lloyd confirmed the presence of a bath. Since indoor toilet facilities were by no means universal at this time, the request was neither so impolite nor unusual as it might seem. There was a bedroom on the top floor, a bathroom off the landing one flight down, and the Lloyds could also use the downstairs living room, where there was a harmonium. Lloyd, an accomplished pianist, professed himself delighted with the arrangements. Margaret sat down

---

* Anti-German sentiment in Britain during World War I led to most Teutonic-sounding names being changed. Bismarck Road became Waterlow Road.

that evening and wrote her mother about the marriage, praising her husband as "a thorough Christian man . . . I have every proof of his love for me . . ."[2] In the letter she also described having a headache and attributed this to the day's excitement. Her husband, though, wasn't so sure, and marched her off to a doctor that very night. Dr. Stephen Bates suspected a mild attack of influenza and prescribed a sedative.

The next afternoon Margaret felt well enough to accompany her husband, first to her bank in Muswell Hill, where she withdrew her life savings of nearly £20, then to a solicitor, where she executed a will making her husband the sole executor and beneficiary of her estate.

That night—December 18—at just after 7:30, the landlady, Louisa Blatch, was ironing in her kitchen when she heard "a sound of splashing. Then there was a noise as of someone putting wet hands or arms on the side of the bath, and then a sigh . . . the sigh was the last I heard."[3]

Thinking no more of it, Miss Blatch resumed her ironing. A short while later the house was filled by the swelling tones of the harmonium. The mournful dirge lasted for several minutes, then ended abruptly, followed almost at once by the sound of the front door slamming.

Another ten minutes passed. Then the doorbell rang. Miss Blatch hurried through. It was Lloyd. His face was almost as red as the tomatoes in his hand—for his wife's supper, he said—as he offered his embarrassed apologies for disturbing Miss Blatch, having forgotten that he had a key. In the hallway he asked if his wife was down yet from the bath. Receiving a negative response, he frowned and headed for the stairs. Halfway up he called out Margaret's name. Getting no answer, he broke into a run. Seconds later he cried to Louisa Blatch, "She's in the bath. Come and help me!"[4] Inside the bathroom, Louisa found Lloyd cradling his wife's naked and lifeless body, which lay in the tub.

Margaret Lloyd's marriage had lasted less than thirty-six hours.

Details of the subsequent inquest found their way into the January 3, 1915, edition of the *News of the World*, a leading London-based Sunday newspaper. Tucked away at the foot of page three was a brief account that read:

"Accidental death" was the verdict returned at Islington on Margaret Elizabeth Lloyd, thirty-eight, who was found dead in a bath at Bismarck Road, North London, the cause of her death being suffocation by drowning. Her husband is a land agent, and they were married at Bath on December 17. They traveled to London the same day, and took furnished rooms at the above address. The wife complained of pains and saw a doctor, who said she was suffering from influenza. It was on the second evening of her residence in London that she was found dead. The landlady at the house said deceased was quite cheerful and happy with her husband, and medical evidence showed that influenza combined with a hot bath might have caused a fainting fit.

Stunned Readers

Two hundred fifty miles away in Blackpool, a guesthouse keeper read the story and gasped. Good God! She cried out for her husband. He too could scarcely believe his eyes. From a drawer they retrieved a well-thumbed local newspaper clipping. A quick comparison removed any lingering doubts. That same day, Joseph Crossley sat down and wrote a letter to Scotland Yard, enclosing the clipping.

Rather closer to London, a Buckinghamshire fruit grower, Charles Burnham, had also been stunned by the *News of the World* report. It had been his daughter, Alice, who had died at the Crossleys' guesthouse just over a year previously. At the time he'd entertained grave suspicions regarding the circumstance of her death; now, following this second tragedy, the conclusion seemed inescapable: a mass murderer was on the loose. Burnham informed his solicitor, who in turn contacted the Aylesbury police.

It is worth considering that just a couple of decades earlier, such lynx-eyed observation by ordinary members of the British public would have been virtually impossible. Mass-market newspapers were a recent innovation, fueled by the Education Act of 1870, which obliged all children to attend school until age thirteen. Within four years, over

5,000 new schools had been founded, and by 1891 elementary education was effectively free. Soaring rates of literacy led to a voracious appetite for any kind of reading matter. As a result, newspapers sprang up like daisies. By the outbreak of World War I, the *Daily Express*, *Daily Mirror*, and *Daily Sketch*, all founded since the turn of the century, were feeding delighted readers a photo-driven mix of populist news coverage. But the undisputed heavyweight champion of the genre was the *News of the World*, a sensational weekly that boasted the highest circulation of any paper on earth. Each Sunday afternoon, millions across Britain curled up on the sofa after the roast beef and Yorkshire pudding to enjoy a lip-smacking dessert of scandal, sex, crime, and gossip.

Had it not been for this short inquest report in a national newspaper, Margaret Lloyd's death might never have aroused suspicion. As it was, two letters wound up at Scotland Yard and, from there, were passed to the desk of Detective Inspector Arthur Fowler Neil at "Y" Division. Neil, a stone-faced copper who rarely smiled, first studied the *News of the World*'s account of Margaret Lloyd's death, then turned to the clipping that Crossley had mailed. It was dated December 14, 1913, and contained the local newspaper report of a coroner's inquest held one day earlier in Blackpool. It told how newlywed Mrs. George Smith of Portsmouth had died at the Crossleys' guesthouse. Apparently, after consulting a doctor and complaining of a headache, Mrs. Smith had been found dead in the bath by her husband. An autopsy performed by Dr. George Billing concluded that the heat of the water had caused either a fit or a faint, and in her helplessness she drowned.

Neil grabbed his hat. There was enough here to justify a trip to Bismarck Road.

Louisa Blatch took Neil up to the bathroom where the tragedy had happened. He measured the iron tub—fifty inches long at the bottom, sixty-six inches at the upper rim—and found it hard to imagine a grown person drowning in such a confined space. Miss Blatch mentioned Lloyd's careful inspection of the tub before he signed the rental agreement. She described him as medium-sized, between forty and fifty, with a bony face and a large, reddish mustache. His most prominent feature—she shivered—were his eyes; not large, but with a horrible staring intensity capable of drilling right through you.

Neil next made his way to 31 Archway Road, Highgate, and the surgery of Dr. Bates. He remembered Mrs. Lloyd being rather lethargic when she and her husband called at his office. Mr. Lloyd—very plausible, apparently—had done all the talking. As for the accident in the bathtub, by the time Bates had arrived, the poor woman was beyond medical assistance. Judging from the white foam at the victim's mouth, he had no doubt that it was a case of drowning caused by a sudden onset of weakness.

Cautiously, Neil asked whether there had been any trace of violence on the person of the dead woman. Bates shook his head. The autopsy had revealed a tiny bruise above the left elbow, though this was not something he would have categorized as a sign of violence, and might easily have resulted from a convulsive movement. Bates did have one other observation. The newly bereaved widower had displayed no sign of grief whatsoever—quite the opposite, in fact. His only concern had been to chisel down the cost of his wife's interment, insisting that a pauper's grave was good enough. Bates had never before experienced such callousness and found it nauseating. Like Louisa Blatch, he had no inkling of Lloyd's current whereabouts.

Neil's first task was to track down the suspect. Discreet inquiries were made among London solicitors, and it wasn't long before a Mr. W. P. Davies, with offices at 60 Uxbridge Road, Shepherds Bush, reported that on January 4, 1915, a Mr. Lloyd had presented his wife's will and asked for it to be proved.

Things now started to move at a pace. Neil heard again from Dr. Bates. He'd received an inquiry from the Yorkshire Insurance Company. They wanted clarification of Margaret Lloyd's fatal accident, as on December 4, 1914, Mrs. Lloyd, then still Margaret Lofty but already engaged to Lloyd, had taken out a life insurance policy for £700, naming Lloyd as sole beneficiary.

Neil told Bates to stall the insurance company while he contacted the Blackpool police to request further information on the Crossley guesthouse tragedy. When the reply came back, even Neil's legendary aplomb wavered ever so slightly: it was a carbon copy of the death of Margaret Lloyd.

On December 10, 1913, someone calling himself George Joseph Smith had booked into the boardinghouse at 16 Regent Road, in the shadow of Blackpool's famed tower, accompanied by his wife, Alice, a pretty but obese woman of twenty-five whose maiden name was Burnham. Smith took the room only after inspecting the bathtub. On moving in, Smith asked Margaret Crossley to recommend a doctor, as his wife was suffering from severe headaches. Dr. George Billing heard minor but insignificant heart murmurs when he examined Alice and prescribed a tonic. The next evening Alice seemed fine and went strolling with her husband after having ordered a bath. Upon their return, Smith accompanied her upstairs. Shortly thereafter the Crossleys noticed a wet patch on the kitchen ceiling. While they were discussing this curious fact, the doorbell rang. It was Smith. Theatrically he brandished two eggs he had bought for the following day's breakfast, then went upstairs. A moment later he shouted down to the Crossleys: "My wife cannot speak to me; fetch Dr. Billing, she knows him."[5]

When Billing arrived he found Smith—left jacket sleeve rolled up—in the bathroom, holding Alice's head above the water, which lapped at the top of the tub. The two men struggled to extricate Alice from the tub and lay her on the floor. All attempts to revive her were fruitless. The next day Billing autopsied the body and found nothing to arouse his suspicions. At the inquest, the coroner returned a verdict of accidental death by drowning. Smith, after quarreling with the Crossleys over the amount of rent owing, promptly vanished.

The report from the Blackpool police expanded on Smith's marriage to Alice Burnham. It all sounded suspiciously familiar. They had become engaged within days of meeting in Southsea, where Alice worked as a private nurse, and fewer than two months later, on November 4, they married. On the eve of the wedding the bride took out a £500 life insurance policy, and on the wedding day itself, Smith wrote to Alice's father, Charles Burnham, demanding the return of £100—

plus interest—which Burnham had borrowed from his daughter. On December 8, two days before the pair left on their belated honeymoon trip, Alice Smith executed a will in her husband's favor. Four days later, she died in the Crossleys' bathtub.

Neil ticked off the similarities between the deaths of Alice Smith and Margaret Lloyd:

1. Both recently married.
2. Both heavily insured.
3. Both married swiftly, then moved some distance from their homes.
4. On both occasions the husband verified that the accommodation had a bath.
5. Both women complained of feeling unwell and visited a doctor.
6. Both wrote letters to their family, praising their husband.
7. While each woman took a bath, the husband went out ostensibly to buy food.
8. Each woman was found dead in the bath by her husband.
9. Both bathroom doors had been unlocked.

Like most experienced detectives, Neil profoundly distrusted coincidences. Until proven otherwise, gut instinct told him that Lloyd and Smith were one and the same person. On January 23 he asked Dr. Bates to send a favorable report to the Yorkshire Insurance Company regarding the death of Mrs. Lloyd. The plan was to flush out Lloyd/Smith, in hopes that he would contact his solicitor as soon as the insurance company agreed to pay.

The offices of W. P. Davies were placed under constant surveillance. Just after midday on February 1, a man matching the description of Lloyd/Smith approached the door. Neil stepped forward. The man, taken aback, cautiously admitted being John Lloyd but denied using the name George Smith. However, when Neil explained that he was merely investigating a suspected bigamous marriage, a crafty smirk lightened the man's dark, glittering eyes, and he said, "In that case I may as well say my proper name is George Smith, and my wife died at Blackpool, but what of that? The entry in the register is not correct, but that is the only charge you can put against me."[6]

Neil sensed that a feeling of profound relief had sparked this unexpected confession, relief at not being exposed as a killer. That night Lloyd/Smith was taken to Kentish Town police station and placed on an identity parade, where several witnesses, including Charles Burnham, picked him out.

With the suspect under arrest, it was time for the H.O. forensic team to begin work. They had been apprised of the case details beforehand, and three days after Smith's arrest—Smith turned out to be his real name—Spilsbury attended Islington Cemetery to supervise the exhumation of Margaret Elizabeth Lloyd. Facing him was one of the oldest conundrums in forensic medicine: had this person drowned by accident or been drowned by force?

Accident or Murder?

As long ago as the thirteenth century, physicians in China had wrestled with this selfsame dilemma. Their findings were incorporated in a book, *Hsi Duan Yu* (the Washing Away of Wrongs, published in 1248), which, with its rudimentary descriptions of how to discern suspicious deaths, is generally considered to be the first recorded application of medical knowledge to the solution of crime.

Even before this, medical practitioners had struggled to define exactly what happens to the human body when it is drowned. In ancient Rome, Galen of Pergamum, physician to Emperor Marcus Aurelius and one of the great medical innovators, thought he knew the answer. His conclusion? The victim died from swallowing too much water, thus excessively distending the stomach.

Galen's ideas went unchallenged until the seventeenth century, when the Dutch anatomist Franciscus Sylvius proposed a radical alternative: that death from drowning resulted from the penetration of water into the lungs. Like so many innovators who rock the boat of received scientific wisdom, Sylvius paid a heavy price for his bravery, being shunned as a lunatic by the academic world, and it was left for the Italian pathologist Giovanni Battista Morgagni, later in the seventeenth century, to demonstrate in a series of gruesome experiments on dogs and cats that Sylvius had been right all along; the lungs did indeed contain a fine white frothy foam after drowning. This is, however, only one common indicator of drowning; these are the others:

1. The lungs become greatly inflated from the inspiration of air and water, giving rise to a marbled appearance.
2. Foreign material, such as vomitus or sand, is found in the air passages, lungs, and stomach.
3. Hemorrhages in the middle ear and mastoid air cell are occasionally seen in bodies recovered from water. Since such hemorrhages also occur in cases of head trauma, electrocution, and mechanical asphyxiation, this symptom should not be taken in isolation.
4. Foreign material in the hands. People drowning tend to grab at anything.
5. Bruising. Victims struggle violently to survive in water and bruise or rupture muscles, particularly those of the neck, shoulder, and chest.

Spilsbury, acutely aware of the difficulties facing him, went over the body of Margaret Lloyd inch by painstaking inch, looking for signs of violence, anything out of the ordinary. Apart from the inconsequential bruise above the left elbow that Bates had mentioned, he discovered only two tiny spots of extravasated blood on the underside of the left arm. Invisible to the naked eye, they provided meager proof of foul play, despite showing signs of having been inflicted within twenty-four hours of death. Thwarted in his quest for visible signs of violence, Spilsbury wondered if anything organic could account for Margaret's abrupt demise. Again, he found nothing, no evidence of either cardio or circulatory disease. From every observable indication, Margaret Lloyd had been a perfectly healthy thirty-eight-year-old woman—until she climbed in that bath.

Even to this day there are no universally accepted diagnostic laboratory tests for drowning, and the problem is made doubly difficult where murder is suspected. Spilsbury knew that homicidal drowning is exceedingly uncommon. Where it does occur, usually there is a marked physical disparity between the assailant and the victim, or a victim incapacitated by disease, drink, or drugs. For this reason he sent samples of the organs to Willcox for toxicological analysis. He also arranged for the fatal tub to be shipped to Kentish Town police station, where he could study it more closely. A few days later Willcox reported back: there had been no trace of poison in the organ samples taken from Margaret Lloyd.

By now the press had smelled blood. Since the Seddon case, reporters had taken to dogging Spilsbury's footsteps, and news of Margaret Lloyd's exhumation first appeared in print on February 5. When, five days later, Spilsbury traveled to Blackpool to conduct the exhumation of Alice Smith, the press was once again hot on his trail. In a futile attempt to shake off his pursuers, Spilsbury supervised this exhumation under cover of darkness. Flashlights illuminated the ghostly scene as the mortal remains of Alice Smith were transported to the mortuary for autopsy, with every step of her journey being recorded by the watching reporters.

Alice Smith had been short—around five feet—and grossly overweight, and thirteen months in the ground had left her corpse considerably more decayed than that of Margaret Lloyd. Nevertheless, Spilsbury was able to draw some conclusions. Again he found no evidence of violence and only very minor indications of drowning. The circulatory organs showed a slight thickening of the mitral valve in the heart, fairly common in someone who, like Alice Smith, had suffered rheumatic fever in childhood, but this was not sufficient to account for an accidental death in the tub. As a matter of course he took organ samples so that Willcox might analyze them, even though he didn't hold out much hope in that area. Somehow—and Spilsbury didn't yet know how—Smith had devised a method of murdering women in the bath that left virtually no trace. Again, Spilsbury ordered the removal of the offending tub to Kentish Town police station.

When Spilsbury returned to London he entered the eye of a newspaper storm. Fleet Street was in uproar. Rumors were buzzing that George Joseph Smith was suspected of *yet another murder*!

A Third Victim

Once again newspaper publicity had flagged the breakthrough. In Herne Bay, on the Kent coast, the local police chief had followed press reports of the London and Blackpool murders with a keener than average eye, and on February 8 he reached for a pen and paper. The letter that landed on Neil's desk detailed a local bathtub death that had occurred in the summer of 1912. But for the origins of this tragedy we need to travel even farther back, to an August day in 1910, when thirty-four-year-old Beatrice (Bessie) Mundy chanced to meet a fashionably dressed man, with a hypnotic stare and a silvery tongue, on the leafy boulevards of Clifton in Bristol.

The stranger doffed his hat and introduced himself as Henry Williams, picture restorer. Although not unattractive, Bessie was a stranger to romance, and nothing had prepared her for the line of mesmerizing flattery that dripped from the stranger's honeyed tongue. In no time at all she was powerless and puppetlike. Her family members would not have been surprised. Soft in the heart and soft in the head was their verdict of Bessie, especially when it came to money. Back in 1904 when her father had died, bequeathing her approximately £2,500 in gilt-edged securities, the family had acted quickly to lock up the funds in a trust, to prevent Bessie from squandering the windfall. The trust, administered by a circumspect uncle, provided an income of just £8 a month.

Williams absorbed all this information as he and Bessie explored the delights of Clifton together over the next few days. Every passing moment increased Bessie's delight. Never before had she met anyone so wildly romantic or beguiling. So beguiling, in fact, that when, after just a few days, Williams begged her to elope and marry, she agreed without a second thought and without packing any baggage.

Williams whisked Bessie off to the seaside resort of Weymouth on the south coast of England, and there they wed at the registry office on August 26. That night she wrote stiffly to her family, "Dear Uncle: I got married today, my husband is writing tonight. Yours truly, B. Williams."[7]

As promised, Smith did contact the family: "Bessie hopes you will forward as much money as possible at your earliest by registered letter. Am pleased to say Bessie is in perfect health, and we are both looking forward to a bright and happy future. Believe me, yours faithfully, Henry Williams."[8]

Appalled by Bessie's madcap behavior and the eye-watering avarice of her husband, Bessie's family hedged and stalled for as long as the law would permit before caving in to the inevitable. On December 13 Williams finally received the surplus interest that had accrued on her securities, £135 in gold. As soon as the funds were in his grasp, Smith absconded, leaving a vile and wholly untrue letter of good-bye to Bessie.

"Dearest, I fear you have blighted all my bright hopes of a happy future. I have caught from you a disease which is called the bad disorder. For you to be in such a state proves you could not have kept yourself morally clean . . . For the sake of my health and honor, and yours too, I must go to London . . . to get properly cured of this disease. It will cost me a great deal of money, because it might take years . . ."[9]

Destitute and possessing only the clothes she stood up in, Bessie trudged back to Bristol and threw herself on the charity of friends. All through 1911 her depression deepened. Early the following year, in an effort to shake off the dreadful torpor that engulfed her, she went to stay with a friend named Sarah Tuckett in the seaside resort of Weston-super-Mare. On the morning of March 14, Bessie stepped out to buy flowers for Sarah. Just minutes later, as if transfixed by a bolt of lightning, she stood rooted to the spot. Her eyes blinked in disbelief. There, on the esplanade, staring pensively out to sea, was Henry Williams.

For some reason most commentators have attributed this meeting to pure coincidence; however, as Sarah Tuckett's subsequent trial testimony makes clear, this was anything but a chance encounter. When Sarah—who met Williams for the first time later that day and loathed him on sight—queried how he had found Bessie in Weston-super-Mare, "I understood him to say that he was told she was there by her brother or uncle."[10] In the ordinary course of events such a reunion, whether by destiny or malevolent design, might be expected to spark verbal fireworks at the very least, but Bessie was a saintly soul with bottomless reserves of gullibility. All was instantly forgiven, even the revolting letter. That very night Bessie returned to the arms of the husband who had so cruelly cast her aside.

For ten weeks the couple meandered across southern England, from the Bristol Channel to the mouth of the Thames. Their wanderings, funded by Bessie's monthly allowance, eventually led them to Herne Bay, where, on May 20, they rented a commercial property at 80 High Street, paying a month's rent in advance. The property had neither a bath nor a bathroom. With a little money that had come in—including £33 of Bessie's—furniture was bought, and a brass plate was fixed on the front door describing Williams as an "Art Dealer."

On June 18 they contacted a local solicitor, Philip de Vere Annesley, bringing drafts of two wills and a copy of the settlement in respect of Bessie's capital. Coaxed by her overbearing spouse, Bessie stammered that she wanted the trust revoked, so that she and her husband could have use of the capital. As such a request far exceeded Annesley's usually daily remit of minor litigation and property conveyancing, he begged leave to seek counsel's opinion.

Two weeks later, back came the opinion: counsel thought it highly unlikely that the trustees would consent to a revocation of the settlement. Moreover, if the wife died intestate, her estate would go to the next of kin, and the husband would get nothing. In amongst the gloom, counsel did offer one ray of hope: if the couple executed mutually beneficial wills, then the surviving spouse would inherit the entire estate, and the family would be cut out of the trust altogether. Unwittingly, the lawyer had signed Bessie's death warrant.

These findings sparked off a flurry of activity. Time was clearly of the essence, because if the Mundys learned what was afoot, they might take steps to tighten the terms of the trust. On July 8, mutual wills were executed. The next day Williams called at an ironmongers and purchased a cheap zinc bath for £2 (curiously enough, when Bessie called back the following day to pay for the tub, she haggled the price down by half a crown to £1.17s 6d). Twenty-four hours later Williams steered Bessie into the surgery of a local doctor named Frank A. French, demanding treatment for a fit she had just suffered. Poor dim Bessie seemed confused. She had no recollection of being ill, but in the end both wife and doctor yielded to the husband's domineering will, and a mild sedative was prescribed.

At 1:30 A.M. on July 12, Dr. French was summoned to 80 High Street; Bessie had apparently suffered another fit. She was in bed. He found nothing amiss: she appeared to have just woken up in something of a sweat; it was a very warm night. Later that day, when Dr. French called at the house, Bessie appeared in perfect health, well enough to write a letter to her uncle describing her illness, lauding her husband's solicitousness, and mentioning that she'd made a will.

The next morning at eight o'clock, Dr. French was breakfasting when a note arrived from Williams: "Can you come at once? I am afraid my wife is dead."[11] The doctor hurried round. An anxious-looking Williams rushed him upstairs, where he found Bessie prone in the bath, her face half-submerged, and her feet "partly out of the water. The legs were straight out . . . the arms were down by the sides."[12] French found no vital signs, and all attempts at resuscitation failed.

The face was bluish and congested with blood, and French noticed a small square of Castile soap clutched in Bessie's right hand.

Williams explained that he had gone out to buy some fish for break- fast and returned to find his wife lifeless in the bath. French decided not to autopsy the body. An inquest decided that Bessie had died from "misadventure" following an epileptic fit. A few days later, Williams re- turned the bath to the ironmonger, having not paid a penny for its use, with an explanation that "he was leaving the neighborhood."[13]

Although the Mundy family strenuously contested Bessie's will, they did so knowing it was a lost cause. Six months later Williams pocketed £2,500 and promptly vanished. And there the matter lay, un- til some two years later when lurid headlines about the "Brides in the Bath" murders resurrected all the old doubts and bitterness.

In almost every detail—save that of life insurance, which wasn't nec- essary because of her trust fund—Bessie Mundy's death replicated those of Alice Burnham and Margaret Lofty. Photographs of Smith, sent to Herne Bay, came back with a positive identification.

Spilsbury made discreet plans to travel down to Herne Bay. But by this time the rumor mill was unstoppable. Peeking through his curtains at Marlborough Hill on the evening of February 17 provided him with an unwanted side effect of his newfound celebrity. "Doorstepping" public figures is a far from recent journalistic ploy, and news of the sen- sational killings meant that a band of reporters was camped outside Spilsbury's home all that night and again early the next morning when he set out for the Kent coast.

Because of the war and its proximity to the continent, Herne Bay was encircled by fortifications and crisscrossed with barbed wire. Just transferring the remains of Bessie Williams from the cemetery on Canterbury Road to the local mortuary proved a tortuous business. In spite of the advanced decomposition, Spilsbury did find one symptom associated with drowning: "goose-skin."[14] More properly known as *anse- rina cutis*, goose skin is a roughening of the skin resulting from rigor or the erector pilae muscles, and is found most prominently on the thighs. Since it can occur in circumstances other than immersion in water,

Spilsbury knew better than to regard this as an infallible indicator of drowning.

What observations he could make, given the advanced decomposition, pointed to a very rapid death by drowning. The heart was well preserved with no circulatory disease, nor was there the slightest trace of any wound, violent grasping, or struggle. After taking careful measurements of the body, Spilsbury asked for the tub to be transported to London.

The plain, slightly rusted iron bathtub arrived in Kentish Town on February 23 and was placed alongside the other two tubs. Each day Spilsbury would visit the police station and puzzle over how three apparently healthy women had met their deaths in these tubs, without any obvious signs of physical intervention. He spent hours with a tape measure, making calculations, formulating theories, only to abandon them when they didn't pan out.

Considering the totality of evidence against Smith, Spilsbury's efforts might seem superfluous, redundant even; after all, what were the odds against a husband losing three wives in three identical accidents? But the reality was very different. Like his fellow investigators, Spilsbury was hamstrung by a peculiarity of the British legal system at that time, which mandated that any defendant—even a suspected mass murderer—should face only a single charge at any one time. And taken individually, each case was legally weak. With no witness to the killing, no evidence that it was anything other than an accident, and absolutely nothing to suggest Smith's participation, any competent counsel—and Smith was ultimately defended by one of the very best—would have the case laughed out of court. Spurred on by the very real and appalling prospect of Smith being allowed to walk free, Spilsbury redoubled his efforts, determined to find out how he managed to kill so deftly and with such anonymity.

The Symptoms of Drowning

Drowning is the suffocation by immersion of the nose and mouth in a liquid, and can occur in surprisingly shallow fluid levels. The mechanics of drowning are complex and usually follow this five-step process:

1. Submersion is followed by struggle, which subsides with exhaustion.
2. Breath-holding lasts until carbon dioxide accumulation stimulates respiration, resulting in inhalation of water.
3. Gulping of water, coughing, and vomiting is rapidly followed by loss of consciousness.
4. Profound unconsciousness and convulsions are associated with the aspiration of water, and consequent heart failure.
5. Death occurs within two to three minutes and is almost invariable when the period of submersion exceeds ten minutes.

Spilsbury pondered all the above and found nothing to account for any of the deaths under investigation. His best chance of cracking this mystery, he decided, was to concentrate on Bessie Williams, who had—or so it was claimed—drowned following an epileptic fit.

Epilepsy is a relatively common disorder, affecting 1 in 200 of the population, and is slightly more prevalent among males than females (about 10:8). However, since more than 70 percent of epileptic individuals have their first attack before age twenty, and since nothing in Bessie's medical or family background hinted at any trace of epilepsy, Spilsbury doubted its presence here. Rather than discard the possibility out of hand, he concentrated on whether it was physically possible for someone suffering an epileptic fit to have drowned in the Herne Bay tub.

Bessie had been five feet seven inches tall, robustly built, and yet she had died in a tub that measured only five feet at its longest point. The tub had a sloping back and a vertical front, which gave a seating length of forty-four inches. Since the first phase of an epileptic fit—the tonic stage—is characterized by "the state of complete rigidity of the body,"[15] this meant that Bessie's head could not have been submerged naturally. On the contrary; given her size and the shape of the tub, the rigidity would tend to push the upper part of her body up the sloping part of the tub, far above the level of the water.

Phase two of an epileptic fit—known as the clonic stage—consists of violent spasms of the limbs, which are drawn up close to the body and then flung outward again. Again, it was difficult to imagine how anyone seated in the tub could possibly end up underwater. Nor was the likelihood of this increased during the third stage of an attack, when the body subsides and the muscles relax.

According to Dr. French, the dead woman was on her back, head submerged, legs extended, and feet protruding above the water. Spilsbury could see no explanation of how Bessie Williams had arrived at such a position. Unless . . .

Spilsbury hastened to his library. There, in the literature on cases of sudden death by drowning, he found the data he was looking for. Scanty, maybe, but enough to convince him that he had hit on the solution.

The vagus nerve is the longest and most complex of the cranial nerves and runs from the brain, through the face and thorax, to the abdomen. It can be astonishingly lethal. According to Professor Keith Simpson, sudden and unexpected vagal inhibition "can kill like a karate chop."[16] Usually this reflex is stimulated by the tightening of a hand or a ligature about the neck, as many an unintending strangler has discovered to his or her cost. But there are other methods of prompting vagal inhibition. Spilsbury uncovered examples where a sudden rush of water into the nasal passages had induced exactly this effect. In such a case, loss of consciousness is usually instantaneous, and death ensues soon afterward, at most within a few minutes. Significantly, an autopsy discloses none of the usual signs of drowning as death is believed to be the result of cardiac arrest induced by impact of water on the back of the pharynx and larynx. Although extremely uncommon in water, death involving vagal inhibition usually occurs when people jump feet-first into swimming pools or rivers, thereby facilitating the sudden ingress of water to the nose. Eyewitnesses report the mystifying absence of struggle on the part of the victim, who is found to be dead even if the body is recovered immediately.

Convinced he had found the cause of death, Spilsbury now set himself the task of establishing how Smith could replicate this effect in a household bathtub. Much the likeliest scenario, he felt, would involve some kind of sexual interaction. As the unsuspecting woman took her bath, Smith, possibly naked also—thereby avoiding any wet clothes—drew near. A few moments' caressing might have followed, allowing the muscular Smith time to ease himself into what Spilsbury thought was the killing position—right hand on top of head, left forearm beneath the victim's knees. One convulsive jackknife movement, heaving upward with the left arm while simultaneously pressing down on the woman's head with the right hand, would have achieved his murderous purpose. As the victim's head slid underwater, a lethal rush of water into the nose and throat would cause virtually instantaneous unconsciousness, thus explaining the absence of injuries and the minimal signs of drowning and asphyxia. Interestingly, a recognized side effect of vagal inhibition is cadaveric spasm—a kind of instant rigor—a reaction that would account for the piece of soap still clutched in Bessie's fingers.

When Neil heard Spilsbury's theory, he decided to conduct a practical demonstration. Various expert female swimmers, all about the same size and weight as Smith's victims, were placed in the three tubs and told to resist Neil's efforts to submerge them. Even when pushed hard on the head and upper body alone, all the women were able to struggle violently and grab hold of either the edges of the bath or their attacker. Then, in a moment of monumental stupidity, Neil upped the ante. Without warning, he abruptly seized one woman's feet and yanked them upward. In a flash she slid beneath the water, hands useless to save her. Neil's sense of triumphant vindication lasted barely a second—the woman was no longer moving!

Panic-stricken, he pulled her from the water. Her head lolled limply to one side. It took a doctor and several minutes of anxious resuscitation to restore the woman to consciousness. When she recovered, all she could recall was suddenly sliding down the bath and water rushing up her nose. Then everything had gone black. Neil's foolishness had almost cost one woman her life, but it did corroborate Spilsbury's theory.

Between January 26 and May 11 Spilsbury and Willcox conferred together on four occasions, their invariable tactic when scheduled to testify at the same trial, trying to anticipate defense strategy and any possible awkward questions. All this came at a hectic time for Spilsbury. In May, much to his relief, Edith gave birth safely to their third child, a healthy boy whom they called Peter. But overhanging the month was the somber news that on May 7, the liner *Lusitania*, en route from New York to Liverpool, was torpedoed by a German U-boat fifteen miles off the Irish coast, with the loss of 1,198 lives, including 128 U.S. citizens. Then, on May 31, came the development that Spilsbury had feared: the first Zeppelin raid over London. It left 28 dead and injured 60 more, and meant that Spilsbury was now busier than ever.

Against this somber backdrop, George Joseph Smith went on trial at the Old Bailey on June 22. London at the time had been enjoying a rare heat wave, with temperatures climbing into the eighties, and inside court number one the atmosphere was equally steamy. Despite unofficial attempts to bar women from attending what was expected to be a sex-laden trial, the public gallery bulged with tremulous female spectators, all eager for a glimpse of England's very own Bluebeard.

As mentioned earlier, under British legal procedure a defendant could face only one indictment at a time, and after much consultation, and to some considerable surprise, the Crown decided to charge Smith with the oldest murder, that of Bessie Mundy/Williams. The reasons were twofold: (a) Smith profited most from this death; (b) the prosecution felt confident that Spilsbury could demolish defense claims that the victim drowned accidentally following an epileptic fit.

In this highest of high-profile trials, Smith was defended by the most famous advocate of the age, Edward Marshall Hall, KC. Erratic but undeniably brilliant, Hall had pulled off some stunning acquittals in his time, and even though pretrial publicity had made Smith the most notorious accused killer since Crippen, Hall still felt confident about securing another famous victory. That belief disintegrated on the opening day. Even though the trial would last eight days—exceptionally long for the time—its outcome became a foregone conclusion when the judge, Mr. Justice Scrutton, decided that details of the deaths of Smith's other "wives" could be admitted as evidence of "system"—provided the jury drew no conclusions as to Smith's guilt in these deaths! It was legal sophistry of the finest kind, a decision still debated and argued to this day, and it ripped the heart out of Marshall Hall's defense. What began as a forlorn cause speedily degenerated into a rout.

Spilsbury's Deadly Demonstration

Even though the prosecution produced 112 witnesses, as the trial transcript shows, only one really mattered. The trial was into its sixth day when Spilsbury took the stand. After briefly outlining the results of his postmortems on the three bodies, he launched a preemptive attack on the anticipated defense strategy. With the Herne Bay bath set up in court alongside him, and after explaining to the jury that Bessie Mundy had been above average height, Spilsbury was asked by Archibald Bodkin, KC, the Crown prosecutor, if it was possible for Miss Mundy to have been submerged in such a small tub.

"I think it is highly improbable,"[17] he replied.

Spilsbury next dealt with the possibility of Bessie having fainted. Had she done so, and then became partially submerged, the water "would have a very powerful effect, and would probably recover the person from the faint . . . the presence of any substance, fluid or solid, in the air passages is a very powerful stimulant to the body and the nervous system."[18] Contrast this, he said, with a sudden and unexpected rush of water into the nasal passages, in which consciousness "would be lost at once."[19]

Spilsbury laid great stress on the square of soap that Bessie had clutched in her fingers. Had she fainted, relaxation of the muscles would have caused the soap to slip from her grasp. "But if death occurred immediately the contraction of the muscles of the hand might pass instantaneously into the death stiffening, and the object might then be retained after death."[20] He cited a recent example of vagal inhibition in which a man, clutching a flashlight, had fallen into an icy reservoir at night. Death had been virtually instantaneous. When he was found three weeks later, the dead man's fingers were still clasped around the flashlight.

Across the courtroom, dwarfed by the enormous wooden dock that surrounded him, Smith sat white-faced and mute as Spilsbury tightened the noose around his neck with every utterance. This interlude marked a rare moment of silence for the defendant. Throughout the trial he'd raved like a madman, interrupting witnesses and court officials alike with a fusillade of abuse and insults, but during Spilsbury's testimony he maintained a deathly hush.

Not even the mighty Marshall Hall, himself the son of a physician and particularly adroit in the art of cross-examining medical experts, could dent Spilsbury's sangfroid. His terse response to Marshall Hall's opening question set the tone for their long exchange: "I am a recognized authority upon health, and I am invariably called in by the Treasury for the purpose of all matters of this kind."[21] Thereafter, his monosyllabic responses were murderously effective in their brevity. Marshall Hall was at his serpentine best, probing and prodding, seeking to gain some concession, no matter how slight, from the witness that the presence of the piece of soap in Bessie Mundy's hand lent support to the theory of epilepsy.

"It is not impossible," was as far as Spilsbury would go. "It is not very likely."[22]

When Spilsbury left the witness stand, his place was taken by Willcox, who essentially duplicated everything the former had said. During his testimony there occurred a raw example of how the courts, and especially the judiciary, preferred Spilsbury's icy assuredness over Willcox's more cautious approach. At one stage Marshall Hall asked Willcox to confirm that if a head were immersed in eight inches of water, "the body would have to be almost flat on the bottom of the bath?"[23]

Willcox's reply of "Not necessarily"[24] induced a scowl from the bench. Mr. Justice Scrutton grouched only semi-humorously: "Some day I should like to have an Act of Parliament by which witnesses who say 'not necessarily' shall be shot."[25]

Nowadays Willcox's circumspection would be applauded. But in an era when science was expected to deliver muscular absolutism, such watchfulness smacked of timidity, not a trait greatly prized in English courtrooms of the early twentieth century.

Marshall Hall called no witnesses, not even the defendant. Instead he reserved his efforts for an impassioned polemic that has reverberated in thousands of courtrooms in hundreds of countries ever since: the overwhelming advantage enjoyed by the State when it comes to expert witnesses. "Had the prisoner not been the pauper he is, had he been possessed of unlimited means like some recent American criminals,* he might have procured experts to say that the cause of death was other than that stated by the experts for the Crown."[26] Marshall Hall, after struggling to extract some advantage from this imbalance, then sharpened his focus, reminding the jury that even "Dr. Spilsbury had said, with all his expert knowledge, that he dare not say that it was impossible for it to have been an accident."[27] This was straw-clutching in the grand manner. One wife dead in the bath, maybe. No jury was going to swallow an "accident" three times over. And so it proved. On July 1, 1915, after a jury deliberation of just twenty-two minutes, Smith was found guilty and sentenced to death.

The case of George Joseph Smith sent shock waves through the British psyche. At a time when Allied troops in Europe were dying at a rate of more than 1,000 each day, the "Brides in the Bath" trial succeeded

---

* The murder trials of New York millionaire Harry Thaw (1907–08), in which expensive medical testimony played a significant part, had aroused great interest in the British press. Reciprocally, Smith's trial was heavily covered by U.S. newspapers.

in relegating these ghastly statistics to the inside pages. To those who had not witnessed it, the scale of death on the western front was unimaginable, whereas the murder of three women in their own bathtubs had a peculiar intimacy and resonance. Readers struggled to fathom how someone's moral compass could skew so violently off course as to regard human beings as nothing more than negotiable assets. In an age when an artisan might count himself lucky to earn £100 per annum, Smith made many times that amount from either fleecing or killing women. He had failed as a baker, a gymnastics teacher, a property speculator, and in the world of antiques, but he was supremely successful at the business of separating women from either their lives or their life savings. Had he remained in the provinces, he might have eluded justice for years to come, possibly forever. Instead, he gambled and took his trade to London, heart of the national newspaper industry. Within weeks he was under lock and key.

Life had turned full circle for Smith, for it was London that had bred him. He was born in 1872, the son of an insurance agent, and had been criminally disposed since childhood. In 1898, whilst between prison sentences, he married his only legitimate wife, Caroline Thornhill. She subsequently fled to Canada to escape his brutality. So far as Neil could ascertain—and the list is by no means guaranteed to be complete—Smith "married" another six women, each time following the same routine: whirlwind courtship, marriage, transfer of assets, followed by immediate disappearance. One "wife," Sarah Freeman, was abandoned at the National Gallery, when Smith made an excuse that he needed to use the men's room. Darting unseen out of an exit, he raced across London to Sarah's lodgings in Clapham, cleaned out her entire belongings, and vanished. Obviously someone who, when he found a successful plan, stuck to it, Smith repeated this trick with another bigamous victim, Alice Reavil, deserting her in a public park and once again fleeing with all her worldly goods.

Oddly enough there was one "wife" whom Smith neither swindled nor murdered. In 1908 he had gone through a marriage ceremony with

Edith Pegler, and not until his trial for murder seven years later did this poor woman discover that the husband who regularly disappeared from their Bristol home on jaunts scouring the country for antiques was in reality a far different kind of collector. Each time Smith returned, pockets stuffed with money, and each time Edith welcomed him home. On the witness stand she had nothing but good to say about this psychopath who'd murdered three women.

Masculine blood pressure, blind to the changes that the women's suffrage movement had wrought, boiled over at the ease and frequency with which a "vulgar and all but illiterate ruffian"[28] like Smith managed to seduce the flower of English womanhood. This wasn't just about the ballot box; centuries of sexual repression were being shed at the same time. For those stuffed shirts too outraged to countenance such radicalism, it became an article of faith that Smith obviously possessed Svengalian powers of hypnotic persuasion; nothing else, they argued, could explain the eagerness with which well-brought-up young women leapt into his bed. Even Smith's own defense team fanned the flames of this particular fire. "He had," said junior counsel Montague Shearman, "a horrible way of looking at one,"[29] while Marshall Hall once terminated an interview with Smith, "convinced that the man was trying to hypnotize him."[30] Indeed, speaking later in private, Marshall Hall—who it must be said had a wonderfully excitable disposition—went so far as to express his belief that Smith employed mesmerism to induce his victims to drown themselves! Spilsbury, typically pragmatic, dismissed such nonsense out of hand.

Clearly, Smith was far from being a commonplace ruffian. Besides oozing sexual magnetism by the bucketload, he played the piano, enjoyed poetry, and was no mean artist. In between bigamous escapades he composed thoughtful letters to local newspapers on a variety of social issues, such as the declining standard of behavior amongst children, inconsistent refuse collections, "inferior literature,"[31] and the need for greater reform of criminals—"this downfallen class,"[32] as he termed them.

Breathtaking hypocrisy, maybe, but it does highlight Smith's singular attitude, and perhaps goes some way toward explaining his sinister appeal. Another point to bear in mind is that he always chose his victims well. Single women, late twenties or early thirties, often plain and unused to flattery, with relatively modest amounts of money to their names were the preferred targets. Any richer and they would have already been snapped up; any poorer and he wasn't interested. Dangling the carrot of matrimony in front of some shelf-bound spinster was, as Smith found out, an almost guaranteed shortcut to loosening the tightest bodice and the tightest purse strings.

Smith was hanged on August 13, 1915. Accounts of his end vary enormously. Gloating press reports claimed that, semi-comatose and with his hair turned white from fear, the cowardly wife killer had to be dragged to the gallows. However, the bishop of Croydon, who visited Smith in the condemned cell, had it on the authority of prison chaplain Reverend G. Stott that Smith died serenely, without struggle, merely saying, "I am innocent"[33] as the trapdoor sprang open. It was a suitably enigmatic end to this most enigmatic of lives.

The "Brides in the Bath" murders had dominated headlines throughout the early part of 1915, and once again, Spilsbury's evidence had been crucial. Thanks to his research, medical science was, at last, beginning to unravel the mysteries of the body's nervous system, discovering how certain reflexes can produce sudden death. Such was the furor created by Smith that the Home Office ordered that henceforth, all deaths occurring in baths would be investigated by an experienced pathologist. For the metropolitan district of London, this responsibility was allocated to Spilsbury.

It was an additional duty he could have well done without. Especially since it came at a time when Willcox's continued lobbying for a more active wartime role had finally paid off. He had secured a position as consulting physician to the army in the eastern Mediterranean. For Spilsbury, having never practiced medicine clinically, such a posting wasn't an option. On July 15, Willcox left London and headed for the Allied base at Moudros in the northern Aegean, where he would tend soldiers blown to bits in the disastrous Dardanelles campaign. His absence doubled Spilsbury's workload, setting him on a solitary treadmill that he would tramp for the rest of his life. Delegation wasn't in his nature. Over the course of his long career he would perform more than 25,000 autopsies, peaking at 1,000 per annum. Each added to his unrivaled experience of sudden and violent death, and each would help cement Spilsbury's global reputation as "England's modern Sherlock Holmes."[34]

1 *Times*, December 4, 1911, 3.
2 Gordon Honeycombe, *The Murders of the Black Museum: 1870–1970* (London: Arrow, 1984), 206.
3 Eric R. Watson, *The Trial of George Joseph Smith* (Edinburgh: Hodge, 1922), 185.
4 *New York Times*, June 29, 1915, 8.
5 Watson, *The Trial of George Joseph Smith*, 153.
6 *Ibid.*, 237.
7 Honeycombe, *The Murders of the Black Museum*, 200.
8 *Ibid.*
9 Watson, *The Trial of George Joseph Smith*, 87.
10 *Ibid.*, 92.
11 *Ibid.*, 117.
12 *Ibid.*, 118.
13 *Ibid.*, 113.
14 *Ibid.*, 204.
15 *Ibid.*, 207.
16 Keith Simpson, *Forty Years of Murder* (London: Harrap, 1978), 45.
17 Watson, *The Trial of George Joseph Smith*, 214.
18 *Ibid.*, 217.
19 *Ibid.*
20 *Ibid.*, 218.
21 *Ibid.*, 219.
22 *Ibid.*, 221.
23 *Times*, June 30, 1915, 3.
24 *Ibid.*
25 *Ibid.*
26 Watson, *The Trial of George Joseph Smith*, 263.
27 *Times*, July 1, 1915, 4.
28 D. G. Browne and E. V. Tullett, *Bernard Spilsbury: His Life and Cases* (London: Harrap, 1951), 263.
29 Edward Marjoribanks, *Famous Trials of Marshall Hall* (London: Penguin, 1950), 291.

30 *Ibid.*

31 Philip H. A. Willcox, *The Detective-Physician* (London: Heinemann, 1970), 107.

32 *Ibid.*

33 Marjoribanks, *Famous Trials of Marshall Hall*, 304.

34 *Washington Post*, March 30, 1938, 3.

CHAPTER THREE

The Butcher of Soho

When German troops stormed into Belgium on the night of August 3–4, 1914, not just Britain but the whole British Empire declared war on the aggressor. Solidarity was the watchword, and no nation embraced this concept more wholeheartedly than did Australia. With the declaration of war punctuating the run-up to a general election, Labour leader Andrew Fisher stormed to victory on the platform that Australia would support Britain to "the last man and the last shilling." This was no empty campaign slogan: out of a population of 4.5 million, almost 10 percent volunteered, and of these, 324,000 would see active service overseas in the Great War.

For many troops, their first point of call in England was Sutton Veny, a sprawling military compound on the edge of Salisbury Plain that doubled up as an Allied training base and a POW camp for captured enemy soldiers. The first Australians arrived in December 1916. By this time it's fair to say the initial glow of patriotic duty to the mother country had dimmed somewhat after the horrors of Gallipoli, where untested Australian troops had been cut to ribbons by Turkish guns.

The disaster might have cost its chief architect, Winston Churchill, his job, but for almost 9,000 Anzacs the price was much, much higher.

Despite this setback, loyal antipodeans continued to pack the recruiting offices, with many prepared to pay their own fare to Europe to join the Australian Imperial Forces in the fight against Germany. Some treated the trip as a kind of vacation, a once-in-a-lifetime opportunity to see the Old Country before they faced the mud-filled trenches of France. Joseph Durkin was typical of the breed. He was twenty-four-years old and came from the small farming community of Kilmore, in central Victoria. A talent for firearms ensured that upon his arrival at Sutton Veny he was attached to the Sixth Battalion and made a Lewis gun instructor.

The tedium of camp life didn't sit well with the fun-loving Durkin. He had a girl back home who wrote regularly, but she was half a world away, and around Sutton Veny there was plenty to tempt the testosterone-fueled recruits. Some local women, many of whom had been encouraged to take in soldiers' laundry, soon found themselves providing rather more than just washing facilities. Durkin's good looks and breezy manner made him a big hit with the ladies, both local and farther afield in Salisbury, where he hooked up with Beatrice Diamond, the wife of a restaurant owner.

When Beatrice's husband died suddenly in October 1917, Durkin wasted no time in warming the widow's bed. All the while he continued to receive letters from his sweetheart back in Australia. Clearly his double-dealing didn't trouble him, as his visits to Beatrice—and hers to him at the camp—became increasingly frequent. On one occasion when he traveled the twenty miles to Salisbury to see her, he was accompanied by a fellow Lewis gun instructor, Acting Corporal Verney Asser. Asser was some six years older than Durkin, much darker in nature, and with a deeply troubled past. If he journeyed to Salisbury expecting any further subdivision of Beatrice's sexual favors, then she speedily disabused him of that notion. Her heart was irrevocably set on Joe Durkin. From all accounts, Asser took the rejection with a sour grace.

In late November Durkin's correspondence from Australia assumed a much edgier tone. Someone—it was never established who—had informed Durkin's fiancée of his duplicity, and she wrote an angry letter demanding an explanation. It arrived on November 27. That night, just after "Lights Out" echoed round the camp at 9:30, a single shot shattered the still November air over Sutton Veny.

Some time later, at around 11 P.M., the duty officer, Sergeant Frederick Smith, was notified that there had been an accident; Joe Durkin had shot himself.

Smith went at the double to investigate. He entered the hut where Durkin was billeted and found it in total darkness. Turning to Asser, who shared the hut and who had reported the incident, he ordered him to fetch a candle. When it arrived, Smith was able to distinguish the shadowy shape of Durkin slumped on the floor at the far end of the hut, lying on his right side in a simple roll-out bed. Blood trickled down from a single face wound, and his head lolled off a makeshift pillow, his kit bag. Smith checked for any vital signs and found none. Beside the bed lay a .303 Lee Enfield service rifle.

Asser explained that he had been "in bed asleep and heard a shot."[1] Startled out of his wits, he had jumped up and blundered around blindly in the darkness until his eyes adjusted to the light. Only then did he discover what had befallen his best friend. Horror-stricken, and without another thought, he had run for assistance.

The arrival of the medical orderlies only confirmed what Smith already knew: Durkin was dead. He was dressed only in his underclothes, his body entirely inside the bed, with the blankets pulled up about his shoulders. A single bullet from the rifle had entered the left cheek, about two inches in front of the ear, then exited behind the right ear. Everything pointed to Durkin having shot himself.

There was just one curiosity: the breech in the rifle was empty. Asser explained that, in grabbing the rifle from Durkin's body, training had taken over and he'd instinctively ejected the spent cartridge in a reflex action. A search of the hut found the expended cartridge on the floor. Also found were two unused magazines, each containing forty-eight cartridges. No more was thought of this discovery at the time.

Daylight brought a fresh development when investigators located the deadly bullet. After exiting Durkin's head, it had passed through the kit bag and a double blanket, then pierced the hut wall before embedding itself in the ground outside.

Later that day, completely oblivious to what had happened, Beatrice Diamond arrived at the camp, as arranged, to meet Durkin. Only now did she learn of the tragedy. For the second time in two months, a man had been taken from her. Broken and distraught, she limped back to Salisbury.

Beatrice's arrival at the camp blew the lid off Durkin's messy personal life, much to the chagrin of the commanding officers, who wanted the whole unsavory incident swept under the carpet as quickly as possible. The official version was that Durkin, driven mad by guilt over the shoddy way he had treated his sweetheart back in Australia, had blown his brains out. At the subsequent inquest the coroner duly recorded a verdict of "suicide from temporary insanity."[2]

Although little discussed at the time, suicides in all branches of the military were by no means uncommon during the Great War; nor was it the prerogative of shell-shocked soldiers in the trenches. Surprisingly enough, training camps took the heaviest toll. Military records show that of the 967 American military personnel who took their own lives during World War I, no fewer than two-thirds died within the U.S.

So on the face of it, the death of Joe Durkin had been one small tragedy played out against a much wider backdrop of unimaginable carnage, and for the sake of camp morale, the authorities decided to draw a very firm line under the affair. But for one man this suffocating blanket of official silence was more than he could stomach. He needed to clear his conscience.

Corporal Peter Milne had been in charge of Hut 31, an ammunition store, on the night of the incident, and, at a few minutes after "Lights Out," he had spotted Verney Asser fumbling with some boxes of bullets. Significantly, the cartridges in these magazines, although intended for Lewis machine guns, could also be used in a Lee Enfield .303.

Asser had mumbled that he was taking three empty magazines and then left. Milne had thought no more of it at the time, not even when, like everyone else in the vicinity, he heard the single shot fired some time later. Because this was a military base, the noise hadn't particularly startled him, although the sound of gunfire at night was unusual.

Only later, around eleven o'clock, did news reach him about the accident. According to Milne, he had gone to the billet and had expressed his skepticism to Asser over the manner of Durkin's death. "He has not shot himself,"[3] Milne said hotly. Asser at first said nothing. But when Milne repeated the claim, Asser rounded on him savagely, snarling that Durkin, whom he called "his best friend," had been "dopey"[4] about Beatrice Diamond, and that the tangled love affair had driven him to suicide.

Officers listened closely to what Milne had to say and compared his words with statements recording the two magazines found in Asser's hut. Milne's belated intervention loosened other tongues. A second soldier came forward to say that, one day before the tragedy, he'd broken up a bitter argument between Durkin and Asser. The fight, he thought, had been over some woman, and he distinctly recalled Asser threatening Durkin with the words, "I will get even for this with you."[5]

Two such claims, coming in quick succession, obviously demanded an urgent reappraisal of the evidence, and this time around, the military brass ceded authority to the local police office. Details of the preliminary investigation arrived at the Home Office, who in turn notified Spilsbury.

Upon his arrival at the camp, he asked for the case notes. Two interesting anomalies jumped out at him: on the fateful night, Asser's bed had not been rolled out; and when he reported the accident he was fully dressed, even to the point of wearing puttees. Neither fact tallied with the purported circumstances. When Spilsbury studied the body, he was immediately struck by the absence of powder burns around the entrance wound. Gunshot suicides generally press the weapon close to the skin before pulling the trigger. This results in a blackening of the skin as smoke and explosive material belch from the muzzle. While it is not unknown for suicides to hold a weapon some distance from the head or heart before firing, it is unusual, and this absence of powder burns was the first indication to Spilsbury that something might be amiss.

These were the early days of ballistics analysis. In London, a society gunsmith named Robert Churchill was taking the first tentative steps in bullet and firearm identification, and had already proved his worth to Scotland Yard. But Spilsbury was beset by a different problem: he needed to know how far away from Durkin's face the muzzle had been when the rifle was fired. Fortunately, assistance was close at hand.

Since 1904 Willcox had been collecting data on this very subject, and when, four years later, he declined the position of Home Office pathologist, he had generously donated his files to Spilsbury. These records tabulated numerous fatalities involving revolvers, rifles, and shotguns, and dealt mainly with Willcox's experiments to determine the angle of fire and the distances from which shots were fired. Microscopic examination of Durkin's entrance wound, cross-referenced to Willcox's data, led Spilsbury to conclude that the closest distance at which the rifle could have been held from the cheek—without leaving the trademark powder burns—was five inches.

Now this posed a conundrum. The Lee Enfield was a long weapon, measuring 44.57 inches overall, with a barrel length of 25.2 inches. To fully depress the trigger required a distance from the muzzle of approximately thirty inches. But Durkin was only five feet seven inches tall, and, as Spilsbury noted, his arms were conspicuously shorter than average for a man of that height. How then was it possible for Durkin to hold and fire the rifle in such a way as to cause the fatal wound?

Spilsbury decided on a practical experiment. Taking the rifle, he lay down on the rolled-out mattress and assumed the deceased's position. Despite being six feet two inches, he could scarcely reach the trigger with his little finger when the muzzle was touching his face. When he held the rifle another two inches away, he was physically unable to pull the trigger.

Spilsbury's reconstruction of the crime scene opened up a yawning chasm in Asser's version of events. When further sifting uncovered yet more evidence of an acrimonious feud between the deceased and Asser over the affections of Beatrice Diamond, the young Australian corporal found himself facing a charge of murder.

In court, the defense persisted with their claim that this was a tragic but obvious case of suicide, and that somehow Spilsbury must have gotten it wrong. When he was in the witness box, Spilsbury agreed with defense counsel that someone lying on their back might have depressed the trigger with their toe, but pointed out that Durkin had been found lying on his right side.

Mr. Justice Avory intervened. "If the deceased had been on his back, might the body have turned over on to the right side?"

"Not lying in bed, sir," Spilsbury replied. "If he was lying on his back he would have been found lying on his back."[6]

Spilsbury's clinching argument against the "toe theory" hinged around the fact that the rifle was found lying alongside the bed. As death would have been instantaneous, had Durkin operated the trigger with his toe, it would have been impossible for him to replace his leg under the blankets, as it was found.

Avory allowed the jury to take the rifle into their deliberations, with the caveat that if they did attempt any "gymnastics" they should remember that the deceased was struggling "in the dark."[7] Like everyone else, the jury was unable to square the physical evidence with Asser's testimony, and on January 16, 1918, at the end of a two-day trial, the Australian private who'd traveled halfway around the world to fight the Kaiser, only to be destroyed by jealousy, was found guilty and sentenced to death.

Most appeals tend to be dry reruns of the original evidence. Asser's was startlingly different. In the first place, he dispensed with counsel and drafted his own petition of appeal. Second, he now claimed to be insane. His dementia, he said, went back to his adolescence, when, under his real name of James Nugent, he had been discharged from his position as a "bugler boy" in the navy at age fourteen because of mental instability. When war broke out he had enlisted under the name of Verney Asser to conceal the time he had spent in a lunatic asylum. Whatever the truth of these allegations, military records at Sutton Veny did confirm that, in July 1916, Asser was admitted to hospital for "mental derangement," brought on, according to the doctors, by "alcoholism."[8] Since insanity had played no part in Asser's original trial defense, the court decided it had no place here, and the appeal was rejected. A panel of doctors convened to gauge Asser's mental competence also found no reason to recommend a reprieve, and on March 5 he was hanged at Shepton Mallet prison.

Three days before Asser met his inauspicious end, another killer, also foreign-born, had been similarly dispatched at London's Pentonville Prison. In this overlapping case, Spilsbury's intervention had also proved critical. But there were signs that he was spreading himself too thinly. The warning bells had first rung in early 1917 when, thoroughly run-down from overwork, he had contracted an infection of his left arm after autopsying a badly diseased body. For someone who'd previously enjoyed the rudest of health, such a setback came as a profound shock. In the ordinary course of events he might have taken extended leave, but these were unusual times and demanded extreme sacrifices. Spilsbury kept on working. For the most part he rarely saw his family at all, just the odd fleeting visit to Malvern, then it was back to London and the remorseless grind of the mortuary.

Since the name of Bernard Spilsbury is synonymous with notorious murder cases, it may come as a surprise to learn that of the more than 25,000 autopsies that he performed in his career, barely 1 percent contained any kind of criminal involvement. Generally his work centered on the more mundane aspects of sudden or inexplicable death, and in wartime Britain all too often this involved tragedies in the weapons workplace. In December 1914 Gilbert Moddy, thirty-five, had collapsed while working on aircraft construction at a factory in Hendon. Spilsbury found extensive liver disease and traced its cause back to the dope, a quick-drying varnish, that Moddy applied to the aircraft wings. Moddy's repeated complaints that the fumes were making him sick had been ignored, and only with his death were steps taken to improve the working lot of those in airplane construction.

Another home-front casualty was Florence Chandler. This munitions worker was only eighteen when she died on January 11, 1917, from TNT poisoning, a victim of sloppy safety regulations and lethal obduracy. Like most of her coworkers, she eschewed the masks and gloves provided, complaining that they made her too hot and uncomfortable, safe in the knowledge that most factory inspectors were prepared to turn a blind eye when it came to the war effort. After the autopsy, Spilsbury recommended that all employees in this dangerous industry be medically examined every two weeks for signs of abnormality, as he felt that Florence might have been saved had her symptoms been diagnosed early enough.

London's First Air Raids

But much the greatest increase in Spilsbury's mortuary workload was due to German aerial bombardment. Oddly enough, it had been the effectiveness of the Allied anti-Zeppelin strategy that inspired this upsurge. When Zeppelins had first appeared over Britain's coastline, the monolithic airships were awesome weapons of terror that struck fear into the bravest heart, but because warfare has a knack of accelerating technological progress, it took no time at all for the Royal Flying Corps to come to grips with the lumbering bombers. Within months the Zeppelin was exposed as a cumbersome anachronism, virtually defenseless against any kind of aerial counterattack and pitifully easy to shoot down.

German technological pride, badly dented by this humiliation, fought back fast, and its engineers and factories now went into overdrive, determined to regain aerial supremacy. What the high command in Berlin demanded was an agile warplane capable of bombing the major British cities, particularly London, and in the spring of 1917 that wish sprang from the drawing board to the runway.

The Gotha G.V. "Bomb Dropper" was a quantum leap forward in aerial destructiveness. Unlike the unwieldy Zeppelin, the Gotha could fly in formation at a speed of eighty-eight miles per hour, defend itself with a movable Parabellum 7.9 mm machine gun, and deliver a 1,200-pound payload of explosives. This was the stealth bomber of its age. The first daylight raid on London came on July 13, when a squadron of fourteen Gothas flew up the Thames Estuary at 16,000 feet—too high to be intercepted—right out of the pages of H. G. Wells's *The War in the Air* and into the homes of a terrified population. Londoners soon learned to flee for safety whenever these dread planes were sighted. Blackouts were imposed, with Londoners ordered to have their blinds and curtains closed by 5:30 P.M. each day.

Forced once more to play catch-up, the RFC again proved equal to the task, soon restricting the Gotha to night missions only. This less-ened the Gotha's effectiveness, but as the raid of Wednesday, October 31, 1917, demonstrated, it could still deliver a lethal payload. That night ten died and twenty-two more were injured as the Gotha's bombs battered London. When the first blasts echoed at 11:15 P.M., a young woman, elfinlike and angst-ridden, dashed from her home just off Regent's Park, looking for sanctuary. Unlike most of her neighbors, she shunned the safety of the nearby tube station and instead disap-peared into the tangled warren of streets that lies behind Tottenham Court Road.

She would never be seen alive again.

At half past eight on the Friday morning, Thomas Henry left home at 17 Regent Square, in nearby Bloomsbury, and set out for the store where he worked as a packer. There had been a heavy overnight storm, and the cobbled streets were still shiny and wet as he cut across the sleepy square. He skirted the small communal garden, with its blunt-topped iron railings, that lay in the middle of the square, then paused. His eyes narrowed. Just beyond the railings, in the deepest shadows, lay an irregular package done up in sacking. Irresistibly curious, Henry decided to take a closer look. Peeling back the sacking, he saw what looked like bloodstained meat. "I thought, at first impression, it was a half of a sheep,"[9] he said later. Closer inspection revealed the fallibility of that assumption. Fighting back the bile that surged up through him, Henry ran for help.

When the police arrived they found that the package comprised four sacks, each measuring approximately four feet by six feet three, tucked one inside the other. On one was stenciled the words "Joseph Rank, Premier Flour Mill, Victoria Docks." Inside the final sack, wrapped in a bloodstained sheet and some scraps of muslin, lay half a human body. It comprised a trunk and arms, but no head, hands, or legs. Gallows humorists present couldn't help but note that one of the muslin scraps was labeled "Argentina La Plata Cold Storage." Since these wrappings were damp rather than wet, it was assumed that the body had been dumped some time after the rain stopped at 4:30 A.M. This time frame was narrowed still further when a road sweeper reported that on his last cleaning visit to Regent Square at 6:15 A.M. the garden had been empty.

As the police extended their search of the garden, a second package, this time done up in paper, came to light. In it were the missing legs. According to the first medico-legal expert on the scene, police surgeon Dr. John Rees Gabe, who examined both the torso and the legs, "The remains were those of a woman about 30 years of age, well-nourished, some 4 ft. 11 in. in height. She had been the mother of several children. There was no trace of disease. She had apparently been dead about 24 hours."[10] Judging from the good-quality underclothes—a white embroidered silk chemise and a ribbed cotton slipover—the victim had come from a comfortable background.

One discovery did puzzle Gabe. Beneath the chemise was a brown paper bag, the type used for fruit. It had been folded in half, and across it, in angular writing, was scrawled "Blodie Belgiam [sic]." As news of this discovery filtered out to the rubberneckers who stood, noses pressed through the railings, it sparked off an angry reaction: obviously the killer had been some villainous Hun, incensed by Belgium's plucky determination to battle alongside Britain in the fight against "Kaiser Bill." Given the recent nightly bombardments, such xenophobia was as predictable as it was misplaced. Fortunately, the detectives investigating the crime were not so easily swayed. They needed to put a name to the body.

Spilsbury entered the case the next day when he was summoned to the Saint Pancras mortuary and asked to perform a full autopsy. He formed the opinion that the dissection showed signs of a skilled hand, not necessarily medical, more someone used to disarticulating carcasses, perhaps a butcher. The lower part of the legs had been severed at the knee joints, the head at the neck, and the arms separated at the wrist. He estimated the victim's height as 60½ inches, and that death had occurred at least forty-eight hours previously but not more than four days. There was bruising on the thighs and the right leg, probably the result of her struggle for life. He recorded that "the trunk of the body was wrapped in a torn white twill sheet, 8'4" × 6'6", nearly new,"[11] and it was this sheet that provided the breakthrough clue. Embroidered into the fabric with red cotton was a laundry mark, "II H." Details of the mark were circulated in the press.

Although evolving domestic patterns means that laundry marks are nowadays rarely seen, at one time they formed an invaluable source of identification for police forces, since every industrial laundry had its own distinctive logo. In this case, it was the proprietors of an establishment in Charlotte Street, a little over half a mile from where the body was found, who came forward to claim ownership of the mark.

Customer records at the laundry steered investigators north another half a mile or so to the eastern edges of Regent's Park, an area of faded tenement buildings, and to number 50 Munster Square. The rambling apartment house was typical of the district and overflowing with residents, one of whom was Madame Emilienne Gerard, who had not been seen since late on Wednesday night. Like thousands of her compatriots, this thirty-one-year-old Frenchwoman had taken refuge in

London at the outbreak of hostilities, eventually gravitating to this cosmopolitan neighborhood in April 1916.

By now overall control of the investigation resided in the hands of Chief Inspector Frederick Wensley, one of Scotland Yard's top detectives and a man destined to work alongside Spilsbury in some of the greatest murder cases of the age. He wasted little time. On the Saturday at 4:30 P.M., police officers descended on Munster Square.

The fact that Emilienne had not been seen for a couple of days had aroused no great suspicion amongst her neighbors. This was a laid-back, no-questions-asked kind of locality, popular with bohemians and transients alike. Mrs. Adelaide Chester, who also lived in the building, described the missing woman as round-faced, short, about five feet tall, with light curly hair, and on the plump side. Oh yes, and the back of her right hand was badly burnt and scarred. Emilienne was, said Mrs. Chester, sad by nature and sad by countenance; hardly surprising for a woman who had lost two children at an early age and whose husband was fighting on the western front. Mrs. Chester said Emilienne told her she was "in receipt of a separation allowance."[12]

Emilienne Gerard was born in Rouen and had married in 1910. Ever since the outbreak of war she had struggled to keep the marriage alive. Her infantryman husband had remained in their homeland, fighting for the French Army, and on more than one occasion she had been permitted to cross the Channel for visits. As Wensley delved further, whispers reached his ears that these trips served as a camouflage for her real purpose, carrying out espionage tasks for British intelligence. It added a nice romantic touch to what was an otherwise tawdry tale, though he never uncovered a jot of evidence to support these rumors.

According to Mrs. Chester, on the Wednesday night as the air raid began, she had yelled out a warning to other tenants in the building. Emilienne had not bothered opening her door at the time, just shouted back that she understood. By the time the all-clear had sounded and the other residents returned to Munster Square, Emilienne Gerard had vanished.

The landlady, Mary Rouse, let Wensley into the missing woman's flat. It was divided into two rooms, a dining/reception area that doubled as a bedroom, and a kitchen. And it didn't take any expert with a magnifying glass to spot the vivid streaks of blood in both rooms. When officers searched the drawers, they found six cotton sheets, all bearing that distinctive "II H" laundry mark. Another interesting find was an old-fashioned Gladstone bag with the initials L.V. tooled into the black leather.

Much the likeliest clarification of these initials came from a promissory note that lay on a table. It showed that, in August 1917, Emilienne had lent £50 to a Louis Voisin, repayable with £2 interest that the borrower had paid in advance. According to Mrs. Rouse, it was Voisin who paid the rent on Emilienne's apartment, and it was his photograph that stared down at Wensley from above the mantelpiece. He had a heavy-jawed, fleshy face, with deep-set eyes and extravagant mustaches that curved upward at the ends.

Coyly at first, then with greater liberty and license, the other residents opened up, admitting that Emilienne and Voisin had been lovers. Everyone agreed it had been a tempestuous relationship. Mrs. Chester recalled that just a few days before her disappearance, Emilienne had been arguing violently outside the building with Voisin, her shrill voice dominating the altercation. That quarrel in itself would have been sufficient to warrant further investigation of Voisin's whereabouts on the night in question, but when it was learned that he worked at Smithfield Market, the center of London's meat and butchery trade, the need to interview him took on added urgency.

It turned out that Louis Marie Joseph Voisin worked as a horse handler for Messrs. Green and Co., a firm of sausage makers in Smithfield Market, and that he usually worked shifts. Tracking him down wasn't difficult. That same Saturday evening, detectives raided a basement flat at 101 Charlotte Street in Soho, not far from the laundry, and there they found the fifty-year-old Voisin sitting in his kitchen with a woman named Berthe Roche, aged thirty-eight.

Both were French, and while Voisin could get by in broken English—
he had lived in London since 1913—Roche had no grasp of any language beyond her native tongue. Her reaction when confronted by the
police officers was a barrage of semicoherent gibberish that left the
newcomers bemused. Voisin, much surlier, impassive almost, watched
her ravings with Gallic disinterest. When he stood up from the table
he wasn't tall, but his chest was deep and he had large, meaty arms
made powerful from years of handling horse teams. The full-length
butcher's smock that he wore harked back to his time as an abattoir
worker. When asked to explain some bloodstained overalls that officers
found in his flat, he shrugged that he had recently slaughtered a calf
around the back of the flat, next to where he stabled the horses. This
also accounted, so he said, for the numerous blood splashes that
streaked the living room and kitchen.

Brutal Fight

While Voisin parried interrogators' questions, other officers went knocking on nearby doors. They reaped a rich harvest. Neighbors recalled
overhearing two women engaged in a ferocious argument late on the
night of October 31. So far as anyone could ascertain, the racket came
from Voisin's flat. Upon learning this, detectives arrested both Voisin
and Roche and took them to Bow Street police station for further
questioning.

Wensley conducted the interviews through an interpreter. Voisin's
first version of events had him denying all knowledge of Emilienne's
current whereabouts. He admitted knowing the missing woman for
eighteen months and that during this time she had acted as his housekeeper. He had last seen her on the afternoon of October 31, in the
company of a woman whom he knew only as "Marguerite." Emilienne
had explained that the pair were setting off that day for France, via
Southampton, and she had asked Voisin to feed her cat during her

absence. This he had done, thus accounting for her apartment key being in his pocket.

Enquiries showed that Emilienne had not been anywhere near Southampton on the day of her disappearance. Not only had she been seen near Munster Square when the air raid began, but a Georges Evrart also came forward to say that he and Emilienne had dined at the Commercial Restaurant in Soho that same evening until 10:30, and at no time had mention of Southampton or France cropped up in conversation.

Events took a decidedly ominous turn when it was realized that, at the time of her arrest, Roche was wearing a distinctive brooch fashioned from three small coins known to have belonged to the dead woman. (Other jewelry belonging to Emilienne was found in a secret recess in the bedroom mantelpiece.) Even when confronted with this, Roche persisted in her denials of ever having met Emilienne. All in French, of course. Privately, Wensley wondered whether Roche's professed ignorance of the English language was not just some ruse, seized upon to gain valuable thinking time and frustrate her interrogators. After all, she'd lived in England for sixteen years, and in 1914 she had married a Soho nightclub owner, also French, who'd subsequently left to fight in the war. After his departure, she'd managed to run the club by herself—dealing with English suppliers—and had only sold it upon learning that her husband had been killed in action.

Over the weekend the cracks in Voisin's story began to widen. According to Mrs. Rouse, on November 2 Voisin had called at the flat, ostensibly to feed the cat, as he claimed. During this meeting Voisin mentioned that Mme. Gerard would be away for a week or two, adding that she was expecting a sack of potatoes she wished to be stored in the kitchen. Wensley had a pretty good idea what that sack really contained.

Then came a major breakthrough. A bloodstained towel was found in Voisin's basement flat, and trapped within its fibers was a single earring identified as belonging to Emilienne. The taciturn Monsieur Voisin could offer no explanation for its presence. Nor could he explain why he had two of Emilienne's bank books, which together totaled £197, in his possession.

On the Sunday morning Wensley played his trump card. In a casual tone he asked Voisin if he had any objection to writing the words "Bloody Belgium." Voisin hesitated at first, then agreed. In his clumsy hand he spelt the two words as they were written on the piece of brown paper found with the body: "Blodie Belgiam." Five times Wensley asked him to repeat the procedure, and each time there was the same misspelling. Nor could there be any disguising that idiosyncratic, angular handwriting. At this point Wensley felt confident enough to charge Voisin and Roche with the murder of Emilienne Gerard. When the charge was translated to Roche, she launched into a hysterical tirade against her companion. Voisin, doleful to the point of near stupidity, merely muttered "C'est malheureux"[13]—"it is all most unfortunate."

The next day Wensley returned to Charlotte Street. In his hand was a bunch of keys taken from Voisin. One of these unlocked a cellar at the rear of the property, next to the basement kitchen. What Wensley found there prompted an urgent call to Spilsbury.

It was just before midday when the pathologist arrived. He was immediately escorted down to the dungeonlike cellar. Dipping his head to avoid the low, arched ceiling, Spilsbury squeezed his way to the rear, where some earthenware jars, baskets, and other ephemera stood alongside a large wooden barrel. The lid of the barrel had been removed. Inside, resting on a bed of sawdust and alum (a meat preservative), lay the head and the hands of a woman.

Spilsbury leaned in more closely. In the right ear was an earring, identical to that found in the bloodstained towel, while on the back of the right hand was the deep scarring, extending along the middle finger, that Emilienne Gerard's neighbor had talked about. With nothing more to be seen here, Spilsbury asked for the remains to be taken to the Saint Pancras mortuary, and there he began the grisly business of piecing the head, torso, legs, and hands back together. They all matched perfectly.

Next, Spilsbury needed to find out how Emilienne had died. So extensive were her injuries that he required no fewer than five of his cards to record them all. She had been struck repeatedly about the head with some kind of blunt instrument. Heavy defense bruises on her right hand were an ugly reminder of how she had fought in vain to fend off the murderous assault. Spilsbury counted at least eight blows—three or four of which would have led to unconsciousness—that had mashed the facial features to a bloody mess, yet failed to fracture the skull or extinguish the last breath in Emilienne's body. An attempt had been made at suffocation, most likely by the towel being stuffed into Emilienne's face.

The body was formally identified by the dead woman's husband. Paul Emmanuel Gerard had been granted compassionate leave to travel to England in his hour of bereavement. This ex–pastry cook turned soldier told Wensley how Emilienne had written to say that she had found a job waiting tables at a restaurant in Charlotte Street. He traced their marital problems back to December 28, 1916, when he had arrived unexpectedly in London from the fighting, only to find his wife and a stranger together at the apartment in Munster Square. The stranger turned out to be Louis Voisin. Over supper that night Voisin had tried to laugh off Gerard's suspicions, assuring him that he normally dined at Emilienne's restaurant, but on this, her night off, she had agreed to cook for him at home. Not even several glasses of wine could assuage Gerard's reservations, and when he returned to the trenches he did so with the heaviest of hearts. In May 1917, Emilienne had visited France and stayed for three months, seeing Gerard sporadically, but the magic had gone, and, at the end of July, she had wished him au revoir for the final time and caught the ferry back to Dover.

Upon hearing this, Wensley's ears perked up. Something that Roche had said. He leafed through her statements. There it was! Just eight days before her rival's unexpected return to England, Roche had moved into Voisin's filthy hovel. Was this, Wensley pondered, the spark that had ignited this tragedy?

In the meantime, Voisin, obviously rattled by the speed with which he had been tracked down and the discovery of his cellar's secrets, now cobbled together an alternative story. This version had him visiting Munster Square on November 1 to feed the cat as arranged, only to find Emilienne's door unlocked. Nervously, he entered the silent apartment. Imagine his horror when, in the bloodstained kitchen, he saw her head and hands wrapped in a flannel jacket and lying on the table. The rest of the body was missing. Fearing that he was the victim of a trap—he neglected to specify by whom it might have been laid—he panicked and, rather than call the police, attempted to clean up the blood, staining his clothes in the process. A quick dash back to Charlotte Street to wash and change was followed by a return to Munster Square to grab the head and hands. His third visit to Munster Square, the next day, had prompted the story of Mme. Gerard's absence and the sack of potatoes. Both were mere expedients, he confessed, fabricated to gain breathing space until he got in touch with Emilienne's husband.

However implausible the story might have sounded, it was not beyond the realms of possibility. Wensley now turned to Spilsbury. What did the physical evidence say? Was there anything to support Voisin's fantastical yarn?

Spilsbury began in the dead woman's apartment. There were small bloodstains on a cloth that covered the kitchen table, where Voisin claimed to have found the head and hands, and they extended up the wall, across the door, and onto the doorframe near the handle. In the bedroom he found more spots and smears. A white counterpane on the bed had a 3½-inch bloodstain in one corner, while the adjacent washstand, the rim of the basin, and the neck of a water jug all showed traces of what looked like blood.

All of these specimens, when subjected to the benzidine test,* reacted positively for blood by turning a deep blue, as Spilsbury expected.

---

* An organic chemical once used to detect the presence of blood, benzidine is nowadays little used because of its carcinogenic qualities.

But every minute he spent in the flat only hardened his belief that Voisin was lying through his teeth. He was certain that Emilienne Gerard had been killed and butchered elsewhere. At a conservative estimate, he reckoned Emilienne would have lost at least two pints of blood—almost 25 percent of her body's total—during the attack and the dissection. This was bloodletting on a grand scale. And nothing in the Munster Square flat suggested that it had hosted such carnage. In fact, everything about the amount and the siting of these bloodstains that Spilsbury now studied had a staged, downright phony appearance to them.

Blood Spatter Evidence

The basement of 101 Charlotte Street told an entirely different story. Here, the squalid back room resembled a slaughterhouse, and there was no faking the distinctive traces of low-velocity blood spatter that fly off a bludgeon's head as the assailant swings it repeatedly in a murderous arc. They painted a ghastly mosaic, up a wall, across the ceiling, onto one of the doors. Larger splashes of blood drenched the floor, then exited through the back door into a small yard before continuing on the wall outside. There were more stains in the kitchen—chiefly on the sink, the draining board, and the gas stove—but Spilsbury concluded that, most likely, these had occurred during the cleanup phase of the killing. The heavy concentration of blood by the back door hinted strongly that this was where the attack on Emilienne had begun, possibly as the terrified woman tried to make her escape. In the drawers and on the walls of the kitchen, Spilsbury found plenty of knives, saws, and other implements that could have inflicted the kind of sharp-bladed dismemberment he'd seen on the body.

Voisin shrugged off these revelations with a dull defiance. Nothing could shift him from his stubborn insistence that all the blood in his apartment was animal in origin, the legacy of that calf he had slaughtered on the Thursday morning. As unbelievable as this story may sound to modern ears, had he made this claim just a decade or so earlier, there is a strong possibility that he would have gotten away with murder.

Ever since Napoleonic times, scientists had searched for a test to determine whether stains or spots found at a crime scene or on a suspect were actually blood or whether they had some more innocent source. Empirical evidence soon taught them that blood quickly loses its typical color as it dries and ages, changing from red to brown, and later on it takes on a greenish yellow hue that in no way resembles blood. But these were just visual indicators and fell some way short of actually *proving* the presence of blood, or that the blood was human in origin.

The legal implications of such an impasse were maddening. Even if a murder suspect were caught literally red-handed, awash in fresh, unmistakable blood, all he or she had to do was claim that the stains had been acquired from some animal, and there was absolutely nothing the authorities could do to prove otherwise. No one will ever know how many killers in the eighteenth and nineteenth centuries managed to thumb their noses at justice courtesy of this loophole, but in 1901 the rules of the game changed forever.

After years of experimentation, a German scientist named Paul Uhlenhuth, working at the University of Greifswald, found that by injecting protein from a chicken's egg into rabbits, then mixing the rabbit serum with egg white, the egg proteins separated from the clear liquid to form a cloudy substance or precipitate. An extension of this process led him to explore the production of rabbit-based serums. His paper, "A Method for Investigation of Different Types of Blood, Especially for the Differential Diagnosis of Human Blood," was published by a German medical magazine on February 7, 1901. Included was the following rather laconic sentence: "It is noteworthy . . . that, after drying blood samples from men, horses and cattle on a board for four weeks and dissolving them in physiological NaCl [salt] solution, I was able to identify the human blood at once using my serum—a fact that should be of particular importance for forensic medicine."

With these few words, Uhlenhuth announced to the world that he had found the Holy Grail of serology: a definitive test for the presence of human blood.

Furthermore, Uhlenhuth's precipitin test worked even on old bloodstains and the tiniest traces. This was a revolutionary development, one of the greatest of all medico-legal advances, equal in importance to the discovery of fingerprint individuality and DNA profiling. Spilsbury used the precipitin test now to test several items found in Voisin's flat: a man's shirt and flannel jacket, and three pairs of butcher's overalls. All tested positive for the presence of human blood, as did a chopping board and a knife in the kitchen. A similar result was achieved on a hearth rug identified as originating from Munster Square found in the stable where Voisin kept his horse and trap, and this came with a bonus: Hairs trapped in the rug fibers were microscopically indistinguishable to those on the head of Emilienne Gerard.

These findings blew Voisin's story clean out of the water.

When confronted with the evidence of Spilsbury's experiments, the French horse handler remained impassive. He persisted in his version of events, though he was gracious enough to add, "I wish to make the declaration that Madame Roche is entirely innocent."[14]

Spilsbury seriously doubted this. To his experienced eye, everything pointed to Berthe Roche being a central player, maybe even the instigator of the murderous assault. In all likelihood, he thought, once the air raid began, Emilienne had run through the danger-filled streets to the apartment of her lover, desperate for shelter. Quite why she chose such a perilous stratagem must forever remain within the realms of conjecture, but jealousy surely played a part. In her heart of hearts she knew that Voisin's affections had swung toward another woman, and when she reached his flat these fears were confirmed in the worst possible way. For Voisin, lying in bed with Berthe, the sudden and violent hammering at his door, overlaid against the din of bombs dropping nearby, must have created a hellish scenario. And it only got worse.

Somehow Emilienne gained entrance to the flat, sparking off a dreadful argument between herself and Berthe. Neighbors could hear their shrieking even above the air raid's cacophony. Spilsbury always believed, as did Wensley, that it was the dangerously unstable Berthe who grabbed a poker or something similar and began clubbing her hated rival in the kitchen. All the head injuries that Emilienne sustained were disfiguring but not fatal. Spilsbury studied the hulking Voisin. In his younger days, the Frenchman had worked as a butcher, and was used to poleaxing cattle with a single blow. Such a man, caught in a murderous rage, would surely have crushed Emilienne's skull to pulp. Spilsbury reasoned that Berthe had beaten the screaming Emilienne to the ground, and that someone, probably Voisin, had grabbed the towel to stifle her screams, ripping out the earring in the process. Slowly the blood seeped out of her body, and slowly she died. Once she fell quiet, the dissection began.

Then came the botched cover-up. The following morning, Thursday, Berthe was seen in the back alley at the uncharacteristically early time of 8:30, drawing water from a tap. She told neighbors that Voisin had butchered a calf and she needed to clear up the mess. After midday, Voisin had visited Munster Square with the intention of making it appear as though the crime had taken place there. His rudimentary attempt to stage a crime scene had fooled no one, least of all Spilsbury. Before leaving, Voisin grabbed one of the bedsheets, which he took back to Charlotte Street and used to wrap the body.

Voisin's workmates at Smithfield Market recalled that on the Friday morning, Voisin had left work at 6:30, as usual, giving him plenty of time to get home by the tube, load the body onto his horse-drawn trap, then drive the mile or so to Regent Square. At 7:40 A.M. he was seen driving his trap in the direction of the square where the remains of Emilienne Gerard were found less than one hour later. When he dumped the body, he attempted to mislead any investigation by scrawling "Blodie Belgiam" on a brown paper bag, little dreaming that it would only worsen events for him.

Presumably at some point Voisin and Roche had intended disposing of the head and hands, only to be undone by the bewildering speed with which they had been apprehended.

At their trial, which began on January 2, 1918, both Voisin and Roche pleaded not guilty. The proceedings were desperately awkward and time consuming, with every scrap of testimony having to be translated into French for the defendants. Spilsbury was once again the premier Crown witness. At his suggestion, the kitchen door from 101 Charlotte Street was brought into court, and he used it to point out to the jurors the telltale streaks of blood. He told how he had tested fourteen different objects from Voisin's flat, and found human blood on all of them. Urged on by a grateful prosecution, he outlined his theory of how the attack had taken place and his belief that Emilienne had died on the kitchen floor.

Then came a bizarre sideshow. The jury asked if they could see 101 Charlotte Street, with Spilsbury as their guide. Mr. Justice Darling acceded to the unusual request, with the proviso that Spilsbury remain mute throughout the visit. Were he to speak outside the presence of the defendant, who remained in court, then that would amount to unfair testimony, leaving Darling no choice but to declare a mistrial.

At firsthand the jurors were able to inspect the hovel that Voisin called home. Spilsbury, the dumb director, could only point and gesticulate. As instructed, he remained silent throughout. When the cavalcade returned to court, the judge dropped a bombshell. In one of the most extraordinary judicial decisions that anyone could remember—and to the dismay of prosecutors and Spilsbury alike—Mr. Justice Darling instructed the jury that the charge of murder against Roche should be dismissed, on grounds that no proof existed to show she had participated in the death of Emilienne Gerard. She would later be charged with being an accessory after the fact.

This left Voisin to face the music unaccompanied. He did so with his customary stoicism. His most telling contribution was to reiterate his earlier declaration that "Mme. Roche is entirely innocent."[15] Three days into the trial, with all the testimony concluded, the judge began his summing up. He used it to hammer home the way that forensic science was changing forever the face of jurisprudence. Dealing with defense claims that the blood in Voisin's kitchen had come from a calf he had slaughtered, Darling told the jury, "It did not matter if he brought home the carcasses of a thousand calves. Not one drop of human blood would have come out of these."[16] It was the most emphatic confirmation possible that Spilsbury's use of the precipitin test had destroyed Voisin's defense.

After Voisin had been found guilty, Mr. Justice Darling, speaking first in French, then in English, sentenced the defendant to death. He took the news without any hint of emotion, merely replying, "I have to say I am innocent."[17] Spilsbury's unease about Voisin's solitary guilt was shared by Sir Basil Thomson, onetime head of CID, who, as recently released government records show, thought Roche equally culpable. "We could not prove that, but that is my belief."[18] (Those same records also reveal for the first time that in 1903, Voisin had been strongly suspected of murdering a Joseph Hardy, whose body was found in a river near Angers. Although eventually no charges were preferred, in all likelihood this incident colored the Home Secretary's decision not to reprieve Voisin.)

On the morning of March 2, 1918, Voisin paid the ultimate price on the gallows at Pentonville Prison. Just one day earlier, the other player in this lethal love triangle, Berthe Roche, had received seven years imprisonment for her part in the death of Emilienne Gerard. At times her courtroom testimony teetered on the brink of psychosis. Despite having lived in the flat for some months, she claimed never to have entered the kitchen where Spilsbury said the murder had been committed. Voisin had expressly forbade her access to the kitchen, she said, because "it was let to an old man,"[19] whom she described as having dyed black hair and a beard. Equally outlandish protestations that she had never seen Emilienne, alive or dead, also failed to impress the court. Once behind bars, Berthe Roche's frail grip on reality crumbled, and she went insane. The following year, on December 12, she succumbed to cervical cancer.

Spilsbury always was a compulsive collector of exhibits and memorabilia from his most infamous cases. Most of these found their way to the pathological museum at St. Mary's. Among them was a scrap of material with a brownish stain, which he kept in a cardboard box. The brownish color was blood, and the scrap of fabric came from the hearth rug found in the basement at Charlotte Street.

As this case and the conviction of Verney Asser make evident, by the end of World War I Spilsbury's status within the crime-fighting community had undergone a radical change. He was now valued as much for his detective skills as for his eminence as a pathologist. Where ordinary mortals failed, he was expected to provide answers, to reconstruct how crimes were committed, to be the final voice. While hardly a desirable state of affairs—after all, no one is immune from error—it does demonstrate the iconic reverence that Spilsbury was beginning to enjoy, especially at Scotland Yard. Police confidence in him, and his in himself, would now lead Spilsbury into the golden age of his career. Through no fault of his own, this was a path that he would tread alone.

Following the cessation of hostilities in November 1918 and his return to civilian life, William Willcox decided to abandon his formal rank as Home Office analyst—a position taken over by Webster—and devote his energies to rebuilding his private practice. For the remainder of his life, Willcox would continue to act as honorary medical adviser to the Home Office, but he always acted in the shadow of his former protégé. Spilsbury's coronation was duly approved by the press. With the war finally off the front pages, Fleet Street wasted little time in reviving prewar levels of crime reporting, and henceforth, so far as the press was concerned, Dr. Bernard Spilsbury was the undisputed superstar of British legal medicine.

He wouldn't have argued the point.

1 *Warminster Journal*, December 21, 1917, 2.
2 *Ibid.*, December 7, 1917, 4.
3 *Ibid.*, January 18, 1918, 3.
4 *Ibid.*
5 *Ibid.*
6 *Ibid.*
7 *Ibid.*
8 *Times*, February 19, 1918, 4.

9 *Ibid.*, November 7, 1917, 4.
10 *Ibid.*, November 3, 1917, 3.
11 *Ibid.*, November 5, 1917, 5.
12 *Ibid.*, November 6, 1917, 3.
13 *Ibid.*, November 21, 1917, 6.
14 *Ibid.*, January 3, 1918, 3.
15 *Daily Express*, January 3, 1918, 3.
16 *Times*, January 19, 1918, 3.
17 *Ibid.*
18 *Public Records Office*, HO 14/2183.
19 *Times*, March 1, 1918, 4.

CHAPTER FOUR

Arsenic Among the Weeds

When the armistice ending the Great War was signed at the eleventh hour of the eleventh day of the eleventh month of 1918, London, like every other major city in the Western world, erupted in a tumult of delirium. Bells chimed triumphantly, bands struck up and marched through the capital, pursued by cheering crowds of soldiers and civilians, fireworks exploded like benevolent bombs. These scenes of frenzied jubilation were duplicated right across the capital—except in one London mortuary. Even at this pivotal moment in history, Spilsbury permitted himself no break from his autopsy schedule. While the rest of the world went crazy, he was hard at work. The details were mundane—a man had died suddenly from heart failure following acute bronchopneumonia—but nothing more vividly portrays Spilsbury's unblinking devotion to duty. In truth, he was busier than at any time in his career; Britain was caught in the grip of Spanish flu. The global pandemic that would eventually claim more lives than the Great War itself—twenty million is the most conservative estimate—had first reached British shores in May 1918, and since that time victims had been dying at the rate of 4,000 per week. Without the benefit of modern refrigeration methods, it meant that bodies were either autopsied at once or not at all. Spilsbury did what he could, but like doctors everywhere, he was working round-the-clock.

Somehow he found time to make some urgent domestic readjustments. After several years of separation, interspersed only by fleeting visits, his family was once again reunited in their London home at Marlborough Hill. Edith soon found herself pregnant, and in the following August, their fourth child, Richard, was born.

Eventually, as abruptly as it had arrived, the Spanish flu vanished, taking with it more than a quarter of a million British lives, but as one battle ended so another began. Crime figures invariably surge in the aftermath of international conflicts, as home-coming soldiers struggle to adapt to the different rigors of civilian life, and Britain was no exception in the early 1920s. Violent crime particularly began to soar, and as the murder crime rate edged upward, detection rates strained to keep pace. This was especially true outside of London. Provincial police forces, lacking the experience and manpower of Scotland Yard's famed Murder Squad, often floundered when it came to homicide investigations. A case in point arose in 1919 when Elizabeth Ridgley, a fifty-year-old storekeeper from Hitchin, just north of London, was found dead on the morning of Monday, January 25. One of the neighbors, Louisa Roach, had heard a dog barking between 8:20 and 9:00 on the Saturday night, followed later by the sound of someone moaning around midnight, only to then dismiss both incidents from her mind until the Monday morning's grim discovery.

Mrs. Ridgley's body was found lying in the doorway between the kitchen and a passageway that connected to her general store on Nightingale Road. The back of her head was a matted, bloody mess; she had cuts to her face, a broken nose, and around her neck was tied a khaki handkerchief. Alongside her lay the cold, stiff body of her Irish terrier. Early indications suggested that the dog had been poisoned. On the floor nearby lay a four-pound weight, the kind used to measure out quantities of food. It was heavily encrusted with blood, and there appeared to be hairs, both human and canine, adhering to its surface.

Although a drawer-cum-cash-register was found yanked open and empty, because money turned up elsewhere in the house, local detectives rejected the notion that this might be a bungled robbery/murder. In fact, they spurned the idea that they were investigating any sort of crime at all, being convinced that Elizabeth Ridgley had died as the result of an accidental fall.

This rather startling conclusion owed much to the fact that, some months previously, Mrs. Ridgley had been found lying comatose in mysterious circumstances that were never fully explained. To skeptical police officers, this was merely a tragic repetition. Certainly there was a peculiar lethargy to the early investigation, which meandered without direction or purpose. But ruffled local sensibilities were not so easily smoothed, and demands began to build for some kind of outside assistance. Stubborn at first, the local police eventually caved in, swallowed a sizable chunk of humble pie, and contacted the Home Office. Such intransigence was nothing new. Turf wars between law enforcement agencies are as old as policing itself, and in England and Wales at this time, some provincial chief constables would rather have walked barefoot over hot coals than "call in the Yard." Fortunately in this instance, cooler heads prevailed.

By the time Chief Inspector Frederick Wensley assumed charge, much of the evidence had gone cold. Spilsbury didn't even get to see the body until more than a week had passed. What he found left no doubt in his mind that this was a case of murder. Mrs. Ridgley's skull had been crushed by four blows to the back of the head, while a string of ugly bruises ran across her back and arms. He judged that the assault had occurred as the woman lay facedown in the doorway, and that she had, at some point, been dragged across the floor by her hair. Since there were no signs of strangulation—no fractured hyoid bone in the throat, or petechiae in the face or eyes—he suspected that the khaki handkerchief had most probably been used as a gag rather than a ligature and that it had slipped down in the struggle. Cause of death was hemorrhaging from the fractured skull. Saddest of all was Spilsbury's belief that the woman had probably lived for several hours after the attack. Had the neighbor been just a tad more inquisitive, then medical assistance on the Saturday night might have saved Mrs. Ridgley's life.

The deeper that Spilsbury dug, the more examples of investigative ineptitude he uncovered. For instance, his examination showed that the dog, far from being poisoned, had also sustained a fractured skull. Despite the presence of the bloodstained weight, Spilsbury wasn't prepared to state categorically that it was the murder weapon, only that it might have been.

Within days of taking over the inquiry, Wensley made an arrest. John Healy, aged thirty-three, was a laborer who lodged at Radcliffe Road, just around the corner from Mrs. Ridgley's store. Barbara Smith, the daughter of his landlady, remembered seeing Healy outside Mrs. Ridgley's store at around 8:15 on the night in question. She further recalled that he'd staggered in that night at 10:30, blind drunk, and, most unusually for him, went straight to bed. The following morning when he came down for breakfast, his hand was bandaged.

In Healy's room, the police discovered a wealth of ostensibly incriminating evidence: a jacket with blood inside the right sleeve and blood smears inside a right-hand trouser pocket. There was also a belt with blood near the buckle. Of the three shirts that Healy possessed, one was stained with blood, as were two bedsheets. At the time of his arrest on February 15, Healy had a deep cut on one finger and six £1 notes in his possession.

Healy denied all knowledge of the crime. He swore that the injury had happened at work, and the money was the residue from a small wartime service gratuity awarded him by the British government on January 31. Official records did corroborate this claim.

Other circumstances darkened the case against Healy. Just one day before the attack, he had stormed off his construction job after an argument over some unpaid wages. This was particularly significant since he'd owed his landlady back rent, which he paid a day or so later.

He told Wensley that the money had come from the government gratuity. Even though the case was borderline at best, Healy found himself standing trial for murder.

At the trial, which began June 17, Spilsbury gave his opinion that tears found on a pair of Healy's trousers might have been made by the dog, as might the faint traces of a bite mark found on Healy's left buttock at the time of his arrest. It was good evidence, but it wasn't the implacable Spilsbury that the courts had come to expect. Many have criticized Spilsbury for his uncompromising self-certainty on the witness stand—and, yes, once his mind was definitely made up he could be as immovable as Everest—but examine his record more closely, go beyond the headline cases, and numerous examples surface of Spilsbury's admitting to misgivings if the circumstances warranted it. This was just such a case. He knew it had been a botched investigation. More importantly, so did the judge, Mr. Justice Darling, who remarked caustically that "every precaution seems to have been taken in the early days to ensure that nobody should be detected."[1]

In his summing up, Darling piled on the sarcasm, saying, "The worst way in which to investigate a case is to make up one's mind how a thing happened, and then look about for evidence afterwards."[2] With prompting like this from the bench, the jury needed only a few minutes to return a verdict of not guilty. No one else was ever charged with the murder of Elizabeth Ridgley, and it remains officially unsolved. But both Spilsbury and Wensley always wondered what the outcome might have been had they been involved right from the beginning.

The year of 1920 brought problems of an entirely different kind for Spilsbury: jealousy. As his influence and celebrity grew, some of those around him became bitterly resentful. To this day, no one is prepared to divulge the full circumstances—if anyone still knows—of the feud that drove Spilsbury to turn his back on St. Mary's, but the flash point came when a fellow faculty member asked Spilsbury to preserve a specimen for him. Spilsbury, feeling the specimen was unworthy of preservation, declined and gave his reasons. A furious row ensued, with the other person demanding that Spilsbury accede to his wishes. By this stage of his career, Spilsbury was unused to having his decisions even questioned, let alone being treated like some laboratory flunky, and he demanded an apology. When this was not forthcoming, he went through the roof.

To his dying day, Willcox regretted not being asked to mediate in the dispute. Nobody knew Spilsbury better than he, and certainly no one would have been better placed to defuse the volatile situation. Instead he remained stranded on the sidelines, as what started out as a professional disagreement degenerated into a brutal vendetta. The matter was referred to the hospital's board of governors. But on November 18, 1920, Spilsbury forestalled their decision and severed all connection with the institution that he had called home for the past twenty years. Even when the governors subsequently sided with Spilsbury and ordered the other party to apologize, it made no difference; Spilsbury's mind was made up, and that was very much that. He received the apology with the same icy reluctance with which it was given, and it is said that the two protagonists never again spoke outside of professional matters. Walking out of St. Mary's for the last time must have been a terrible wrench for Spilsbury, but one that he bore with his customary fortitude. Besides, he already had his next position lined up: a short move across town to St. Bartholomew's Hospital and the post of lecturer on morbid anatomy and histology.

With its 800 years of history, St. Bart's might have been the oldest teaching hospital in London, but in terms of medico-legal status and gravitas, it languished some distance behind St. Mary's. The hiring of Spilsbury was supposed to make good the deficiency. As it turned out, his addition to the faculty did little to bolster the pathology school's lackluster exam results. Spilsbury was not a natural or even a very good teacher. He had a flat, impersonal lecture style—strong on substance, short on interest—that students found all too easy to ignore. But this deficiency told only part of the story. Frequent absences on Home Office duties inevitably ate into his faculty responsibilities. All too often Spilsbury found himself caught in the middle of a tug-of-war: St. Bart's on one side and the whole British crime-fighting apparatus on the other. It was no contest. The police were not prepared to abandon what had become their most powerful weapon. They needed Spilsbury's expertise on call at all times. And in January 1922, they needed his talents more than ever; something very murky, indeed, had emerged on the Welsh borders.

The facts had come into focus the preceding Christmas Eve, when the director of public prosecutions, Sir Archibald Bodkin, had called at Willcox's surgery in Welbeck Street to discuss suspicions that a solicitor in Wales had attempted to poison a rival, and might even have poisoned his wife. Willcox was incredulous. Why, it was only twelve months or so since he had given evidence at the trial of *another* Welsh solicitor, Harold Greenwood, also accused of wife murder! On that occasion, inspired advocacy from the defense counsel, Sir Edward Marshall Hall, KC, had won a startling "not guilty" verdict. Bodkin didn't want any more fiascoes.

His consultation with Willcox resumed the day after Christmas, and this time lasted for several hours. Willcox studied depositions, police reports, statements from local doctors, and a long report from Scotland Yard that had been compiled in secret. At the end of the meeting, Bodkin stood up, ready to depart. "What about it?"[3] he asked.

As always, Willcox weighed his words like gold dust before speaking. What he would say resulted in British legal history being made.

Armstrong Arrives in Town

Herbert Rowse Armstrong was thirty-six years old when he moved to the small town of Hay on the England-Wales border in 1906. Nowadays this picturesque hamlet in the Wye Valley is internationally renowned for its antiquarian bookshops and annual literary festival, but when Armstrong arrived, it was a drowsy little backwater where not much of anything ever happened. Armstrong would change all that. Plymouth-born and Cambridge-educated, he had more than a decade's legal experience behind him when he took up a position as managing clerk for an elderly solicitor named Edmund Cheese. He settled in quickly and, with his finances in good order and prospects bright, was at last able to marry his longtime fiancée Katherine Friend, a printer's daughter, also from his home county of Devon. For five years the couple lived in a modest-sized house in the nearby village of Cusop; then in 1912—with Armstrong now a full partner in Cheese & Armstrong—they moved to a far grander property called Mayfield, which came with a retinue of servants. Shortly after this they had their first child; two more followed in quick succession.

Armstrong was a walking paradox. To the world at large, he was a neatly made, dapper fellow, bursting with that air of rather strained confidence that so often hallmarks the small man. He dressed expensively and well, and exuded a strutting self-esteem that owed much to his role as a reservist officer in the Territorial Army. At home it was a different story. Here he was cowed and submissive, like a whipped dog. Katherine ran the house with iron-fisted malice. Husband, children, shopkeepers, servants, all felt the lash of her acid tongue, though most of her venom was directed at the hapless Armstrong. Told what to eat, what to drink, where and when he could smoke, constantly rebuked in front of the servants and friends, his life became insufferable. His only escape from Katherine's bullying was Mayfield's large garden. Even here he was beset with problems. Weeds. Dandelions, mostly. To combat their rampant spread, he, like most other contemporary gardeners, treated them with arsenic, in his case purchased from the local pharmacist.

As it did for everyone, 1914 brought huge changes to Armstrong. First, in April, old Edmund Cheese died and was followed to the grave within twenty-four hours by his wife. This unexpected vacuum allowed Armstrong to become sole proprietor of the practice. The future had never seemed so bright. And then the world exploded. Like most of his countrymen, Armstrong volunteered for war service. His age, though, told against him, and he was restricted to a reserve position in the Territorial Army. This didn't prevent him spending some time in France, where, freed from the suffocating restraints of life at Mayfield, he appears to have enjoyed himself immensely. Everything points to this being the time when Armstrong's carnal juices began to flow. What we do know is that, after the armistice, when he returned to Hay to pick up the threads of his life, the little solicitor was not a happy man.

Absence had done nothing to improve Katherine's vile temper. She managed to find fault in everything that Armstrong did. Even his greatest perk from the war—an official sanction permitting him to retain his wartime rank of major—backfired horribly. At dinner parties Katherine's stentorian cry of "No wine for the Major!"[4] was an oft-heard and much-mimicked cry on the Hay social scene. Armstrong, being Armstrong, meekly complied and sipped his cordial. Defiance was not an option. Although in many respects Katherine was a devoted wife and mother, and much esteemed locally, her overbearing bossiness did sway most observers to naturally sympathize with her henpecked husband.

As if home life were not trouble enough, Armstrong also found headaches at work. Directly opposite from his office in Broad Street lay the premises of Hay's only other solicitor, Robert Griffiths, who had just recently taken on an energetic young partner, Oswald Martin. This was a pride-wounding development for Armstrong. For years he'd dreamed of amalgamating the two practices, thereby creating a lucrative monopoly on legal advice in the area; now, overnight, those plans had blown up in his face. Even worse, Martin turned out to be a real hotshot. Unusually for a small-town solicitor he knew the income tax laws inside out and was especially adept in drawing up trusts and other Treasury-defeating instruments. Soon, farmers and businessmen alike were flocking to his office, all searching for ways to reduce their crippling postwar tax liabilities. Martin's success at tackling the Revenue had a knock-on effect: not only did the locals entrust him with their tax returns, they now also instructed him in the more mundane matters of land conveyancing and will making—the very core of Armstrong's fast-dwindling business.

In truth, the major had always struggled to make his mark in the community. Like Martin, he was an outsider, and there the resemblance ended. In business discussions, Armstrong's bumptious tone really grated on the nerves, while his younger rival's affable, altogether more easygoing manner cut easily through the barrier that often exists between lawyer and layperson. One thing was certain: Martin's arrival triggered an alarming decline in Armstrong's fortunes, and without his wife's private annual income of £2,000, he would have struggled to keep up Mayfield and its large, expensive staff.

Thoroughly chastened by events both domestic and business, in the late spring of 1920 Armstrong began manufacturing reasons to absent himself from Hay. Mainly these trips were to London, where, freed from the oppressive and censorious gaze of village life, the henpecked major shook off his inhibitions. He revived an acquaintance with a woman whom he'd first met in 1915 while on army service. Since this liaison apparently never developed beyond the platonic, as subsequent events made plain, Armstrong obviously used these jaunts to find other ways to satisfy his burgeoning sexual curiosity.

In between these excursions to London a strange event occurred. On July 8, 1920, out of the blue, Armstrong rewrote his wife's will. Under her original testament, made three years earlier, she had bequeathed her husband £50 per annum until 1933, and thereafter £100 annually. The residue (apart from certain minor bequests) was left to her children. Under the terms of this new will, which was irregularly witnessed by two servants who did not actually see Katherine sign the document, the children were pointedly excluded from any legacy, as her husband became the sole beneficiary and executor. Although it was never proved categorically that Armstrong forged this will, all the evidence suggests that he was both author and signatory of the document.

Another curious development at this time was a sudden explosion in Armstrong's horticultural problems, if his purchases of arsenic-based weed killer from the local pharmacy were anything to go by. On August 4 he bought three cans of powdered weed killer, to top up the four gallons he'd bought the preceding May. Coincidentally, it was around this time that Katherine's physical and mental health suddenly went into free fall. She had always been a hypochondriac, but there was no faking the violent biliousness that first began on August 15. Even more alarming were the episodes of delusional behavior, mixed with feelings of guilt and abject inferiority, that accompanied these attacks. So precipitous was this decline that her doctor, Thomas Hincks, had little hesitation in signing forms that committed her to the Barnwood Asylum in Gloucester.

Although Armstrong acted the dutiful husband, visiting his wife regularly, acquaintances in Hay couldn't help but notice a decided loosening in his behavior. He drank alcohol at social functions, even smoked in public, and there were mild complaints from some flushed females that, after a cocktail or two, the major's approaches were rather less than gentlemanly. All in all, Armstrong seemed to be relishing his newfound freedom.

So it came as something of a shock when, during January 1921, he petitioned the asylum to release his wife in order that she might return to Mayfield. Even more intriguing was the fact that, just eleven days before Katherine's homecoming, Armstrong had purchased a quarter of a pound of arsenic. The local pharmacist who'd sold Armstrong the arsenic had briefly marveled at the unseasonable vigor of Mayfield's weeds in the middle of winter, and then just as quickly banished the thought from his mind.

Agonizing Death

The improvement Katherine had shown in the asylum didn't endure. Inside a month she was worse than ever, fighting for her life, bed-bound, vomiting, raddled with diarrhea. On February 22, at the age of forty-seven, her tortured, frail body finally gave out. (Armstrong's sole diary entry for that day read, "K. died.") Dr. Hincks certified the cause of death as gastritis, noting heart disease and nephritis as contributory factors. Three days later, Katherine was buried in the churchyard at Cusop.

After her death, life at Mayfield went on very much as before, except that Armstrong was now master in his own home, and he had an extra

£2,278—the proved amount of Katherine's will—in his bank account. It should have been the best of times. Unfortunately for Armstrong, a new and potentially ruinous problem had reared its ugly head.

It concerned a long-running land transaction that dated back to the fall of 1919. At that time Armstrong, acting for the vendor in the sale of a local estate, had taken a deposit of £500, pending the outcome. A completion date set for February 1920 came and went, as did several more throughout the remainder of that year. Every time the transaction was on the verge of being sewn up, Armstrong would conjure up some legal spanner to throw into the works, or so it seemed.

When one of the prospective purchasers died in July 1921, his frustrated former partners decided to switch solicitors. They settled on Oswald Martin. He enjoyed no more success with Armstrong than had his predecessors. Every approach was rebuffed. Eventually, the purchasers, their patience exhausted, set a deadline: either complete by October 20, or the deal was off and the deposit would have to be refunded. With the seller desperate to sell, and the buyer eager to buy, it should have been a done deal. Except that Armstrong again dragged his feet. When the deadline passed unmet, Martin flew into a temper. He immediately sent Armstrong a registered letter canceling the deal and demanding the return of the deposit. (With the Hay grapevine already humming with rumors of Armstrong's financial difficulties, Martin privately wondered if the £500 had disappeared into his rival's personal account.)

Armstrong's response was to contact Martin and invite him round to his house to discuss the matter over tea and scones.

The meeting took place on the evening of October 26. Armstrong was congeniality personified, pouring out the tea and handing Martin a buttered scone with the apology, "Excuse fingers."[5] Martin, somewhat taken aback by the culinary indiscretion, took the scone anyway. Amazingly, Armstrong then managed to navigate his way through the rest of the meeting without once mentioning the disputed land sale, and when Martin left at a few minutes past 6:30 he was none the wiser as to the possible outcome.

Fretful and frustrated, Martin returned home to work on some documents with his clerk. An hour or so later, a strange gnawing sensation started deep in his belly. By 9:15 he was prostrated in the bathroom, doubled over with pain, pulse racing wildly, awash with sweat. Martin's agony lasted all through the night. When Dr. Hincks called early the next day, he diagnosed "a bilious attack brought on by overwork and lack of exercise."[6]

News of Martin's illness whistled through the close-knit community. Later that morning, and repeatedly throughout the day, Armstrong pestered Martin's office, constantly inquiring after his health. He was equally solicitous the following morning, when he made the short journey to Martin's house. When told by Constance Martin that her husband was much better, Armstrong's eyes began to blink furiously behind his spectacles, and he blurted out, "Oh! Better?"[7] Mrs. Martin thought she detected an element of surprise. Armstrong left without seeing his stricken colleague, promising—rather oddly, given the circumstances—to do everything in his power to ease Martin's professional obligations.

Over the next few days, Martin responded well to Hincks's treatment. Well enough for him to return to work on November 1.

By then, though, events in Hay had begun to gather pace.

The catalyst for this activity was Martin's father-in-law, John Davies, who just happened to be the pharmacist who'd sold all that arsenic and weed killer to Armstrong over the past few years. At the time of Katherine's death, Davies had felt a vague tremor of unease, though not sufficient to mention to anyone else. On the morning of October 27, hearing that his son-in-law had been laid low after visiting Armstrong, Davies could bottle up his suspicions no longer. He went straight round to Hincks's surgery and unburdened himself. When Hincks declared his belief that Martin had suffered nothing more than a bilious attack, Davies wasn't convinced. "Are you sure he has not been poisoned? I must put you on your guard because it is always easy to be wise after the event."[8]

Hincks tried to brush off Davies's concerns as unthinkable—for God's sake, man, solicitors don't go round poisoning their colleagues!—but the pharmacist was not someone easily deflected. He went to see Martin for himself. One glance at the stricken man, doubled up over the toilet, retching horribly, convinced Davies that this was a case of poisoning, and he warned the couple against accepting any further invitations to Armstrong's house, or even accepting any gifts from him.

At this the Martins exchanged nervous glances. Constance explained: on September 20, an anonymous package, with a postmark too faint to read, had arrived at their house. Wrapped in brown paper, it contained no message, just a one-pound box of Fuller's chocolates that appeared to have been opened and resealed, judging from the haphazard way the ribbon had been retied. After eating a couple of chocolates from the box, they had set the gift to one side. It was next produced on the evening of October 8, when the Martins hosted a dinner for some relatives. After the meal Martin's sister-in-law helped herself to the proffered chocolates. No one else partook. That night Dorothy Martin was violently ill, with a racing pulse and high fever, and only recovered after days of misery. Like Martin's, her illness had been diagnosed as a bilious attack.

By chance the Martins had kept the remaining chocolates, and when Davies examined them he found two that showed obvious signs of tampering. Chocolates in hand, he returned to Hincks's surgery. When confronted by this, Hincks immediately dug out the medical literature on poisoning. Like most GPs he had no practical experience of toxicology, and what he read confirmed Davies's suspicions: Oswald Martin displayed all the symptoms of arsenical poisoning. Reading further, he noted numerous similarities to the mysterious ailment that had afflicted Katherine Armstrong before she had been committed to Barnwood, and her recurrent illness upon returning home.

At Davies's urging, Hincks took a urine sample from Martin, and on October 31, this was sent to the Clinical Research Association in London for analysis. After some inexplicable and inexcusable bureaucratic procrastination, the urine sample and the chocolates were eventually sent to the H.O. analyst, John Webster.

All through November and into December a lethal game of cat and mouse was played out across Broad Street in Hay. Almost daily, Armstrong peppered Martin with invitations to tea. Thinking up diplomatic and nonsuspicious reasons why he could not attend became a full-time ordeal for Martin, whose nerves soon began to fray under the pressure.

Davies and Hincks, too, needed to tread carefully. If Armstrong was guilty, they could not afford to alarm him. On the other hand, if he was innocent and news broke about their behind-the-scenes maneuvering, then both faced professional and financial ruin. Falsely accusing a solicitor of attempted murder could result in a career-terminating damages award if it went to a civil action.

After an anxious month for all concerned, Webster's report came back on December 3: he'd found $1/33$ of a grain of arsenic in the urine—not a huge amount, but more than normal—and evidence that, of the thirty-two remaining chocolates, two had indeed been tampered with. Each had been injected with more than two grains of arsenic each, a fatal dose for most adults. Deeply suspicious though this might have been, there still wasn't a shred of evidence to connect Armstrong to the lethal package. Clearly, the authorities still needed to proceed with the utmost caution.

On December 9, Hincks was summoned to a meeting with officials from the director of public prosecutions (DPP). During this interview, Hincks, ashen-faced and with his nerves almost shattered by the clandestine events of the past six weeks, blurted out that Armstrong was mentally abnormal, someone who kept a revolver at the side of his bed, a homicidal maniac. "If he gets to know about the police inquiries he might murder himself, his children and me."[9]

However grandiloquent Hincks's description of Armstrong's mental state might have sounded, it was rooted in more than mere hysteria. For the past year he had been treating the major for syphilis, and he feared that the disease might have driven Armstrong mad. In this re-spect Hincks was guilty of blatant overreaction and poor medicine. Mental deterioration due to GPI (general paralysis of the insane) is a side effect of syphilis that manifests itself only after many years of in-fection, and Hincks knew better than anyone—patient excepted—that Armstrong's infection dated from the time of his wife's incarceration, just twelve months previously.

During this course of treatment the major did let slip one revealing comment. While being injected one day, he asked if the shot contained any arsenic and, when told that it did, queried Hincks as to what might constitute a fatal dose. "Two or three grains," the doctor replied, in-stantly provoking an astonished expression from Armstrong, who said, "Wouldn't one be enough?"[10] Hincks, amused more than surprised, shook his head. In light of subsequent events, that interlude now as-sumed a new, more sinister quality.

Whilst sufficient evidence existed for the DPP to proceed in the matter of Martin's poisoning, the case was by no means ironclad. To strengthen its hand, it wanted proof that Armstrong had poisoned his wife as well, and for that it needed confirmation that her symptoms prior to death were consistent with arsenical poisoning. Hence Archibald Bodkin's visit to Willcox over Christmas 1921.

Of all the medico-legal experts attached to the Home Office, Will-cox was the most experienced clinically and had made a special study of toxicology. Just six months earlier, national recognition for Willcox's immense contribution to forensic medicine had come in the form of a knighthood. It would be his call. Bodkin waited anxiously.

At long last Willcox raised his eyes from the bundle of paperwork and nodded. "Mrs. Armstrong undoubtedly died of acute arsenical poisoning,"[11] he said.

This was all Bodkin needed. On New Year's Eve, Chief Inspector Alfred Crutchett, together with two other officers, traveled to Hay and strode into Armstrong's office. The major seemed surprised to see them. Surprise turned to jaw-dropping incredulity when told that he was being arrested on suspicion of having attempted to poison his rival solicitor, Oswald Martin. "I am quite innocent,"[12] he protested. When asked to turn out his pockets, Armstrong sheepishly handed over a small folded sachet. It contained white powder. Analysis showed it to be arsenic, 3¾ grains in all, more than enough for a lethal dose. When Armstrong's house was searched, twenty more of these lethal little packets were discovered.

The news that one of Hay's most prominent citizens had been arrested for attempted murder hit the little town like a thunderbolt, as did the revelation next day that no less a personage than Dr. Bernard Spilsbury would supervise the exhumation of Katherine Armstrong's body.

Dusk in the Graveyard

Darkness had already fallen by the time Spilsbury arrived at Cusop graveyard on January 2, 1922. Those who knew the pathologist well might have detected a slight stoop in his previously ramrod-straight frame. The hardships of his job—the relentless traveling and harrowing investigations such as this, carried out in the bitterest weather, often in the middle of the night—had started to take their toll on his health. His lower back was knotted up in constant pain, and he had begun to lose his sense of smell. This latter affliction proved to be a double-edged sword. On the one hand it allowed him to work in conditions that others found physically sickening; the trade-off came with a diminished capacity to differentiate between the dreadful but informative odors that can emanate from a dead body.

But Spilsbury came from the old school, trained from childhood not to betray emotions or pain, and standing now, at seven o'clock on a freezing January night in a snow-filled Welsh graveyard, there was little to suggest the discomfort he was feeling. Beyond the cemetery walls reporters and townspeople jostled for a better view of the eerie scene, as hurricane lamps flickered through the sacking screens that had been erected around the open grave of Katherine Armstrong.

Spilsbury studied the oak coffin in situ and was struck by the new-ness of its appearance. A little polish had gone; other than that it looked funeral-parlor fresh, with no sign of disintegration. He gave a nod to the sexton, and ropes were threaded beneath the casket, which was then slowly raised. At Spilsbury's direction, a police officer lowered himself gingerly into the grave and began scraping soil samples into specimen jars. Once the coffin had been formally identified by the undertaker, it was placed on a hand bier and trundled to a nearby cot-tage that had been readied for the purpose.

Onlookers bared their heads as the ghostly cortege passed in the darkness. Inside the cottage more sacking obscured the windows to keep out prying eyes. Because there was no heating or light, except the handheld lamps, Spilsbury decided against performing an autopsy that night. When he announced that he would complete his examination the next day, the cottage was cleared of officials, the door locked, and a police guard posted to dissuade any overzealous spectator from sneak-ing a closer look at the coffin.

The following day at 10 A.M. Spilsbury returned. Alongside him were Hincks and Dr. William Ainslie, another local practitioner on hand to represent Major Armstrong. All three watched silently as the coffin lid was unscrewed. The face of the corpse was hidden by a hand-kerchief, the trunk and limbs were covered with the coffin lining, and a towel lay over the legs and feet. Removal of these items revealed a body clothed in a partially rotted nightdress and stockings.

As in any exhumation, the legal niceties had to be observed. Formal identification of the body fell to Humphrey Vines Webb, the under-taker. There could be no mistaking Katherine Armstrong's prominent teeth or the long plaits of dark hair tied with light-colored ribbon that lay on either shoulder. Once Hincks confirmed the identification, the way was clear for Spilsbury to begin. Oblivious to the abominable con-ditions, the substandard lighting, the cramped space, little ventilation, and nonexistent washing facilities, Spilsbury was instantly absorbed. He began, as always, with a full-body visual examination. Although the exposed parts of the corpse showed considerable decomposition—

the eyeballs had collapsed, and the soft tissue on the hands and feet was gone—the corpse was virtually intact, even after eleven months in the ground. Testifying later in court, he would say, "The body of Mrs Armstrong was in an unusually well-preserved condition . . . The external appearance was that of a body which had shrunken from loss of fluid and which was undergoing mummification rather than that of a body in which putrefaction was taking place in the normal manner."[13]

Visual inspection over, it was time to open up the body.

Assistants removed the cadaver from the coffin and placed it on a trestle table. Spilsbury wasted no time. Starting with the head, he found that the hair came away easily, and the right plait was immediately removed and placed in a bottle. Inside the cranial vault, the brain had turned to a soft, greenish pulp, with no signs of disease. At each step of the way, Spilsbury placed samples in his jars for future analysis.

Next, he opened the chest cavity to reveal the heart and lungs. The heart was slightly reduced in size, and there was some thickening of the mitral valve and slight disease of the aorta, but nothing that would have hastened death. He found fluid in the lungs, which were also marginally undersized, and again he took samples. No disease was detected.

It was the same story with the liver and kidneys; some fatty degeneration, nothing out of the ordinary. The stomach was normal in size and contained a small amount of fluid, as did the large and small intestines.

Spilsbury worked with his customary deftness, totally engrossed, wielding his scalpel with artistic efficiency. Right or left hand, it made no difference. Since childhood, when an accident had slightly impaired the use of his right arm, he had been ambidextrous. Unlike some later pathologists, who boasted of completing a full autopsy in ten minutes flat, Spilsbury always took his time, studying, dissecting, taking samples, committing every detail to memory for notation later on those ubiquitous little white cards. Sometimes the clock ticked on for hours. But he would not be rushed. Those who engaged his services did so at bargain-basement rates, and the biggest beneficiary of all was the Home Office. For an annual retainer of £100 and just over £3 per autopsy, plus traveling expenses, they enjoyed the services of not just the world's premier pathologist but an unbeatable expert witness. It was quite a deal.

Had Hincks and Ainslie known how poorly recompensed Spilsbury was for his services, their already dumbstruck admiration might have been greater still. As it was, they watched like fascinated schoolboys as the great man worked. When it was done, Spilsbury stood back and announced himself finished.

He informed Hincks that there was nothing organic to account for the wretched vomiting and diarrhea that had ravaged Katherine Armstrong in her final hours. This was not intended as a slight on Hincks's professional expertise. Arsenic is a lethal mimic. Because its symptoms replicate those of so many illnesses, without organic analysis it is impossible to say that someone has ingested arsenic. While a corpse in unusually pristine condition may be an indicator of arsenical poisoning, this is only evident after months or even years of interment. And because very few doctors expect their patients to be poisoned, Hincks, like countless other physicians before and since, acted on the visible symptoms and diagnosed accordingly. Where his true qualities really shone through was when, presented with all the circumstantial evidence regarding Armstrong's weed killer purchases and the results of the laboratory analysis, he had the common sense and, more importantly, the courage to seek more expert opinion.

Those organs surplus to analytical requirements were replaced inside the body, which was then stitched and returned to the coffin. Spilsbury gathered his samples together—six jars of bodily samples, sawdust and shavings from the coffin, and the aforementioned samples of soil adhering to the coffin—then hurried off to catch his train back to London that night. He always seemed to be in a rush. The sexton and undertaker were equally busy. Even before Spilsbury's train chugged out of the station, they had returned Katherine Armstrong's body to the cold ground of Cusop cemetery.

When Spilsbury reached Paddington, despite the lateness of the hour, he went straight round to nearby St. Mary's, where he handed over the samples to Webster for analysis. The schism between Spilsbury and his alma mater had in no way affected his warm relations with most faculty members, as was further evidenced later that same night when, just before retiring to bed, Spilsbury phoned Willcox at home to discuss his findings. What he had to say must have comforted the older man. Gut instinct—and it could be nothing more until Webster's results were back—allowed Spilsbury to tell Willcox that he had been right: Katherine Armstrong had died from arsenical poisoning.

On the day that Spilsbury autopsied Mrs. Armstrong, the dead woman's husband was arraigned on a charge of attempting to murder Oswald Martin. In the packed little courtroom where Armstrong had spent so much of his professional life, he heard the Crown state ominously that further charges might be levied against the prisoner, who was remanded in custody.

Now it was up to Webster and his new assistant, Dr. Gerald Roche Lynch. Could they find any trace of poison in Katherine Armstrong's organs? It is a sobering thought that, for most of recorded history, arsenic, like all poisons, was completely untraceable in the human body. Such anonymity means that no one can even hazard a guess as to how many unsuspected victims of arsenical poisoning lie buried in the world's graveyards. The first great toxicological breakthrough came in the late eighteenth century when a chemist named Johann Metzger discovered that if substances containing arsenic were heated and a cold plate held over the vapors, a white layer of arsenious oxide would form on the plate. While this "arsenic mirror" could establish whether food had been laced with arsenic, it could not tell if a body had already absorbed arsenic.

The solution to this problem came a few years later when Dr. Valentine Rose at the Berlin Medical Faculty took a human stomach with its contents, cut them up, and boiled them into a kind of stew. After filtering the stew to remove any traces of flesh, he treated the liquid with nitric acid. This converted any arsenic present into arsenic acid, which could then be subjected to Metzger's "mirror" in the usual way.

But much the greatest advance occurred in 1836, when a London chemist, James Marsh, devised a means of detecting even the smallest quantity of arsenic. Basically he employed Metzger's method, but instead of allowing the vapors to rise up to the cold metal plate—with most of the gases escaping into thin air—the process took place in a sealed U-shaped tube that forced the vapors to exit via a small nozzle. The sample was dropped onto a zinc plate covered with dilute sulfuric acid to produce hydrogen. Any arsenine gas was then heated as it passed along a glass tube, condensing when it reached a cold part of the tube to form the "arsenic mirror." In a refined form, the Marsh test remains in use today.

Webster was the most brilliant chemical analyst in Britain, thoroughly conversant with the Marsh test, which he ran on all the Armstrong samples that Spilsbury had provided. The results staggered him: never, in more than 300 similar cases, had he found so much arsenic in a dead body, about 3.5 grains. And that was just the broken-down residue; the actual dosage must have been many times greater.

The presence of more than two grains of arsenic in the liver and kidneys confirmed that a poisonous dose had been administered in the last few days of life. But Katherine had been poisoned a long time before this, as Webster was able to tell by analyzing her hair and fingernails.

Because arsenic gets into hair via sweat and other sebaceous secretions and binds strongly to the keratin molecules, and because hair grows at a fairly predictable rate—about half an inch per month on average—it provides an identifiable record of contamination. If traces of arsenic are found, say, two inches along a hair, then it is a powerful argument for saying that that person ingested arsenic some four months previously. Similarly with fingernails. They can also record when poisoning first took place, and what Webster detected in Katherine's hair and fingernails provided irrefutable proof that she had been systematically poisoned for several months, long before she was admitted to hospital. But he needed to be cautious. Just because hair shows traces of arsenic, this is far from being an infallible barometer of deliberate poisoning. Arsenic is the twentieth most abundant element in the earth's crust and can easily migrate from the soil into a human body once the coffin has begun to crumble. Although Katherine's coffin had shown no signs of decay, this was why Spilsbury had taken soil samples from her grave; he needed to be certain that the earth in Cusop cemetery did not have elevated levels of arsenic, levels that defense counsel might seize upon as the source of any contamination.

Spilsbury's circumspection was justified by Webster's results: there was nothing out of the ordinary about the arsenic levels in the grave. However the arsenic got into Katherine's system, it didn't originate from her final resting place.

Once Webster's full results were in, the DPP decided to act. On January 19 all the shilly-shallying came to an end: Armstrong was charged with wife murder.

Copycat Killing?

When the news broke it caused a sensation, not least because lawyers in Britain have so rarely been charged with murder. The most notorious incidence, as mentioned earlier, came in November 1920 when Harold Greenwood, a Welsh solicitor from Carmarthenshire, stood trial for his life, charged with poisoning *his* wife with arsenic. The newspapers had been stuffed full of his ordeal. Acquaintances in Hay recalled Armstrong obsessively devouring every word of coverage, and his shiny-eyed glee when, against all odds, Greenwood was acquitted. Such preoccupation prompted many to wonder if Greenwood's good fortune had encouraged the major along his murderous path.

On February 12, Spilsbury called round to Welbeck Street to discuss the analysis results with Willcox. While their testimony could be informed by Webster's findings, it would be restricted to their own fields of expertise: pathology and clinical diagnosis. The meeting lasted for two hours. By its conclusion both men were agreed: the liver and kidneys showed characteristic changes due to metallic poisoning, the unusual degree of corporeal preservation was strongly indicative of arsenical poisoning, and the sudden onset of Katherine's mental distress was most probably due to arsenic acting on the brain (encephalopathy).

Armstrong's trial began on April 3, at the Shire Hall, Hereford, in the midst of an unseasonable snowstorm. While the blizzard raged outside, within the ancient courtroom the entire first day was given over to legal arguments concerning the admissibility of evidence relating to the attempt on Martin's life, and the lethal box of chocolates. In the end, Mr. Justice Darling decided to permit the introduction of evidence regarding Martin but disallowed any testimony relating to the chocolates, as they could not be linked in any way to Armstrong.

While the lawyers wrangled, that same day Spilsbury, Wilcox, and Webster—the prosecution's big guns—traveled down to Hereford by train. They all stayed in the same hotel, and that night held a council of war with Attorney-General Sir Ernest Pollock, KC, who was leading for the Crown, and representatives of the DPP. As always in these meetings Spilsbury yielded the floor to Willcox, content to let the latter dominate proceedings. Spilsbury never quite shook off his sense of inferiority when in the presence of his mentor. Willcox was the great all-rounder—a first-rate pathologist, accomplished analyst, and experienced clinician. More importantly, he was highly respected by his academic peers. Spilsbury, for all his newspaper eminence, never enjoyed anything more than peripheral status within the medical community. For the most part this lack of recognition was a self-inflicted wound. He was always threatening to write the great textbook on medical jurisprudence, yet somehow he never quite got round to it, due principally to his crushing caseload. "Publish or perish" goes the old academic saw, and Spilsbury was one of its most notable victims, which is why, in this Hereford hotel room, he sat and listened while Willcox polished the prosecution strategy. The next day, of course, the roles were reversed. It was Spilsbury, immaculately attired as always, with the inevitable red carnation, who captured the eye and the ear.

He told the court what he had found at autopsy, then gave his opinion, informed by Webster's tests, that "a poisonous dose, possibly a fatal dose, must have been taken certainly within 24 hours of death."[14]

When it came time to elaborate on the condition of the body, Spilsbury adopted a novel ploy. Because jurors often became confused by the medical terms, he'd overseen the drawing of a diagram that showed the human alimentary system, with organs highlighted in different colors. Like a teacher in the classroom, Spilsbury led his jury box pupils through the lesson, pointing out those areas from which he had taken his samples.

Thus far it had all been fairly straightforward. But the defense was led by Sir Henry Curtis-Bennett, KC, one of the most ferocious cross-examiners at the British bar, and he came at Spilsbury with all guns blazing, determined to prove that Katherine Armstrong had committed suicide. This strategy was rooted in a strange remark uttered by Mrs. Armstrong to a nurse treating her: "Would it be possible to kill oneself by jumping out of the attic window?"[15]

For the strategy to succeed, Curtis-Bennett needed to undermine Spilsbury's claim that a lethal dose of arsenic had been administered within twenty-four hours of her death. This was difficult, as Hincks had already testified that in the last six days of her life Katherine was bed-bound, having lost all use of her limbs, and would therefore have been unable to get her hands on any poison. Curtis-Bennett manufactured a neat solution to this problem. He put it to Spilsbury that the medical literature recorded instances where doses of arsenic had been ingested as much as seven days before death, and where large quantities of the poison were later found in the corpse. Spilsbury acknowledged the existence of such cases.

So far, so good. Was it not possible, then, Curtis-Bennett asked, that Mrs. Armstrong might have ingested the arsenic seven, ten, even fourteen days before her death, only for the immediate symptoms of arsenical poisoning to abate and then reappear in the final hours of her life?

Cautiously, Spilsbury conceded the possibility. Curtis-Bennett expanded his theory, suggesting that this remission of the symptoms might have been caused by the arsenic becoming encapsulated with mucus in the stomach, and therefore not fully dissolving. Might this not cause the violent symptoms of poisoning to abate temporarily, only to restart when the arsenic finally worked its way free? While agreeing that instances of encysted arsenic had been reported, the most that Spilsbury would commit himself to was that he would ". . . not like to exclude it entirely."[16]

As the cross-examination wore on, the exchanges became noticeably more heated. When Spilsbury refused to budge from his original opinion that Katherine Armstrong had been poisoned, Curtis-Bennett looked heavenwards and rolled his eyes, sighing, "You are putting it now, that the whole of the symptoms are due to arsenic?"

Spilsbury glared at his interrogator and snapped, "Yes, of course I am."[17]

Such courtroom vehemence was entirely out of character for Spilsbury and gives some indication of the pressure he was under. Deep down, Curtis-Bennett must have quaked. His strategy had backfired badly. By goading Spilsbury into such adamantine intransigence, all he'd achieved was a strengthening of the witness's standing with the jury. Not that they really needed it. For more than a decade this collection of farmers and businessmen would have devoured details of Spilsbury's exploits in their daily newspapers. They expected him to be right, and to hear that opinion expressed so forcibly must have been wonderfully reassuring.

Curtis-Bennett, a vast, hulking man, took on the appearance of an enraged bull as he charged Spilsbury's testimony from every angle, only to by swept harmlessly aside by the adroitly placed matador's cape. It was a magnificent contest, and one that Spilsbury won hands down. When the pathologist finally vacated the witness box, Armstrong must have heaved a profound sigh of relief to see the back of his main tormentor.

Everything now rested on his own testimony. As one would expect from someone so used to legal procedure, he handled himself assuredly and well throughout most of his six-hour ordeal. He might have hedged over his reasons for wanting Katherine released from the asylum, and there were certainly some discrepancies in his statements to the police, but all things considered, it was an impressive performance, and as Armstrong prepared to step down from the stand, experienced courtroom watchers were still shading the odds in favor of an acquittal.

Until the judge called him back.

Mr. Justice Darling had a few questions that he wanted to put to the defendant. The next few minutes of Armstrong's life were the most uncomfortable he had ever known. He wriggled like a hooked fish as Darling picked apart his unorthodox methods of weed control. In particular, the judge wanted to know why Armstrong hadn't poured arsenic directly from the container onto the weeds. Armstrong's response, that he preferred to make up packets to treat each weed individually, prompted a baleful look from the bench. Darling, who rather fancied himself as something of a legal wit, was uncharacteristically grim and unsmiling as he crystallized his doubts in one question: "Why make up twenty little packets, each a fatal dose for a human being, and put it in your pocket?"

Armstrong floundered for a moment, then spluttered: "At the time it seemed to me the most convenient way of doing it. I cannot give any other explanation."[18]

Most observers were agreed that Darling's intervention changed the course of the trial. Although Armstrong's ordeal was not yet over—the merciless interrogation from the bench droned on for some considerable time—he never fully recovered from that single, deadly question. The jury needed less than an hour to find him guilty, and a sentence of death was passed.

Armstrong's spell in the condemned cell gave him plenty of time to curse his failed attempt on Martin's life. Had he restricted his arsenical dabblings to uxoricide, he could have spent the rest of his life congratulating himself on having committed the perfect murder; instead—on May 31, 1922—he earned the dubious distinction of being the only British lawyer ever to be hanged for murder.

As was now customary, newspaper headlines lauded Spilsbury's brilliance and that of his colleagues. But he derived little personal pleasure from the triumph. How much longer, he wondered, could medico-legal experts in England keep pulling the rabbit out of the forensic hat? He'd read about the huge advances in medical jurisprudence being made abroad—particularly America, which after a slow start was fast gaining ground on the rest of the world—and he lamented the lack of a cohesive strategy in his home country. In numerous speeches he argued for the formation of a medico-legal institute where students, properly funded, could acquire the knowledge that he, Willcox, and others were so ready to pass on. His own student years had been marked by financial difficulties, and he feared that the notoriously poor pay scale associated with the pathology profession was stifling the flow of fresh blood into the discipline.

His arguments fell largely on deaf ears. The official attitude seemed to be: "We've already got the best forensic pathologist in the world; why do we need another?" with the result that Spilsbury continued to shoulder the burden of three men. Colleagues marveled at his financial selflessness. On one occasion Willcox reportedly said, "Spilsbury is a fool: he'll kill himself with work done for nothing."[19]

It wasn't so far from the truth. From the early 1920s Spilsbury's health was always a cause for concern, due in no small measure to a three-packs-a-day cigarette habit. But on a personal level, there was one great triumph. In December 1922, he received notification from Downing Street, informing him that in the New Year's Honors he would be awarded a knighthood.

---

1 *Times*, January 18, 1919, 9.

2 *Ibid.*, January 19, 1919, 9.

3 *The Medical Detective*, 171.

4 Robin Odell, *Exhumation of a Murder* (New York: St. Martin's Press, 1989), 17.

5 Philip H. A. Willcox, *The Detective-Physician*, (London: Heinemann, 1970), 172.

6 Odell, *Exhumation of a Murder*, 44.

7 *Ibid.*

8 *The Medical Detective*, 173.

9 *Ibid.*, 174.

10 *Ibid.*, 176.

11 *Ibid.*, 171.

12 Odell, *Exhumation of a Murder*, 2.

13 *Ibid.*, 87.

14 *Ibid.*, 155.

15 *The Medical Detective*, 180.

16 Odell, *Exhumation of a Murder*, 157.

17 John Rowland, *Murder Revisited* (London: Long, 1961), 82.

18 *Ibid.*, 91.

19 D. G. Browne and E. V. Tullett, *Bernard Spilsbury: His Life and Cases* (London: Harrap, 1951), 244.

CHAPTER FIVE

The Human Jigsaw

"Call Sir Bernard Spilsbury!"

For almost three decades there was no more exhilarating phrase in the English courtroom. For jaded reporters in the press box it was the cue for some brisk pencil sharpening; for the jury it represented a probably once-in-a-lifetime opportunity to observe a national icon; for the quaking defendant in the dock it meant a sudden and drastic parching of the lips and throat. Everyone knew that when Spilsbury took the stand the crucial point in the trial had been reached. With the exception of Andrey Yanuaryevich Vyshinsky, the pitiless prosecutor at the stage-managed Soviet Great Purge trials of the 1930s who operated in a grotesque and wholly different arena, no single figure of the twentieth century ever wielded so much courtroom power. As the Jazz Age sparkled and capered, Spilsbury, an unreconstructed Victorian if ever there was one, regularly found himself voted among the top twenty of the most famous living Englishmen. It was a time when, in the words of one contemporary, "He [Spilsbury] could achieve single-handed all the legal consequences of homicide—arrest, prosecution, conviction and final post-mortem—requiring only the brief assistance of the hangman."[1]

No case better demonstrates Spilsbury's omnipotence than the one he described as the most challenging in his career. Speaking later, he said, "It gradually took shape as in building up a jigsaw puzzle."[2]

The first pieces in that puzzle were slotted into place on a rainy Thursday night in April 1924. A cloudburst had broken over West London, drenching Ethel Duncan as she battled her way along the rain-slick streets of Richmond. The foul weather matched her mood. She was flat broke, out of work, and soaking wet, and all she wanted was to get home to her sister's house, just over the Thames in nearby Isleworth. As she trudged past Richmond train station and into George Street, a man dropped in beside her and began chatting. In her thirty-two years Ethel had become well-accustomed to male attention, so she was neither shocked nor scared by the stranger's forwardness, just intrigued. He sounded decent enough, well-educated almost, very articulate, and he was undeniably attractive, with those deep-set brown eyes, thinnish face, square jawline, and twinkling smile. When she mentioned that she lived in Worple Avenue, he offered to accompany her home. Ethel felt herself wavering. After a moment's hesitation, she agreed.

As they crossed Richmond Bridge, the stranger gave his name as Pat and told her that he also lived locally. Soon he began leaking details of his unhappy marriage, "a tragedy"[3] he called it. This was something Ethel could relate to. She'd been married once, but that had gone sour, and she was now reduced to living off her sister's charity. Right now, she said, all her hopes were pinned on landing a waitressing job at a Lyon's Corner House. Pat rubbed his chin thoughtfully and said he might be able to help. They chatted almost to Ethel's front door, at which point Pat tipped his hat and made to leave. Almost as an afterthought, he asked if they might go out for dinner one night. Ethel agreed and gave him her address. Pat said he would get in touch, most probably the following Wednesday.

He was a day early. On the Tuesday afternoon, April 15, Ethel received a telegram that read, "Charing Cross 7 tomorrow sure—Pat."

Ethel didn't need any second bidding. The next evening, done up in her best finery, she made her way into London. Seven o'clock found her inside Charing Cross station. For almost an hour she paced the concourse, searching for a familiar face among the throngs of homeward-bound commuters, growing ever more fearful that she had made a fool of herself. Then, at a few minutes before eight, Pat hurried into view, all smiles as usual, effusively apologetic, blaming his lateness on a delayed train. Without the fedora he was even more handsome than Ethel had remembered, a shade under six feet, with thick brown hair—longer than average—just showing the first flecks of gray. She noticed that his right wrist was bandaged. His explanation had a suitably heroic ring: he had sprained it, apparently, saving an elderly lady from falling off a bus.

The date went well. Over drinks, Pat casually mentioned that he had borrowed a friend's bungalow—"rather a charming place"[4]—in Eastbourne; perhaps Ethel would care to spend the upcoming Easter holiday weekend with him? She agreed. The tryst was sealed with a toast. Only then did Pat glance at the time and realize that he'd missed the 10 P.M. train back to Eastbourne. After booking a single room at a nearby hotel, he accompanied Ethel to Waterloo station, where he saw her onto the 10:36 to Isleworth.

The next day, Thursday, Ethel received a telegraphic money order for £4 and a telegram that said, "Meet train as arranged—Waller."[5] It was her first indication of Pat's surname.

On April 18—Good Friday—she journeyed down to Eastbourne on the south coast of England, arriving just before two o'clock. As promised, Pat was waiting at the station. After lunch the couple took advantage of the glorious weather to visit the local sights and that evening dined at the Royal Hotel. All through the meal, Pat kept flashing a large roll of bills. At around ten o'clock they left the hotel and took a taxi some three miles along the coast to a village called Langney and a row of holiday bungalows that nestled up against the English Channel. Pat's bungalow was set apart from the rest, a reminder of the days when it had served as the local coastguard station, a connection still reflected in its name, the Officers' House.

The house looked out over the Crumbles, a long skein of shingle beach interspersed with scrubby grass that stretches from Eastbourne to Pevensey Bay. Ever since the nineteenth century, the Crumbles had been plundered for its shingle for use in hardcore and ballast, and the ugly scars of that legacy were still visible in the abandoned old shovels, iron bars, and bolts. Hardly "brochure material" when it came to romantic destinations, but for couples intent on an illicit weekend it did have the attraction of being marvelously isolated.

The house itself was a single storey whitewashed affair, with half a dozen rooms. The main bedroom was the first left off the hallway, and as Ethel set her luggage down, she immediately detected the presence of another woman: a tortoiseshell brush and some cosmetics lying on a chest of drawers. Pat laughed off her concerns, explaining that these belonged to his wife, who had stayed the previous week. Setting aside all thoughts of the absent Mrs. Waller, the couple slipped between the sheets.

When Ethel awoke the next morning, her gaze was drawn toward a pair of ladies' buckled shoes. Again Pat said these were his wife's: she intended picking them up after the Easter break. That Saturday afternoon the couple went in to Eastbourne, and while Ethel had her hair fixed, Pat headed for Plumpton races.

They met up again that evening and, after dinner, returned to the bungalow. On the mat, waiting for them, lay a telegram. It read: "Must see you Tuesday morning nine Cheapside. Lee."[6] Pat sighed his regrets. Unfortunately this meant ending the weekend early and returning to London on Monday. Ethel pulled a face. Her disappointment might have been keener still had she known that the sender of the telegram was Pat himself. He had wired it from Plumpton Racecourse. Obviously a change of heart was setting in. But not quite yet, as he steered her into the bedroom . . .

Early the next morning, as Pat was getting dressed, Ethel noticed a cluster of bruises across his shoulder and down the back of his upper arm. She didn't give it another thought. Pat, meanwhile, busied himself trying to change the lock on the adjacent bedroom. In between the hammering and the muttered curses, he explained that a friend had stored some valuable books at the bungalow, and he was concerned about security. When Ethel peeked over his shoulder and into the room, she glimpsed a bed, washstand, and trunk. At that moment the chisel that Pat was using slipped and took a chunk out of his left hand. After Ethel bandaged the wound, Pat abandoned his lock-changing plans and instead screwed the door shut.

After another night of dining, drinking, and carousing, the couple caught the train back to London on Easter Monday, took in a theatre show, then kissed good-bye at midnight on the platform of Richmond station. Pat said he would be in touch. Still glowing with memories of the weekend, Ethel Duncan burrowed into the darkness over Richmond Bridge, confident that her recent run of ill luck had turned at last. Dame Fortune, however, had other plans.

The Bloody Bag

Eleven days later, on the evening of Friday, May 2, 1924, a plainclothes police officer, Detective Constable Mark Thompson, was staking out the left luggage office at Waterloo station. There had been a report of a suspicious package. Apparently, a few days earlier an ex-railway policeman turned private investigator named Jack Beard had been hired by a woman to conduct a matrimonial inquiry. It was a bread-and-butter job for Beard, the core of his business: husband rarely home, serial womanizer, anxious wife desperate to know what he was up to. Anxiety had finally given way to anger with news that the previous weekend, a friend had seen the husband in the betting ring at Plumpton races, wagering large amounts of cash. Infuriated by this discovery, the woman had searched her husband's suit pockets and found a left luggage ticket. This she gave to Beard, along with the suspicion that her wastrel of a husband was using left luggage facilities to stash book-making paraphernalia.

When Beard presented the ticket at Waterloo station cloakroom, he was given a locked Gladstone bag, the kind that medical practitioners used to carry. Easing the sides apart tentatively, he managed to peek in-side. Moments later he was hotfooting it from the station. He had left the bag, with instructions that on no account should it be released. Then he called on the worried wife, set her mind at ease on the book-making score, and told her to replace the ticket in her husband's pocket. What Beard kept to himself was that he had contacted Scot-land Yard. And what he told them had prompted this round-the-clock surveillance on the cloakroom.

At 6:40 on that Friday evening a fellow wearing a light gray tweed suit and fedora and carrying a rolled umbrella strolled up to the counter and presented a ticket numbered J.2413. It was for the Gladstone bag. As the stranger made his way to the exit, DC Thompson moved for-ward and asked, "Is that your bag?" The man leveled a cool stare at Thompson, then replied in a cultured voice. "I believe so." When Thompson said he wanted to look inside the bag, the other man shrugged and said, "I haven't got the key."[7] Dissatisfied with this re-sponse, Thompson marched the man into the nearest police station.

The inside of police stations was familiar territory to the stranger, and once there he freely admitted his identity: Patrick Herbert Mahon.

He had been raised in Liverpool and had a criminal record dating back to 1911 when, only one year after marrying, he had whisked an-other woman over to the Isle of Man with £120 obtained by forged checks. The following year brought a twelve months' sentence for em-bezzlement. After being released from prison he flitted from town to town until settling in Sunningdale, deep in the Surrey stockbroker belt. On the night of April 18, 1916, he set out to rob the Windlesham branch of the London and Provincial Bank. Next door to the bank lived the manager, and Mahon reckoned that his best chance of gaining access to the bank vault was through this house. When he broke in through a window and a maidservant began screaming at the top of her lungs, he first silenced the woman's cries by clubbing her insensible with a hammer, then tried to revive her with kisses, fondling, and apologies. Immune to his blandishments she raised the alarm, and Mahon was imprisoned once again, this time for five years.

Throughout all this turmoil the one constant in Mahon's life was his long-suffering wife, Jessie. Each time he came out of prison she took him back, and in 1921 she even secured him a salesman's position at the company where she worked, Consols Automatic Aerators, which made soda fountains. With his quick smile and quicksilver tongue, Mahon proved an excellent acquisition for the company, which paid him accordingly, almost twice the national average. But old habits died hard. And Mahon's increasingly erratic lifestyle began to erode Jessie's patience. Then came news of that trip to Plumpton races . . .

By 9 P.M. Mahon and the still unopened bag were delivered to Scotland Yard, where he was interviewed by Chief Inspector Percy Savage. After Mahon admitted ownership of the bag, Savage opened it carefully. Inside were a torn and bloodstained pair of bloomers, two pieces of bloody white silk, a scarf, a cook's knife, and a brown canvas tennis-racket bag initialed E.B.K. Everything had been liberally sprinkled with disinfectant, presumably to mask the offensive smell.

Asked to account for these contents, Mahon replied, "I'm fond of dogs. I suppose I carried home meat for dogs in it."[8] When Savage snorted his disdain, Mahon fell moodily silent.

It's worth bearing in mind that at this point, Savage had absolutely no idea what crime, if any, had actually been committed. All he had was a bag full of bloodstained clothing and a knife. It could have been nothing, but gut instinct told him otherwise. Mahon sat slumped, head resting on one hand, probably more silent than he'd ever been in his life. For fifteen minutes the impasse lasted. Then he looked up. "I wonder if you can realize how terrible a thing it is for someone's body to be active and one's mind to fail to act."[9]

Savage said nothing.

Another half an hour passed in total silence, while Mahon wrestled with his inner demons. Then he spoke again. "I'm considering my position."[10]

Fifteen more minutes ticked by. Finally he sighed, "I suppose you know everything. I'll tell you the truth."[11]

The truth and Patrick Mahon might have been rare bedfellows for most of his life, but what he had to say that night—corroborated by a police visit to the Eastbourne bungalow the following day—convinced Scotland Yard that it was time to contact Sir Bernard Spilsbury.

Early on the Sunday morning Spilsbury found himself heading south from London, deep into the Sussex countryside, down to the Crumbles. He was no stranger to the area. Almost four years earlier on this same stretch of lonely beach, a seventeen-year-old typist, Irene Munro, had been battered to death and robbed. Spilsbury's participation in that case had been more advisory than integral, after two other doctors had disagreed in their findings. His reading of the medical notes brought some much needed clarification to the disputed time of death and led to two thugs named Jack Field and William Gray being hanged.

Today also marked something of a watershed in Spilsbury's career; for the first time he was accompanied to a crime scene by a personal assistant. Hilda Bainbridge was the widow of Professor Francis Bainbridge, a colleague of Spilsbury's at St. Bart's, who had died in October 1921. After her husband's death she had applied to the hospital for any kind of work, and found herself in the pathology department alongside the illustrious medical examiner, taking dictation as he worked. Any worries that Spilsbury may have entertained regarding Mrs. Bainbridge's possible squeamishness were soon allayed by her steely nerve in the autopsy room. Clearly she had a strong stomach, which was just as well, considering what awaited them both inside the Officers' House.

The Road to Eastbourne

To find the origin of the events that brought Spilsbury to the Crumbles, it is necessary to travel back some ten months to the summer of 1923. By this time, Consols Automatic Aerators had gone bust, but the firm of chartered accountants—Robertson, Hill and Co.—brought in to act as liquidators were so taken with the outgoing Mahon that they kept him on as sales manager and made his wife, Jessie, company secretary.

One side effect of this promotion meant that Mahon was called upon to regularly attend the company headquarters in London's financial district, and it was during one of these visits that his wolfish gaze fell upon a secretary named Emily Beilby Kaye. There was plenty to like in her appearance; she was tall and athletic looking, with fair bobbed hair that framed a roundish face, handsome rather than pretty. Friends knew her as fiercely independent, if somewhat shy in the company of men. Mahon soon began chipping away at her reticence. He learned that she had moved to London from her native Manchester just the previous year and boarded at a women's club in nearby Bloomsbury. She also told him that she was single and aged twenty-eight. The first statement was true; the second was not. She was actually ten years older than she claimed, but vanity being what it is, perhaps she feared that the thirty-four-year-old Mahon might be deterred by the idea of an older woman.

An important caveat: for the following account of how their relationship progressed we are entirely dependent on Mahon's statements, and it should be remembered that every word he uttered was designed to save his own neck. That being said, attempts made in some quarters to portray Emily as this dewy-eyed innocent seduced by a heartless lothario simply do not hold water. At no time did Mahon attempt to deceive her about his wife—pointless anyway since Emily spoke frequently to Jessie on the phone at work—and there can be no doubt that

Emily was a strong-minded woman who knew exactly what she wanted and pursued that goal with singular resolve.

According to Mahon, Emily was relentless in her hounding, constantly badgering him for a date. In August, his resistance worn down at last, he yielded to her invitation for an afternoon on the Thames. The intimate nature of this meeting left Mahon in no doubt that Emily was "a woman of the world,"[12] someone well used to sexual contact. Friends of Emily would later react angrily to Mahon's depiction of her as a woman of casual and easy virtue. Strong-willed? Definitely. Promiscuous? Never.

For his part, Mahon fought to keep the relationship casual and loose. Regular sex was the only dish on the menu, as far as he was concerned. But for Emily, with the passing of another birthday and middle-aged spinsterhood looming large, nothing less than marriage would do. Her desire to possess Mahon became all-consuming.

The final months of 1923 treated Emily roughly. In October she was made redundant by Robertson, Hill and Co. As she'd always been thrifty—her savings amounted to more than £600, a considerable sum at the time—she had enough to tide her over, so she opted to take a few weeks off. But no sooner had she recovered from this setback when, at Christmastime, her brother died and she had to hurry north to attend his funeral. The new year saw her back in London, where she found temporary employment with a financier. Still determined to make a life with Mahon, she began realizing her financial assets and banking the proceeds. On February 16, 1924, she cashed a check for £404, receiving the money in four £100 notes and four £1 notes. It was money she desperately needed, as one day beforehand she had been thrown on the employment scrap heap for a second time, after the original secretary had reclaimed her job at the financier's.

In March she fell victim to a bout of influenza and spent a week recuperating in Bournemouth, though how much her discomfiture owed to illness is a moot point, for it was around this time that she received confirmation of the suspicion she'd harbored for weeks: She was pregnant.

Emily was no fool. Thirty-eight-year-old, single expectant mothers could expect no mercy in the pitiless moral climate of the day, and she knew her life was at a crossroads. That she loved Mahon is beyond doubt; that he wanted to ditch her is equally certain. This had been one affair too many, and he scrabbled frantically to find an escape route. In the ordinary course of events, desertion would have been his preferred option—he'd done it often enough before—but the writer Edgar Wallace always claimed to know why Mahon shunned this option: blackmail. According to Wallace, while Emily was relining a drawer in the women's club where she lived, she stumbled across an old newspaper that, by an extraordinary fluke, contained details of Mahon's 1916 conviction for bank robbery and assault. So the story goes, Emily threatened Mahon with exposure unless he acceded to her demands. By this time Mahon had completely rebuilt his life. No one at work knew of his criminal past, and he was making good money; if exposed as an ex-con, he stood to lose everything. The veracity of Wallace's claim cannot now be proven, but it does have the whiff of truth about it. Mahon was a heartless womanizer, firmly entrenched in the hump 'em and dump 'em school. Only something well out of the ordinary could have persuaded him to stay with Emily. And stay with her he did.

Whatever the reason for Emily's vacation in Bournemouth, at week's end she was joined by Mahon, and the couple moved along the coast to Southampton. Here they sealed their devotion with a diamond and sapphire cluster ring bought from a local jeweler—using money from Emily's savings—and that night shared a double room in the South Western Hotel, signing the register as Mr. and Mrs. Mahon. Emily's blind devotion to her lover can be gauged from the fact that she also entrusted him with £300 of her savings, ostensibly to speculate in the currency markets.

For Emily this was a last-ditch attempt at romance, security, and happiness. But still she couldn't persuade the reluctant Mahon to leave his wife. In a self-serving statement published later, he claimed that "she [Emily] reproached me on several occasions as being cold, and told me plainly she wished my affection, and was determined to win it if possible."[13] Central to this determination was her desire that they should run off to South Africa and start life anew. When Mahon quibbled, Emily hedged her bets; in that case, why not, she said, attempt a "love experiment"?[14] Either they could go on vacation together or else rent a small house, so she could act as his wife, "doing the cooking and everything,"[15] and at the end of the experiment, Mahon could make up his mind whether to return to his wife or stay with Emily. Mahon promised to consider the idea.

When the couple returned to London, the corner that Mahon had painted himself into began tightening by the day. News reached him that Emily had taken to flaunting her "engagement ring" in front of friends, boasting that she and her fiancé intended emigrating to South Africa, where Pat had a good job waiting. In anticipation of the great adventure, Emily began scanning the classifieds in search of a suitable venue for their "love experiment." In early April she struck residential gold; there was a bungalow for rent on the Crumbles.

On April 5, Mahon, using the name Waller and giving a false address and references, agreed a two-month tenancy with the owners of the Officers' House. Two days later, an ecstatic Emily left the women's club for the last time and moved down to the Kenilworth Court Hotel in Eastbourne, there to await Mahon's arrival. Her itinerary was all worked out: Eastbourne first, then Paris for a few days, before setting out on the long sea voyage to a new life in South Africa. The happiness that had eluded her for a lifetime now seemed within touching distance.

Mahon adopted a decidedly cooler approach. On April 11 he took possession of the bungalow and—avoiding Emily, who was blithely unaware of his presence in Eastbourne—traveled back to London, back to Richmond, and back to Jessie and their daughter.

The next day—Saturday morning—Emily excitedly threw her clothes into a suitcase and prepared to meet the man she loved. In the hotel foyer she left instructions for any letters to be forwarded to "Poste Restante, Paris." The receptionist, Jessie Richards, noticed that Emily was looking radiant in a smart gray costume, gray suede shoes, and a fur coat with a dark collar. Just a few hours later Emily threw herself into Mahon's arms when he arrived at Eastbourne train station, and from there the couple went by cab to the Officers' House.

The events of the next few days are mostly shrouded in mystery. On the Sunday a butcher delivering meat to the bungalow saw a woman's face through the window, and a neighbor, Mrs. Florence Tate, confirmed that a woman she later identified as Emily Kaye had knocked at her door that day and asked to borrow some milk. After that all sightings of Emily Kaye dried up. Only Mahon knew what had become of her. He made three statements to the police about that weekend, with crucial variations in each, but the version he finally settled on was this:

Far from the idyllic tryst that Emily had dreamed of, the weekend degenerated into a bad-tempered debacle. She demanded to know why, when they were planning to emigrate, Mahon had not obtained a passport for himself, as promised. To placate her, he said, they returned to London on the Monday morning, intending to acquire the necessary passport. Again he shirked the task. (It is worth noting that this alleged visit to London was uncorroborated by any independent witness.) On the train journey back to Eastbourne, Mahon said, Emily's mood blackened, and that night they argued fiercely.

The fight spilled over to the next morning, April 15, and flared up and down for most of the day. That evening the air became as chilly as the mood between them, and Mahon decided that a roaring fire might raise their collective spirits. Collecting the coal scuttle from the dining room, he brought it to the lounge and, using a small wooden-handled ax, broke up some large lumps of coal. Unthinkingly he chanced to lay the ax down on the table where Emily sat writing farewell letters to friends at the women's club. She glared up at him. "Pat, I'm determined to settle this matter one way or the other tonight,"[16] she snapped, then hurled the letters in his face. "These letters and my actions mean that I have burned my boats."[17] From this, Mahon assumed that she had quit the club. The harangue crescendoed. "Can't you realize, Pat, how much I love you," she screamed, "and that you are everything to me, and that I can never share you with another?"[18]

For once Mahon's silvery tongue failed him. There were no words he could muster to quell this tempest. At the end of his tether, he threw up his arms in exasperation and announced that he was going to bed. As he reached the bedroom door, Emily gave a maniacal howl and threw the ax with all her might. It struck his right shoulder blade, then clattered into the doorframe with such force that it snapped the shaft in two. Then she flew at him, clawing at his face and neck.

"We struggled backwards and forwards, and I realized in a minute that I was dealing with a woman almost mad with anger. I tried to keep her off, but I realized she was getting the better of me . . . In an almost despairing throw I pushed Miss Kaye off and we both fell over the easy chair on the left of the fireplace. Miss Kaye's head hit the cauldron [coal scuttle] and I fell with her; she was underneath. She had gripped me by the throat and I had gripped her by the throat. We were locked together."[19]

At this point, Mahon said, he fainted from fear and shock. When he came to, Emily was lying unconscious by the cauldron, blood pumping from her head. Frantically he attempted to revive her, without success. Then panic took over. He ran from the house in a daze, mad with grief. When finally he plucked up the courage to return indoors, he dragged Emily's body into the second bedroom, laid it on the floor, and covered it with her fur coat.

Then he traveled into Eastbourne for breakfast.

In the midst of all this madness, Mahon claimed, he suddenly recalled the date he had made with Ethel Duncan the week before. They had arranged to meet at Charing Cross station that very night. Never one to forgo a chance of sexual gratification, Mahon duly kept his appointment. The next day, before heading back to Eastbourne, he bought a saw and a knife in London and returned to the Officers' House, suitably primed for the disposal of Emily Kaye.

No one could accuse Mahon of a lack of compartmentalization. When Ethel joined him on Good Friday, his joking demeanor gave no hint that he'd spent the morning disarticulating a human body. Similarly that night. In the same room where Emily had so recently slept,

Ethel detected "nothing whatsoever"[20] in Mahon's manner to suggest that she was sharing a bed with a murderer.

A couple of days later, once Ethel was out of his hair, Mahon resumed the dissection. It was much messier and took far longer than he had imagined. And, of course, there was still a fretful wife to placate. On April 28 he decided to take a break. He traveled up to London, deposited his bag at Waterloo station, and went to see Jessie. He had gone back to collect the bag four days later, intending to return to Eastbourne and complete the gruesome task. Instead, he had been arrested.

Spilsbury at the Bungalow

So what would Spilsbury make of Mahon's story? More importantly, what would the evidence inside the Officers' House say? When Spilsbury's car pulled up, crowds of onlookers surged forward. Judging from the lurid thirty-six-point headlines, Fleet Street was throwing the kitchen sink at the "Bungalow Murder," and as always, when news of Spilsbury's involvement leaked out, the rubberneckers multiplied exponentially. Here they hung over the whitewashed wall like spectators in the center-field bleachers, all desperate for the best possible view. Spilsbury hurried into the pebbled, high-walled courtyard through a porch overhung with roses. A pace or two behind, muffled up in a large fur coat and a hat that almost covered her eyes, was Hilda Bainbridge.

Her entrance caused a sensation. Although the Women's Police Volunteers dated from 1914,* female officers were still scarcer than snowballs in August, and none had thus far breached the exclusively male bastion of crime scene investigation. For most of the grizzled police veterans present, the sight of this impeccably turned out middle-aged

---

* In 1915 this title was changed to the Women's Police Service.

lady striding confidently into their domain must have been a real eye-opener. Without even thinking about it, Mrs. Bainbridge had struck a formidable blow for feminism.

As Spilsbury entered the Officers' House, he already knew what to expect—Mahon's statement had gone into lavish and explicit detail—but nothing had prepared him for the stink. The whole house reeked of rotting flesh. Even his defective sense of smell provided no immunity to a miasma that had seeped into the building's very fabric.

It took a moment for his eyes to adjust to the gloomy interior. The house had no electricity, and heavy green curtains over the windows—drawn to keep out prying eyes—necessitated a reliance on oil lamps for illumination. The sitting room looked ordinary enough with its sofa, some chairs, and a table, until one noticed the incongruous two-gallon metal tureen that stood in the hearth, next to the fireplace. The fireplace itself was filled with ash. Three small glasses holding some faded flowers were lined up on the mantelpiece, and there was a plate of oranges on the corner cupboard. Thus far there was little to arouse any suspicion. Except that stench.

Spilsbury didn't touch anything just at the moment, but rather moved from room to room, hands pushed firmly into pockets—his invariable attitude at any crime scene—all the while dictating his findings to Mrs. Bainbridge, who recorded them on a notepad.

In the dining room another large saucepan stood in the hearth, alongside a more conventionally placed coal scuttle. Like its counterpart in the sitting room, the grate was also filled with ash, and thick globs of grease were smeared across the fender.

Moving into the main bedroom Spilsbury found nothing out of the ordinary. Next door, in a bedroom where the doorframe showed signs of having been tampered with, he saw a square hatbox, a leather kit bag, and a large fiber trunk monogrammed with the initials E.B.K. A rusty tenon saw, its teeth clogged by grease, lay on the bed.

In this room, the smell was stomach churning.

Still Spilsbury reined in his curiosity, determined to complete his "big picture" analysis. Experience told him the importance of this procedure, how it could inform his autopsy findings. Looking more closely, he saw a bag that contained a tortoiseshell toilet set, a black fur stole, some opera glasses, a gold ring, a necklace, a pendant, and a watch. In the same bedroom, hanging in a recess, were a fur coat, some hats, the smart gray costume that Jessie Richards noticed at the Kenilworth Court Hotel, and a black lace evening dress. Many of the clothes showed traces of blood.

The bungalow had no bathroom as such, just a converted scullery that housed a sink and a galvanized tub. Both were heavily coated with grease.

With his initial inspection of all six rooms complete, Spilsbury decided to set up a temporary laboratory in the small courtyard because of the better light. Canvas boards were hastily erected atop the courtyard walls to afford more privacy. While the kitchen table was being moved outside to act as a lab workbench, Spilsbury continued his interior inspection. The sheer scale of human devastation that he uncovered over the next few hours transcended anything in his experience.

He began in the dining room, and that two-gallon tureen. It was half-full of a reddish fluid, topped with a thick layer of congealed fat, beneath which floated a chunk of boiled human flesh that still had some skin attached. Spilsbury suspected, though he could not say for certain at this point, that the grease on the fender was human in origin, and he reached a similar conclusion with a saucer of fat that stood on the hearth. Sifting the ash in the grate, much like a prospector panning for gold, he recovered innumerable fragments of bone. As the flimsy scuttle or cauldron had figured prominently in Mahon's statement, Spilsbury paid it special attention. It was cheaply made, bulbous in shape, with three hollow legs, one of which showed signs of damage. Peering more closely, Spilsbury saw two pinpricks of blood.

In the lounge where Mahon said the fight had occurred, Spilsbury went over every inch of the door with a magnifying lens. There was some rubbing where the paint had flaked off, but nothing, no mark or indentation, to support Mahon's claim that the ax had struck the door with sufficient force to snap its handle. What he did find were bloodstains on the bottom right corner of the door, which had spread onto the adjoining floor. Like its cousin in the dining room, the second tureen also contained a by-now-familiar stew of human remains.

But it was the second bedroom that housed the most grisly secrets. Inside the fiber trunk lay a headless human body, obviously female, minus the limbs. Also in the trunk was a biscuit tin, jam-packed with various human organs. The hatbox held no fewer than thirty-seven pieces of a female body, five with pubic hair attached. All had been boiled and some had been wrapped in heavily soiled clothing.

Only now did Spilsbury don his trademark long white apron and rubber gloves. He asked Savage if he and his men could bring all the items from inside the house out to his ad hoc laboratory in the courtyard.

What Spilsbury saw next appalled him. Without a second thought the officers merely rolled up their sleeves and grabbed hold of chunks of putrid flesh, tossing them into buckets, as if they were sorting fish on a quayside. He summoned Savage and delivered a stern lecture on the dangers of infection, ending, "Are there no rubber gloves?"[21] Savage looked at him blankly and explained that his officers never wore any form of protective gear when processing crime scenes. Spilsbury raised his eyes in disbelief and got on with the job in hand, but at the back of his mind was an idea, one that he would revive later.

For the next eight hours he labored, mostly outside in the bright sunshine, only occasionally ducking back indoors to double-check some finding. The woman's torso had been quartered, and, unlike most of the other remains, these pieces had not been boiled. Whoever sawed through the spine did so painstakingly and with some precision. When fitted together, the four pieces of the human trunk formed a unified and identifiable female body. Much the most interesting area on the torso was a patch of discolored skin, some two inches square, at the back of the left shoulder. Spilsbury incised it carefully and decided that it bore all the hallmarks of a very recent bruise, most probably inflicted during the life-and-death struggle that Mahon had mentioned.

Dusk was beginning to fall when Spilsbury finally packed away his instruments and declared himself finished. He supervised the collection of all the ash from both grates and from a dustpan found in the kitchen, and this, together with the accumulated body parts, was then dispatched to his laboratory at St. Bart's.

Over the next forty-eight hours, Spilsbury scarcely got a wink of sleep as he toiled to discover how Emily Kaye had met her death. From the various piles of ash, he recovered almost 1,000 pieces of calcined, pulverized bone. Some were recognizably human, others were not, and it was a case of trial and error as he attempted to put together this human jigsaw puzzle. Piece by piece the charred skeleton took shape. It was a fantastic feat of reconstruction, one that few other pathologists at the time—if any—could have duplicated. By the time he was finished, the framework of Emily Kaye's grossly abused body lay before him, minus the skull, the upper part of the neck, and the lower portion of one leg.

Across town at St. Mary's, Webster had also been burning the midnight oil, analyzing various artifacts from the Officers' House. These included the coal cauldron, a section of the sitting-room door, two pieces of flooring, a strip of carpet, and some felt that acted as a carpet underlay. In many instances the samples were too degraded for accurate analysis, but the flooring and the carpet showed definite traces of human blood. He also examined the ax that had been found in two pieces, the head under some coal in the coalhouse, the broken shaft in the scullery. Tests on the saw and the cooking knife were disappointing, as they were on some scraps of material. All the samples were just too contaminated.

Back at Bart's, Spilsbury, having assembled the skeleton, was now studying it for clues as to how Emily Kaye had met her death.

Apart from some adhesions around the right lung, most likely the legacy of an attack of pleurisy, there was no organic disorder or any sign of an inherent disease. In spite of the uterus and one ovary being absent, the condition of the mammary glands led Spilsbury to conclude that Emily had been about three months' pregnant at the time of her death. While the bruise on the upper shoulder was consistent with a fall, it told Spilsbury absolutely nothing about how Emily Kaye had died. Nor did anything else that he found. Testifying later at the inquest, he said, "The absence of any cause of death in the parts which I have examined indicates, in my view, that the cause of death would have been found in the head or neck, which are missing."[22]

Such a conclusion prompted a renewed drive to find the missing body parts. For the first time in its history, Scotland Yard used sniffer dogs in a victim search. They combed the scrubland around the cottage, but whatever secrets the Crumbles held, it kept to itself. Not a single further trace of Emily Kaye was ever found. (Mahon claimed that he had made some body parts up into small packages and thrown them from the train between Waterloo and Richmond.)

Without the victim's head, Spilsbury, by now thoroughly conversant with the demands of criminal law, pondered whether sufficient evidence existed to convict Mahon of murder. As unlikely—and as macabre—as Mahon's story sounded, it might just be the truth: a man overwhelmed by dreadful circumstances, driven to insane folly. So Spilsbury was asked to turn detective, to decide whether the physical evidence found at the house made a liar out of Mahon.

Spilsbury's task was eased somewhat by the discovery that Mahon's first statement to the police was littered with falsehoods. Much the most damning was his claim to have bought the knife and saw two days after the tragic accident. Inquiries revealed that on April 12—*three days before the probable death of Emily Kaye*—Mahon had entered a kitchen supply store near Victoria station at lunchtime and purchased a tenon saw, a knife with a ten-inch blade, and a knife cleaner. All three implements were found at the Officers' House. When asked to explain this discrepancy, Mahon spluttered some guff about not having received an inventory of cutlery at the bungalow, and that he'd made the purchases because he thought the kitchen lacked a carving knife. He had simply been confused over the date. When the allegedly missing inventory subsequently turned up in Mahon's belongings, more hasty contrivance became necessary. This version had him suddenly recalling that he'd really bought the items because a bedroom lock needed fixing. None of the excuses was good enough. No matter how much Mahon wriggled, the cutler's records provided clear proof of premeditation.

And then there was that meeting with Ethel Duncan. Not the pre-arranged date that Mahon had claimed, but a last-minute assignation confirmed by a telegram sent at 3:40 P.M. on April 15 from Hastings. Its message was damning: "Charing Cross 7 tomorrow sure—Pat." Clearly, when he wired this telegram, Mahon was not expecting to be encumbered by the presence of Emily Kaye.

Courthouse Fights

If the Central Criminal Court at the Old Bailey was to dominate Spilsbury's early career, then in the mid-1920s that stage would switch to the Sussex County Assizes in the market town of Lewes. No other regional courthouse has hosted such a sensational string of trials. When Mahon's trial opened on July 15, 1924, the street outside court was jammed with thousands of people, all fighting to gain admittance to the public gallery. Coats were torn and hats were battered in the crush, and seats changed hands for as much as £5, more than a week's wages for most people. In the end, just 200 spectators were admitted, and they weren't disappointed. As Sir Henry Curtis-Bennett, KC, this time appearing for the prosecution, outlined the Crown's case, the graphic details were too much for one juror, who fainted clean away. When he came to he had the unusual—some might find unsettling—experience of realizing that his medical attendant was none other than Dr. Spilsbury! After a few minutes' treatment, the man was well enough to continue, only to faint a second time. This time he was re-placed, and the trial continued. One of the first witnesses was Ethel Duncan.

For months this young woman had been hounded from one hiding place to another in an effort to avoid the barrage of hate mail that winged her way. The press had made her life a misery, publishing las-civious and grotesquely one-sided accounts of her fling with a married man. "Jezebel!" and "Harlot!" were just two of the tamer insults that reddened Ethel's ears as court attendants elbowed her through the baying mob. The price paid for that single weekend with Mahon was evident now as Ethel raised her veil and stood, hollow-eyed and sobbing, in the witness box. Speaking in little more than a whisper, she relived the humiliation one more time. Even so, nothing could dislodge her from her assertion that she saw four distinct bruises on Mahon's right shoulder. His account claimed that he had been struck on the shoulder by the flying ax, but that was just a solitary blow. In the event, Ethel Duncan was treated far more kindly by the court than by the crowds outside, who jeered and hissed as she was whisked from the building off into merciful obscurity.

After Webster had outlined his findings, it was Spilsbury's turn to testify. The entire court sat hushed as he recounted the horrors of the Officers' House. He had found nothing organic to account for the death of Emily Kaye, which strongly indicated that she had died from some kind of head or neck trauma. The relative absence of blood at the bungalow led him to say, "I do not think Miss Kaye died by having her throat cut."[23] He was not prepared to exclude the possibility of strangulation or some kind of bludgeoning.

At an earlier hearing he had been shown the ax handle and asked if it was "likely to break through being thrown across the room with considerable force and hitting the door?"[24] He had expressed doubt then, and did so now, clearing the way for the Crown to explore the anticipated defense claims that Emily Kaye had died by striking her head on the scuttle. "In your opinion, could Miss Kaye have received rapidly fatal injuries by a fall on the coal cauldron?"

"In my opinion . . . no fall upon the coal cauldron which has been produced would have been sufficiently severe to cause fatal results without crumpling up the cauldron."[25] In a single sentence, Spilsbury crystallized the Crown's case; Emily Kaye's death was physically incompatible with the defendant's statement.

So what would Mahon have to say? He took the stand, smartly dressed in a new plum-colored suit with a mauve silk handkerchief folded carefully in the breast pocket. He looked the very picture of health, courtesy of a fake tan, apparently acquired in the belief that it would impress the jury. All his life Patrick Mahon had traded on his glib charm, and he oozed confidence that the court would swallow his patter one more time.

He was guided through his testimony by J. D. Cassels, KC, a top-class defender and someone not easily duped, especially by his own clients. For instance, he noticed that when Mahon vividly described the death struggle between himself and Emily—breaking off his testimony for some body-wracking sobs—it was a cheap linen square that the witness pointedly used to mop his tears rather than the expensive silk handkerchief. Only a little conceit, it's true, but potentially deadly if spotted. Cassels could only pray that the jury's antennae were not as acute as his own.

Mahon slipped easily between outright lies and shaded facts. Probably the most truthful statement he uttered came when Cassels asked him why, when there was a dead body in the second bedroom, he had taken the almost suicidal step of inviting Ethel Duncan to the bungalow. "The damned place was haunted. I wanted human companionship. I was afraid to go back to the bungalow. I couldn't bear to go back to it."[26]

What the court didn't know was that Cassels had a unique insight into Mahon's mental state. Before the trial, in private consultation, Mahon had related a dreadful incident. Having dismembered the body, he decided to burn the parts, and had built a big fire in one of the bungalow's grates. Once the flames were roaring, he tossed in the severed head. He watched, almost hypnotized, as Emily's thick, fair hair flared and caught alight. Then came a moment of pure Grand Guignol horror. As the extreme heat got to work, tightening various muscles, suddenly the eyelids lifted and the dead eyes fixed themselves on Mahon. At that very moment an almighty clap of thunder exploded overhead. Terrified out of his wits, Mahon fled in his shirtsleeves out to the lonely, rainswept shore. Hours later, when he returned, the head had been consumed by the flames. Using a poker, he broke up the remaining brittle bones on the hearthside, then scattered them along the shingle beach.

By coincidence, when Mahon gave his testimony, it was a sultry, oppressive day, and as he neared the end of his examination-in-chief, a summer storm could be heard rumbling in the distance, ready to play a decisive counterpoint to Cassels's final question to Mahon: "Did you desire the death of Miss Kaye?"

"Never at any time,"[27] Mahon answered confidently. Right on cue, a crack of lightning flooded the courtroom with a ghostly light, and a clap of wrathful thunder shook the building to its foundations. Mahon cringed like a cornered animal, one fearful arm hooked skywards to fend off the vengeful intruder. In that single instant all his bluster and confidence evaporated.

The next day he stumbled his way through a cross-examination that destroyed him. The self-professed "broth of a bhoy"[28] was exposed as a heartless psychopath who had first seduced Emily Kaye, made her pregnant, fleeced her of her life savings—she had a shade over £71 left at the time of her death—then killed and butchered her when she refused to end the affair. Mahon's witness box performance was every bit as inept as his attempt to conceal Emily Kaye's body. Lies littered his every utterance. One glaring example was his protestation that, for sentimental reasons, he had used the bungalow's carving knife to dismember the body, as he couldn't bring himself to use the razor-sharp knife he had purchased because Emily had used that knife to carve a chicken for their Sunday lunch!

Immediately the prosecution recalled Spilsbury to rebut Mahon's claim. He said, "In my opinion the carving knife could not have cut up the body as I saw it. The flesh would not have been so cleanly cut by the carving knife."[29] Holding the carving knife aloft, he told the jury, "If this knife had been used to cut up a dead body it must have been plunged deeply into the flesh. Blood would have been present, not only on the blade but around this junction of the steel and the handle, and, in order to remove it, it would be necessary to clean around there particularly carefully."[30] He had examined the knife, and in that crevice had found only cooking fat and washing powder, indicating that it had been used solely for domestic purposes. Tellingly, there *was* blood on the cook's knife.

All of Spilsbury's earlier doubts about the strength of the case against Mahon were dispelled on July 19, when he was found guilty of murder and sentenced to hang.

Spilsbury might not have been able to say exactly how Emily Kaye met her death—an impossibility—but what his outstanding feat of reconstruction did achieve was the total demolition of Mahon's story. Without Spilsbury, Mahon may well have escaped with a plea of manslaughter. As it was, he came up against a brilliant pathologist at the peak of his powers. Indeed, so impressed were the authorities by Spilsbury's work in this case that they took the highly unusual step of awarding him an ex gratia payment of 50 guineas (£52.10s) for his services.

Even after the trial, interest in Mahon still sizzled. A band of entrepreneurs of dubious taste but sound business instinct took over the lease of the Officers' House and charged members of the public one shilling a head for guided tours of the cottage. As the lines grew longer, cold drinks could be purchased by the front gate. Local outrage at such commercial opportunism resulted in a forty-strong mob of self-styled "British Fascisti" storming the bungalow on August 30 and demanding its closure. Just two weeks later the bungalow reopened with an increased entrance fee, as coachloads of the curious continued to flock to the most notorious holiday cottage in the country.*

Spilsbury's First Execution

Spilsbury, too, was not yet finished with Mahon. On the morning of the execution—September 3—he slipped almost unnoticed through the large crowds that milled outside Wandsworth Prison, in through

---

* The Officers' House was eventually demolished in 1953.

the wicket gate. He was there to autopsy a condemned felon. Following any execution, the law demanded that an inquest be held within the prison walls, and the medical examiner was a vital cog in this judicial process.

Mahon's execution was notable for two reasons; it was the first time that Spilsbury had been called upon to act in this capacity, and it also triggered rumors about some kind of "incident" on the gallows, a story that found its way into Curtis-Bennett's biography, in which the writers claimed that Mahon had been "doubly hanged."

Determined principally by the weight and general muscularity of the prisoner, judicial hanging in the U.K. was a remarkably precise business. It not only required that the length of drop be calculated to the last half inch—too short and the prisoner might strangle slowly, too long and there was the risk of the head being torn off—but also that the condemned person stand in exactly the right place on the trapdoor, which was composed of two heavy-hinged wooden leaves, held in place by bolts. A chalked T-mark on the trapdoor indicated where the condemned's feet were to be placed; heels on one leaf, balls of the feet on the other. When the lever was pushed, the trapdoor fell open, and the prisoner plunged through. Overwhelmingly, executions passed off without incident or struggle, due mainly to the lightning speed of the process; most prisoners were motionless at the end of the rope within twelve seconds of the hangman entering their cell. But, so the story went, Mahon refused to go quietly. As the trap was sprung, he tried to jump clear and, instead of falling cleanly into the pit, swung pendulum-like, striking his back and snapping his spine in two. That alone would have killed him, but half a second later his neck was also broken by the jerk of the rope, hence the comment about being "doubly hanged."

For decades this story was dismissed as prison scuttlebutt, due principally to the insistence of certain writers that Spilsbury's autopsy card for Mahon showed only a dislocation between the fourth and fifth cervical vertebrae, with no mention of any damage to the lower spine. But half a century on, fresh evidence appeared, and this suggested that Spilsbury's little white card didn't tell the whole story.

Albert Pierrepoint was the third member of his family to hold the post of chief executioner in the U.K. The Pierrepoints were legendary for their breathtaking speed and technical expertise, and between them they hanged an estimated 850 persons in the first half of the twentieth century. In his autobiography, published in 1974, Albert finally clarified the Mahon legend. It had been his uncle, Thomas Pierrepoint, who'd officiated on that September morning in 1924, and he gave Albert the inside story, which he passed on in his book. "Mahon jumped forward with pinioned feet as my uncle released the bolts, and his body pitched backward so that the base of his spine crashed against the platform edge, but death was instantaneous."[31]

Even more intriguingly, a closer study of the contemporary records reveals confirmation for the Pierrepoint version originating from the most reliable source possible: *Spilsbury himself.* An account of the inquest, published one day later, has Spilsbury telling the court that the spinal column had been broken in two places. "That's rather unusual?" queried the coroner, Ingleby Oddie. "Yes, I believe it is," replied Spilsbury. "The particular compression of the spinal cord was between the fourth and fifth [cervical] vertebrae. The first, second, and third were not affected. The other dislocation was between the six and seventh [thoracic] vertebrae."[32] So here we have it in Spilsbury's own, unequivocal words: Mahon had indeed been "doubly hanged." Spilsbury's ambiguous report card betrays the heavy-handedness of the Official Secrets Act, which cloaked—or attempted to cloak—all British executions in a veil of impenetrable secrecy. What this execution did do was spark Spilsbury's intense interest in judicial executions; after all, how many pathologists get an opportunity to study postmortem effects on a still-warm human body when the exact time of death is known? Information gleaned in the execution chamber was transferable to his other work, and Mahon's was just the first of more than fifty such autopsies that Spilsbury would perform in his career.

Where Spilsbury differed from those prison doctors who had gone before was in the thoroughness of his autopsies. His was no fleeting autopsy, rushed through to fulfill legal requirements, but a full and exhaustive examination of the body. From these experiences he concluded that fracture dislocation of the spinal column at the second and third cervical vertebrae would provide the instant death that the Home Office desired, and this led him to recommend, on humanitarian grounds, that the scale of drops be increased by three inches.

Many years later, Spilsbury's close friend and colleague Dr. W. Bentley Purchase, the coroner of the North London District who assisted him in this research, was asked to testify before the Gowers Royal Commission Report on Capital Punishment (1953). Data gathered from autopsies performed on prisoners executed at London's Pentonville Prison between 1943 and 1950 all showed severance of the spinal column at the 2/3 cervical vertebrae, a uniformity that Purchase proudly attributed to the revised tables recommended by Spilsbury and himself.

Such bombast did not please Albert Pierrepoint. All his drops were the product of personal experience and calculated in his head, not extracted from some dry H.O. table, and he later wrote sourly, "If every execution between 1943 and 1950 was perfect, I must modestly claim that it was because of my experience and not Sir Bernard's three inches."[33]

A far less contentious outcome of the Mahon case was the introduction of Scotland Yard's famed Murder Bag. Spilsbury's abhorrence of the indifferent hygiene that he'd witnessed at the Officers' House prompted a thorough review of procedures. What it uncovered was alarming and went far beyond mere rubber gloves. Police officers were hopelessly ill-equipped for the efficient performance of their duties. If they wished to preserve human hair on clothing, or soil or dust on boots, they simply picked it up with their fingers and put it on a piece of paper. They had no tapes to measure distances, no compass to determine direction, no apparatus to take fingerprints, no first-aid outfit, no instrument to find the depth of water, no magnifying glass. In short, they had no appliances whatsoever for immediate use at the crime scene.

Appalled by these deficiencies, Spilsbury and Dr. Aubrey Scott-

Gillett, a Wimpole Street doctor who doubled as a police surgeon, put their heads together, and in consultation with Detective Superintendent William Brown from Scotland Yard, the first Murder Bag came into being. Designed to accompany any detective on a homicide inquiry, in its first incarnation the Murder Bag included rubber gloves, a hand lens, a tape measure, a straightedge ruler, swabs, sample bags, forceps, scissors, a scalpel, and other instruments that might be called for. (Some officers were rumored to include a flask of whisky for those nippy winter investigations!) Gradually the Murder Bag was improved to the point where any clue could be safely preserved and any task undertaken with the correct apparatus. Nowadays, with the advent of the specialized criminalist, the Murder Bag has been largely consigned to the history books.

1 Richard Whittington-Egan and Molly Whittington-Egan, *The Bedside Book of Murder* (Newton Abbot, England: David & Charles, 1988), 164.

2 Iain Adamson, *A Man of Quality* (London: Muller, 1964), 73.

3 *Times*, May 31, 1924, 9.

4 Adamson, *A Man of Quality*, 85.

5 *Times*, May 31, 1924, 9.

6 *Ibid.*

7 *Ibid.*, May 28, 1924, 11.

8 *Ibid.*, July 16, 1924, 5.

9 Adamson, *A Man of Quality*, 74.

10 *Ibid.*

11 *Times*, May 23, 1924, 19.

12 *Ibid.*

13 *Ibid.*

14 *Ibid.*, July 18, 1924, 11.

15 *Ibid.*

16 *Ibid.*

17 *Ibid.*

18 *Ibid.*

19 *Ibid.*

20 *Ibid.*, May 31, 1924, 9.

21 Tom Tullet, *Murder Squad* (London: Triad/Granada, 1981), 66.

22 *Times*, June 7, 1924, 9.

23 *Ibid.*, July 18, 1924, 11.

24 *Ibid.*, June 12, 1924, 7.

25 *Ibid.*, July 18, 1924, 11.
26 Adamson, *A Man of Quality*, 85.
27 *Ibid.*
28 *Ibid.*, 75.
29 *Times*, July 19, 1924, 7.
30 Adamson, *A Man of Quality*, 84.
31 Albert Pierrepoint, *Executioner: Pierrepoint* (London: Coronet, 1977), 182.
32 *Daily Express*, September 4, 1924, 3.
33 Pierrepoint, *Executioner: Pierrepoint*, 201.

CHAPTER SIX

A Question of Suicide

In 1924 Spilsbury's career reached its high-water mark. He was at the peak of his fame and influence, unopposed and autonomous, dominating headlines as he glided effortlessly from one sensational murder trial to another. Whilst investigating the Crumbles Murder, he also figured prominently in another cause célèbre, when a French radio technician, Jean-Pierre Vacquier, stood accused of poisoning his mistress's husband, who ran the Blue Anchor Hotel at Byfleet, Surrey. This steamy love triangle and the defendant's unpredictable courtroom antics—he had to be physically manhandled from the court, bellowing like a bull, after being sentenced to death—generated an avalanche of press coverage, as did Spilsbury's involvement in deciding just how much strychnine the body of Alfred Jones contained.* In truth, like most toxicology cases, this was another instance where most of the credit should have gone to the chemical analyst involved—in this case John Webster— but Spilsbury's was the big marquee name, the one guaranteed to boost

---

* Just three weeks before Mahon was hanged at Wandsworth Prison, Vacquier met his end on the same gallows.

newspaper circulation, so once again he was the forensic expert who reaped most of the acclaim.

Spilsbury's third notable case of 1924 occurred in Bristol when George Cooper Jr., thirty-four, was charged with murdering his father. Cooper Snr., a drunken, wife-beating bully, had attacked his son with a hatchet, and as the two men grappled, the elder Cooper had sustained grievous head injuries that killed him. Horrified by what he had done, Cooper ripped up the floorboards in the sitting room and buried the body several feet deep. Following a tip-off, five months later—on January 31, 1924—police visited the house and dug up the remains. Louisa Cooper's immediate response was to shoulder the blame for her son's actions, a decision that led to both being charged with murder. (When the truth finally emerged, she was cautioned and released.) By the time Spilsbury saw the body it was barely recognizable as human, having been wrapped in sacking and doused with a mixture of quicklime and tar. Still, there was enough to show that this had been a brutal attack. In court, he shared his knowledge with the jury by dramatically producing the dead man's skull and pointing out the nine sharp-edged fractures, any one of which would have ended Cooper's life. After listening to all the harrowing circumstances of this tragedy—the son had been brutalized since childhood by his violent father, and this was the first time he had ever defended himself—the jury rejected the murder charge and returned a guilty manslaughter verdict. Sentencing Cooper to seven years, the judge said, "I cannot get over the evidence of Sir Bernard Spilsbury, who, not for the first time, has been of great assistance in the administration of justice, always fair and always dependable; and in this case his evidence was so fair that it was immediately accepted by the defense."[1]

Such accolades from the bench were now commonplace for Spilsbury, virtually his due at every trial he attended. But behind the scenes it was an entirely different story. Already the first dark mutterings of discontent had begun to surface about Spilsbury's privileged status. There is no doubt that he deserved his eminence; by sheer weight of personality and peerless talent he had made himself the foremost figure in English medical jurisprudence. To the public at large, forensic science and Sir Bernard Spilsbury were indivisible, and while this perception might not have been of his making, he certainly never bothered to correct the misapprehension. The backlash came from other pathologists. Some resented his intolerance of any contrary opinion; some craved his spotlight; some felt slighted as doors of opportunity slammed shut in their faces; some—mostly those who knew him only from a distance—found his chilly insularity jarring. What unified them all was a genuine concern over the reputation for infallibility that Spilsbury had acquired, both in the courts and, more dangerously, among the public from whom all juries were chosen.

Chief among the critics, and certainly the noisiest, was Dr. Robert Matthew Brontë. A distant relative of the literary family from Yorkshire, Brontë was born in Armagh, Northern Ireland. Originally he served for a short period as Crown analyst to the government of Ireland, but after the establishment of the Irish Free State, he moved to London and took up a position as pathologist to the Harrow Hospital and the Samaritan Free Hospital. From there, he wheedled his way into an appointment at the Coroner's Court of the Western District in London, where he soon raised eyebrows and hackles by describing himself, quite erroneously, as a Home Office pathologist.

Brontë was just three years younger than Spilsbury and came from similar middle-class stock, but in terms of temperament and personality the two might have inhabited different planets. Spilsbury's glacial assuredness provided stark relief to the hotheaded flights of fancy that often blighted Brontë's work, and the courts made their preference plain. By the mid-1920s Spilsbury had ruled the forensic roost in England for almost fifteen years, and he wasn't about to yield that position to some pushy parvenu. Brontë was relentless, and as frustration gave way to corrosive resentment, he scrabbled for ways to engineer his hated rival's downfall. Ironically, he had the highest regard for Spilsbury's professional ability, even to the point of publicly acknowledging him as "the greatest expert pathologist,"[2] and however grudging this praise might have been, at least it was genuine. This feeling was not reciprocated. Spilsbury despised Brontë as a forensic mountebank, someone prepared to cut corners, slapdash in his methodology, lavish in his conclusions. For the most part Spilsbury kept his feelings bottled up behind a mask of tight-lipped politeness, but Brontë's gadfly petulance always rankled. Never more so than in the early part of 1925, when, after years of trying, the voluble Irishman was finally able to muster some allies and launch a full-scale assault on "Fortress Spilsbury."

Backbreaking Struggle

It might have been the Roaring Twenties, but little of the infectious glitz and glamour that lit up the rest of the Western world had illuminated the drab and unprofitable corner of Sussex countryside that John Norman Holmes Thorne called home. In the two years that Norman Thorne—everyone called him Norman—had run Wesley Poultry Farm, life had been one long, backbreaking struggle. His run of misfortune began in 1918, when he had joined the Royal Naval Air Service as a mechanic at age seventeen, and looked well set to survive what little remained of the Great War, only to be blown up just three weeks before the end of hostilities. Despite recovering quickly—he later described the scars as more mental than physical—demobilization the following year brought a harsh reality check. It soon became painfully obvious that the "Land Fit for Heroes" promised by the politicians had little call for someone with his elementary mechanical skills. By the summer of 1921 he had joined the swelling queues outside the dole office.

What set him apart from the thousands of other out-of-work exservicemen was having a father able and willing to toss him a financial lifeline. It came in the form of a £100 loan that Thorne used to purchase a 2½ acre plot of land just outside the Sussex village of Crowborough. The intention was to raise Leghorn chickens, sell the eggs, then sit back and bank the profits.

No one could ever accuse Thorne of laziness. From dawn to dusk he slaved, sawing wood, hammering nails, trying to cobble together the coops and chicken runs that he needed to fulfill his dream. Come nightfall he trudged wearily back to his lodgings nearby. His social life, skimpy though it was, came on the weekends when he would bicycle the forty-two miles to London to briefly visit his young lady, then cycle wearily back again.

Viewed from more than one perspective, Thorne could be considered a minor pillar of the community. He was a regular chapel-goer, with a strong moral conscience that expressed itself in membership of a temperance organization called the Band of Hope, and he cheerfully carried out volunteer work with the Boy Scouts. And, of course, he was prepared to work every hour under the sun to make a success of his business.

Much of this resolve went into converting one of the chicken coops into habitable living quarters. It wasn't much, just twelve feet by seven, but it was somewhere he could call home, and meant he no longer had to pay rent. Most significant of all, it allowed his girlfriend to travel down from London to see him.

Elsie Cameron was two years older than Thorne. With her hair pulled back into a schoolmarmish bun, spectacles, pinched little face, and an air of hand-wringing angst, she was no head-turner; indeed, most men found her far too highly strung for prolonged contact. But not Thorne. The couple had met in 1920 at Kensal Rise Wesleyan Church in North London, where Elsie taught Sunday School. Thorne soon made plain his interest, and the couple began walking out. Elsie could scarcely believe her good fortune: the man by her side was good-natured; handsome to her way of thinking, with his thick brown hair and penetrating eyes; industrious; and God fearing. Unsurprisingly, she fell head over heels in love with this stranger who had burst into her life, and told anyone who cared to listen that she had found the man she intended to marry.

As soon as Thorne's living accommodation was completed, Elsie began catching the weekend train down to Crowborough. It made a welcome break from the office where she worked as a typist, and of course, it spared him all those marathon cycle rides. Like most young ladies of the age, Elsie was fiercely protective of her reputation and, on these visits always made a point of putting up in boarding houses, taking care to visit Thorne's farm only during daylight hours. All the while she implored Thorne to name the day when they would marry.

He kept fending off all her entreaties. Not because he didn't love her, but because he was up to his eyes in debt. The scruffy tangle of chicken wire and mud called Wesley Farm had turned into a bottomless money pit that barely provided enough for him to survive, let alone support a wife and probable family. Undeterred, Elsie kept on pushing. In December 1922, her persistence finally paid off when the couple announced their engagement.

Less than one month later came a major setback: Elsie was fired from the firm where she had worked for nine years. The anxiety that had plagued her since childhood now went into overdrive, bad enough for her to attend a Dr. Andrew Elliott in Crowborough, whose rather unoriginal diagnosis concluded that she was suffering from "a not very stable nervous system."[3] Elsie Cameron was now fixated on the idea of marriage to Norman Thorne. Nothing else mattered. She drifted in and out of a string of jobs, with employers constantly complaining of her moodiness and forgetful nature. As the time on her hands multiplied, she became a more or less permanent fixture at the converted chicken coop, and in June 1923 came the biggest step of all: she gave herself physically to the man she loved.

Sexual Awakening

Thorne later tried to downplay the significance of this incident. "We became on intimate terms, that is feeling one another's person and from that it went [sic] that I put my person against hers, but in my opinion I did not put it into her. This practice continued on almost all the occasions when Miss Cameron came to the hut. We had previously made up our minds that she should not become pregnant."[4]

Elsie Cameron's first sexual experience, at age twenty-five, deep in the midst of a mental crisis, served only to double her determination. Whole nights were now spent in Thorne's bed, as she pleaded with him to marry her.

Still he could not bring himself to take that step. His indecision wasn't solely self-inspired; there was also family pressure to contend with. His father, the man who had financed the poultry farm, made no secret of his dislike for Elsie. In letters to Thorne, she complained bitterly of this parental interference:

"Oh lovie, I think your Dad is hateful. What he means by causing trouble between you and myself I can't imagine. I believe he is trying to find out my faults, and if he can't find out he makes them up [sic] . . . our love for each other will never die, whatever happens, will it, pet?"[5]

More letters followed. "If only we could get married . . . We can manage in a little hut like yours; your Elsie is quite well now and there is no fear of any children for three or four years."[6]

And so it went, for month after month, until a year had passed. In August 1923 she took a job in Crowborough as a nursery companion, again staying in lodgings. True to form the position only lasted two weeks. Her nerves, by now, were in free fall. One night, in a state of collapse, she begged her landlady to take her to Thorne's hut, a brazen request that speaks volumes about her desperation. Elsie spent that night with the man she loved, and the next day he accompanied her back to London. They were met at Victoria station by Elsie's sister, Margaret. Thorne took Margaret to one side. On the journey, he said anxiously, Elsie had threatened to throw herself from the train if he didn't agree to marry soon. On hearing this, Elsie's family insisted that she consult their own physician in Kensal Rise, Dr. Watson Walker. He diagnosed neurasthenia—a debility of the nerves, causing fatigue and listlessness—and put her on a course of sedatives.

The year of 1923 brought happiness tinged with heartbreak for Elsie as she watched her brother and sister both get married. A fortune-teller had predicted that she herself would be married by December, but as Christmastime rolled around and she was no closer to her dream of a wedding date, her always perilous mental state inched dangerously toward the psychotic.

Still, the candle of hope flickered inside. Her letters reveal the pathetic buoyancy of her expectation, and she continued to visit the farm at every opportunity. All pretense at modesty was now abandoned. Neighbors became used to Elsie's frequent overnight visits, and she was commonly regarded as Thorne's "young lady."[7] Thorne's ardor, meantime, was cooling rapidly. Irritated by Elsie's mood swings and what he perceived to be harassment, he wanted to wash his hands of her. His testiness was exacerbated by an ever more parlous financial position. Each day the chickens seemed to eat their weight in corn, without ever once threatening to produce the anticipated egg bonanza. By the spring of 1924, teetering on the brink of bankruptcy and weighted down by the emotional millstone that was Elsie Cameron, he was close to throwing in the towel and going abroad, hoping to find a fresh start.

Then fate intervened.

Elizabeth Coldicott was a local dressmaker, bubbly, warm, very attractive, and, above all else, reassuringly stable. She lived in South View Road, Crowborough, about a mile from Thorne. The couple had met at a village dance, and it didn't take long for the romantic sparks to fly. They began dating, though taking care to conceal their affections on the one occasion when Elsie met Elizabeth. At no time did Elsie suspect that she was in the presence of a rival.

Thorne and Elizabeth took full advantage of Elsie's ignorance. Most days saw them in each other's company. Doubtless during that summer of 1924, like most people in Britain, they would have discussed the sensational trial of Patrick Mahon that was headlining in nearby Lewes, some fourteen miles away. It was the biggest case to hit the region in years. Thorne, particularly, seemed fascinated by the story, carefully clipping columns from the newspapers and storing them in his hut, where they were later discovered. In light of subsequent developments, it's tempting to wonder if Thorne was studying Mahon's homicidal template, perhaps with a view to finding ways in which it might be improved.

By summer the couple were discussing possible wedding dates, and come September, Elizabeth was even visiting Thorne at his hut. Given the shack's primitive squalor, it says much for Thorne's magnetism that he was able to induce two young women to spend so much time in such wretched surroundings.

Elsie, in the meantime, unaware of any duplicity, continued to struggle with her demons. That September saw her being sent home from her place of employment because of a nervous breakdown. No longer did the sedatives iron out her fluctuating moods; one moment she was screaming hysterical abuse at anyone in earshot, the next found her mired in lethargic silence. Only in one trait was she consistent; her demands on Thorne.

When Elsie showed up in Crowborough in late October, she lodged with friends for a week, and during this visit, according to Thorne, the couple never had sex. That same month he escorted Elsie to the British Empire Exhibition at Wembley in North London, a hugely popular event that attracted thousands of visitors. Among the many pavilions was one for the Alliance of Honor, an organization devoted to promoting premarital chastity. Presumably in the belief that no matter how long beforehand the horse may have bolted, it was never too late to shut the stable door, Thorne renewed his membership and suggested to Elsie that she might want to join the women's section. He later explained away his hypocrisy thus, "She was growing very passionate."[8]

After kissing Elsie good-bye in London, he returned to Crowborough and the arms of his other woman. November saw Elizabeth spending almost every evening, from 8:30 to 10:30, at the hut. By her own admission they passed their time in "lovemaking and talking."[9] Much of that talk centered on Thorne's determination to break off his engagement to Elsie, thus clearing the way for Elizabeth and him to emigrate to America. He agonized over how best to broach the subject. Then events conspired to force his hand.

In early November, Elsie visited Dr. Walker, and what she heard there left her convinced that she was pregnant. She immediately wrote to Thorne. He was staggered by the news, which he found frankly unbelievable. It was now that the iron in his soul surfaced. Writing back by return, he said, "There are one or two things I haven't told you for more reasons than one. It concerns someone else as well . . . I am afraid I am between two fires."[10]

Elsie's clouded mind struggled to make any sense of what she read. "Really Norman, your letter puzzles me, I can't make it out. Why are there one or two things you haven't told me and in what way does it concern someone else? . . . What do you mean by you are afraid you are between two fires?"[11] She amplified her anxiety. "Please arrange about getting married as soon as possible. I feel sick every day and things will soon be noticeable to everybody and I want to be married before Christmas and Christmas Day is only a month from tomorrow."[12]

If Elsie was guilty of willful head-burying in the sand, Thorne's next letter, written on November 27, jerked her eyes wide open. "What I haven't told you is that on certain occasions a girl has been here late at night, I am not going to mention her name, nobody knows. When you gave in to your nerves again and refused to take interest in life I gave up hope in you and let myself go [sic]; this is the result. I didn't know last week what I know now . . . I must have time to think, she thinks I am going to marry her of course, and I have a strong feeling for her, or I shouldn't have done what I have."[13]

This letter hit Elsie like a howitzer shell. Her reply was a heartfelt cry of anguish. "You have absolutely broken my heart, I never thought you were capable of such deception . . . So I am to take it that you have got this other girl into the same condition which you have got me?"[14]

What Elsie didn't know was that Thorne had lied; the story of the second pregnancy was a myth. (He later told the police that, although he had "at times put my hand up her [Elizabeth's] skirt and touched her private part, I have never had sexual intercourse with her.")[15] The lie had been fabricated and calculated to loosen Elsie's grip. Except that Elsie had no intention of quitting: "Your duty is to marry me. I have first claim on you . . . I expect you to marry me and finish with the other girl as soon as possible. My baby must have a name."[16]

On November 30 Elsie traveled down to Crowborough and demanded an explanation. Who was this woman? Was she pregnant? And why hadn't he posted the banns if they intended to marry? With his bluff called, Thorne quickly backtracked. He went on a charm offensive, soothing her fears, cooing that it had all been a big mistake, and promising that they would be married before Christmas. That evening he saw her onto the London train. Once it had steamed out of the station, he returned to the warm and willing Elizabeth, who showed up at the shack as normal at 8:30 P.M.

Three days later John Thorne arrived at the farm to discuss his son's shambolic domestic situation. He listened gravely as the mess unfolded. When Norman expressed doubts about Elsie's pregnancy, John Thorne advised stalling until after Christmas, just in case Elsie was trying to trick him into marriage. That same day Thorne wrote Elsie another letter, outlining his father's advice and his decision to follow it.

Elsie read this and exploded. She could feel Norman slipping away. The next day—Friday, December 5—she bought a new sweater, had her hair styled, threw some items of clothing, including a baby's frock, into a small attaché case, and set off by train for Crowborough, this time determined to stay with Norman until he married her.

It was cold and already dusk when the train arrived. A timetable mix-up meant that Elsie alighted at Tunbridge Wells and then had to catch a bus to Crowborough. The driver, Cecil Copplestone, set Elsie down some half an hour's walk from where Thorne lived. The time was approximately 4:45 P.M. when Elsie struck out for Wesley Farm, eager to begin her new life as a married woman.

Frantic Parents

Five days later, Thorne received an anxious telegram from Elsie's father, Donald Cameron. "Elsie left Friday have heard no news has she arrived reply." Norman's answer came by return: "Not here—open letters—cannot understand."[17] This referred to letters sent by Thorne to Elsie. One, dated Sunday, December 7, began, "My own darling Elsie, Well, where did you get to yesterday? I went to Groombridge and you did not turn up."[18]

On reading this, Cameron wasted no time in contacting the police. A constable dispatched to Wesley Farm found the proprietor pale with worry. Thorne volunteered a photograph of his fiancée and agreed to attend the local station, at which time he provided an account of his movements on the day that Elsie disappeared. He had gone out early that morning, not getting home until 3:45 P.M., just in time to feed the chickens. After supper, he had stayed in until 9:45 P.M., then went to meet Elizabeth Coldicott and her mother. They had been shopping in Brighton for the day and he had agreed to meet their train and escort them home from the local station. He was back in his hut by 11:30 P.M. The next morning—Saturday—he'd gone to Groombridge station to meet Elsie as arranged, except she did not arrive. He had then returned home, as baffled as anyone else by her nonappearance. When Superintendent Isaac Budgeon asked, purely as a matter of routine, if he could search the farm, Thorne readily agreed. A cursory examination of the hut and a few other outbuildings revealed nothing.

By now Elsie Cameron's strange disappearance had become a national story, and within days Wesley Farm was overrun with reporters. Thorne welcomed the media with open arms, reveling in all the attention being lavished upon him, always eager to discuss various theories that might explain the mystery. "They [the police] are welcome to dig every inch,"[19] he declared with a laugh. Only once did he let his cheerful guard drop, savagely kicking a chicken several feet into the air when its clucking at his heels threatened to interrupt one impromptu press conference. This sliver of unthinking cruelty prompted more than one reporter to wonder what really lurked inside Norman Thorne. When photographers asked him to pose, he thought for a moment, then pointed to the chicken run and suggested a shot of him mournfully scattering seed to his Leghorns. Even more poignant was the photo that showed him in rough work clothes and high-laced muddy boots, donning headphones over a crystal radio set to anxiously await news of his missing fiancée. His desolation seemed total. Each day he called at the police station, and each day he heard the same story: still no sign of Elsie.

What made this response doubly puzzling was the fact that the police were already in receipt of information from two local men regarding some interesting developments on the day of Elsie's disappearance. George Adams, who lived in nearby Black Ness, put the time at between 5 and 5:20 P.M. when he'd passed a woman whom he knew to be Thorne's young lady walking down the road that led to Wesley Farm. Admittedly, he had not seen her turn in at the farm gate.

His companion, Albert Sands, a carnation grower, said the young woman was carrying either a suitcase or an attaché case. Although he didn't know her name, he also recognized her as Thorne's lady friend. Like Adams, he couldn't confirm that the woman had entered the gate that led to Wesley Farm.

Astonishingly the local police shelved both statements. Whether Adams and Sands were considered to be unreliable we don't know, but so far as the authorities were concerned, Thorne's open-faced responses were those of someone who had nothing to hide, and they didn't even question him on the matter. As Christmas came and went without any sign of the elusive Miss Cameron, media interest inevitably waned, and reporters left to cover other stories. Soon all mention of Elsie Cameron vanished from the newspapers. And then, suddenly, there came a breakthrough.

Annie Price was a local woman who'd been away from the district for some time and knew nothing of the mysterious disappearance, so when she returned home in early January 1925, she was eager to catch up on all the local news. Naturally this was dominated by the Elsie Cameron saga. Mrs. Price cast her mind back. Thorne's farm was on Luxford Lane, a road she regularly walked when visiting a friend. She recalled that on December 5, she had been walking along Luxford Lane at around five o'clock, and in the gathering gloom ahead were two men—obviously Sands and Adams—walking in the same direction. As they reached Thorne's smallholding, she saw, coming in the opposite direction, a young woman carrying a small case, who, after passing the two men but before reaching Mrs. Price, had turned into the gate that led to Wesley Farm.

When Mrs. Price took her story to the local police, the effect was electric. Whereas they had disdained the statements of Adams and Sands, corroboration from a third witness was too much to ignore. Belatedly they contacted Scotland Yard.

Chief Inspector John Gillan motored down from London. He arrived at Crowborough on January 14, acquainted himself with the details of the case, and that afternoon paid Thorne a surprise visit. He stated bluntly that Elsie Cameron had been seen in the vicinity of the farm on the day of her disappearance. Thorne's protestations of ignorance sounded thin, and he was taken to the local police station where he gave a statement that took most of the night. Exhausted by his ordeal, Thorne snatched some much-needed sleep while a team of officers returned to Wesley Farm. This time they were carrying spades.

Just after daybreak, diggers found an attaché case that had been buried about two feet deep near the gate. Inside was a fawn costume, two new nightdresses, a pair of stockings, a pair of shoes, a hairbrush, and a broken pair of rimless spectacles. Donald Cameron identified the glasses as those worn by his daughter when she had left their home in London. Confronted by this revelation, Thorne lapsed into a brooding silence that lasted most of the day. Finally, at 8 P.M., he made a revised statement. Even before the details that fleshed out Thorne's change of heart reached the farm, searchers had already found Elsie's damaged wristwatch, some jewelry, and a bracelet, hidden in a large can. Thorne's new statement told them to train their flashlights onto a plot some thirty yards from where the case had been buried.

At 11 P.M. the search for Elsie Cameron came to an end. Her body lay directly beneath the spot where Thorne had insisted on having his photograph taken. The unsuccessful chicken farmer now abandoned all pretense and decided to come clean.

On the evening of Friday, December 5, he said, Elsie had arrived out of the blue, demanded that he marry her, and announced that she wasn't leaving until he did. He agreed that he would marry her if she were pregnant, convinced in his heart of hearts that this was not the case, as they had never fully consummated their relationship. The couple ate around six o'clock, a meal that was followed by a fierce argument when Thorne announced that he had to leave at 9:30 P.M. to pick up Elizabeth Coldicott and her mother, as arranged. When he returned two hours later and entered the hut, he found Elsie hanging from a beam.

His statement continued, "I cut the cord and laid her on the bed. She was dead. I then put out the lights. She had her frock off and her hair was down. I laid across the table for about an hour. I was about to . . . go for the police when I realized the position I was in, and decided not to do so.

"I then went down to the workshop and got my hacksaw and some sacks and took them back to the hut. I tore off Miss Cameron's clothes and burned them in a fireplace in the hut. I then laid the sacks on the floor, put Miss Cameron (who was then naked) on the floor and sawed off her legs, and the head, by the glow of the fire. I put them in sacks, intending to carry them away, but my nerve failed me and I took them down to the workshop and I left them there. I went back to the hut and I sat in the chair all night. Next morning, just as it got light, I buried the sacks and a tin containing the remains in a chicken run. I then went to the hut and had some coffee and tried to build up evidence to clear myself."[20]

Worn out by the efforts of the night, Thorne first cleaned up, then revived his flagging spirits by taking in a movie with Elizabeth Coldicott.

Accidental death, panic, gruesome dismemberment, hasty cover-up—so far as the police were concerned, it sounded like "The Mahon Story: Part 2." Few laypersons had studied that case more closely than Norman Thorne, so better than most, he must have realized the peril of his position, especially when told by a reporter that Sir Bernard Spilsbury had been drafted in to perform the autopsy. Thorne's response was characteristically confident: "I'm not worried about him."[21]

Disputed Autopsy

On January 17, Spilsbury spent four hours at Beacon Hill mortuary in Crowborough studying the remains of Elsie Cameron. Whatever criticisms might have been leveled at Spilsbury, scamping the evidence was never one of them. It didn't matter whether the body on the slab had been killed in a road accident, had died in hospital, or was a suspected murder victim; all received the same meticulous autopsy. He worked slowly, using instruments that had been in his case since his student days. He had little time for many newfangled innovations. When something genuinely useful came along—such as the probing forceps that he pioneered—it was added to his bag; otherwise, he stayed with the familiar implements that had become second nature to him.

The remains were in four pieces, and the head, with its freshly styled dark brown hair, had been stuffed so tightly into a biscuit tin that just removing it was a feat in itself. All the parts had been dismembered by clean cuts through the soft tissue and sawing through the bones, and there were clear signs of extensive physical trauma. The skull itself was unusually thin, and there was one bruise on the right rear that measured about 2½ inches by 1½ inches, and another—slightly larger—on the right temple, extending down the right cheek almost to the level of the mouth. The left eye was blackened by yet another contusion. The remaining four bruises that Spilsbury found were on the back, legs, and the left ankle. All looked to have been caused shortly before death. Despite the extent and severity of these contusions, he found no accompanying evidence of any fractured bones.

In light of Thorne's statement, Spilsbury devoted special attention to the neck and the area beneath the ears. The neck is one of the most vulnerable areas of the human body, for it is here, unprotected by any sheath of bone, that the three principal routes for survival—blood supply to the head, air supply to the lungs, and the nervous supply connecting the brain to the rest of the body via the spinal column—are most at risk. Interruption to any or all of these can cause death.

Blood Supply

A continuous pressure of just 11 psi—about the same as exerted by someone sitting down and resting his or her neck against a noose—is sufficient to block the carotid artery, the principal blood supply to the brain and face. Even less pressure—approximately 4.5 psi—will prevent the jugular vein from doing its job of draining blood from the brain. Both of these factors can contribute to cerebral hypoxia. When starved of oxygen, the brain will suffer irreversible damage in about four minutes, if the pressure is uninterrupted, and begin to die. Another factor is the vagus reflex (see chapter on George Joseph Smith). As noted earlier, stimulation of this reflex can lead to cardiac arrest and almost instantaneous death.

Air Supply

When a body is suspended by the neck, the root of the tongue, the soft palate, and the roof of the mouth are often pressed together, blocking the airway. This, too, will result in hypoxia, though not as quickly as when caused by interrupted blood supply.

Spinal Fracture

Finally, a long drop, rarely seen in suicides and more often the preserve of judicial executions, can cause death by fracturing the spinal column. Until recently, most medical examiners believed that such a fracture resulted in instantaneous death, but British government files released in 2000 tell a different story. Secret tests conducted on Nazi war criminals executed in 1946 showed that, in some cases, even twenty-five minutes after being hanged, the hearts were still emitting recordable impulses on an electrocardiograph. (Practical as always, and with a conveyor belt of condemned prisoners to deal with—sometimes as many as seventeen in one day—the Brits overcame the problem by injecting 10 cc of chloroform directly into the heart immediately after the drop was operated. This stopped the heart instantly.)

Spilsbury brought all his experience to bear on Elsie Cameron's neck. He saw some marks, but only the normal creases found in human skin, the result of folding and unfolding, certainly nothing that resembled a rope impression. This was borne out by the internal inspection of the body. There were no visible signs of hanging: no asphyxia, no congestion of the brain, no discoloration of the face, no petechiae in the eyes. Having found absolutely nothing to substantiate Thorne's claim that Elsie had hanged herself, Spilsbury now wondered if it were possible to learn when she had died.

For this he turned to the stomach contents. Since food evacuates the stomach at a fairly predictable rate—a process that ceases at death—if the timing of the final meal is known, this can often provide an indicator of the time of death. As one eminent pathologist puts it, "Very little interferes with the law of the digestive process."[22] According to Thorne, he and Elsie had eaten at around 6 P.M. From what Spilsbury found in Elsie's stomach—several ounces of partly digested food—he thought she had died no more than two hours after eating her last meal. So unless she ate another meal immediately after Thorne left the shack that night at 9:45—not likely but not impossible, either—she must have been dead by eight o'clock. If this were the case, Thorne's whole story had been blown out of the water.

Spilsbury attributed death to shock caused by injuries sustained in some kind of physical assault. Most likely, he thought, Elsie had been attacked from the front and, in falling backwards in the cramped hut, struck her head on either the bedstead or the floor, causing the bruise to the back of the head. He felt that the victim had been dead for several hours prior to dismemberment, as Thorne had claimed. His saddest finding confirmed Thorne's suspicion: Elsie Cameron was not pregnant at the time of her death. Whether she was simply deluded or willfully manipulative, it was impossible to say.

On January 26, a sad funeral cortege gathered outside the house in Clifford Gardens, Kensal Rise, where Elsie had lived. Among the many floral tributes was a wreath from Thorne's parents; another came from the teachers at the Sunday School where she had taught. Just before the procession set off, yet another wreath arrived bearing the words "Till we meet again—Norman."[23] Angry family members removed the card but allowed the now-anonymous wreath to be placed on the grave at Willesden New Cemetery.

While on remand, Thorne remained remarkably upbeat. Even when told that Spilsbury had found no evidence to substantiate his claim of suicidal hanging, his self-possession remained intact. Indeed, he became quite belligerent, insisting that there *had* been bruises around Elsie's neck: he had seen them!

Against the advice of counsel—who privately felt that Thorne's best chance of escaping the gallows lay in a plea of manslaughter—Thorne demanded a second autopsy, one that would, he said, exonerate him. "There's nothing against me except Spilsbury's evidence," he boasted, "And we'll soon knock that down. You see if we don't."[24]

An application was made to the Home Office for the exhumation of Elsie Cameron's body. It took place just after daybreak on February 24, and acting on behalf of Thorne was none other than Dr. Robert Matthew Brontë.

In what must have resembled a scene from dueling days gone by, Brontë took up a position on one side of the open grave, while across the gaping hole stood the lofty figure of Sir Bernard Spilsbury. He maintained a courteous silence as Brontë, assisted by Dr. John Gibson, went about his work. Between the two factions, acting as an unofficial umpire, stood Chief Inspector Gillan. At no time did Spilsbury attempt to interfere with Brontë, nor was there any indication of the contempt he felt for the other man's ability.

In the month that had passed since Spilsbury's previous autopsy, the body had undergone marked putrefactive changes, due in large part to water contamination. Even so, Brontë spotted two marks on the neck, one above the Adam's apple, the other directly over it. (Although far more prominent in males, the Adam's apple—the angle between two cartilage plates in the throat—is still present in females.) Spilsbury had also noticed these marks during his examination but, after making an incision, had decided that they were natural creases, and had not bothered to take any sections.

What happened next would drive an irrevocable wedge between the two men, severing a professional relationship that had never been close, and would henceforth be venomous. Spilsbury always maintained that when he gave his opinion that these were the natural creases or folds so often found in the human neck, Brontë agreed with him. It was a claim that Brontë would later repudiate outright. This was why, he said, he excised several sections of the skin and underlying tissues for further analysis. As a courtesy, he handed half the sections to Spilsbury, so that he might make his own laboratory inspection.

In all other aspects, the rest of his examination concurred with Spilsbury's findings, even down to the stomach contents. With the exhumation complete, the two protagonists parted company, and the remains of Elsie Cameron were returned to the cold February soil. So far as Spilsbury was concerned, nothing in either autopsy supported Thorne's claim that Elsie had committed suicide by hanging.

Nor did the police believe that Elsie had taken her own life. On January 18 Gillan had conducted some experiments inside the shack. Three main beams ran across the hut. The highest was very dusty, covered with undisturbed cobwebs, and obviously hadn't been touched in months. The two lower beams doubled up as hat racks and storage spaces for paperwork. Gillan checked for any marks or indentations that might have been caused by a rope supporting a heavy weight. He saw none.

Police Experiments

Six days later Gillan returned to the hut with some thin rope, similar to the washing line that Thorne said Elsie had used. He was curious to find out if the spindly beams would support the weight of the dead girl. The rope was tied over the lowest beam, then attached to 112 pounds of weights, roughly equivalent to the body weight of Elsie Cameron. In the first experiment the weights were raised gradually to avoid a sudden pull on the rope. This left perceptible fiber traces on the beam. When the experiment was repeated, this time dropping the weight suddenly to simulate the jerk of a suicide stepping off a chair, the rope cut deep into the upper angles of the beam, leaving two distinct marks.

The results seemed unequivocal: Elsie Cameron could not have hanged herself in the manner that Thorne described. So far as the Crown was concerned, the case looked open and shut.

On Wednesday, March 11, 1925, when Thorne stepped into the same Lewes courtroom dock that Patrick Mahon had occupied just eight months previously, a heavy sense of déjà vu hung in the air. Once again, Sir Henry Curtis-Bennett, KC, led for the Crown and found himself opposed by J. D. Cassels, KC. The only significant change in personnel was the judge, William Finlay, whose job it would be to mediate the often fractious exchanges between counsel.

In his opening speech, Curtis-Bennett outlined the prosecution's case in the simplest terms: Thorne had murdered and dismembered one girlfriend to make room for another, and proved himself a very accomplished liar in the process. To the Crown's way of thinking, anyone so ice-cool in the face of such media attention was patently capable of anything. Quite early in the proceedings, the two lower beams from the hut were brought into court, and Gillan detailed the experiments conducted by himself and his fellow officers. Although not sturdy, the beams were strong enough to support someone of Elsie's weight. He pointed out to the jury the two indentations made by the rope he had used. Just as the beam was about to be put away, Cassels asked: "May I also have the privilege of having the marks pointed out to me?"

"Yes, certainly," said Curtis-Bennett. Then he added, "Don't have a grievance, Mr. Cassels."

Cassels fired back: "I've no grievance. When I have a grievance there's no mistake about it."[25]

This testiness spilled over into Cassels's cross-examination of Gillan.

After some exploratory sparring with the witness about possible defects in the wood, Cassels's focus suddenly sharpened. "Was anyone present representing the defense when your experiments took place?"

"No," replied Gillan.

"Had the defense any notice of the fact that you were making the experiments?"

"No."[26]

With these two questions, Cassels ignited a legal powder keg. Hitherto the integrity of police investigations had gone virtually unchallenged in the British courtroom, and, although unstated, Cassels's subtext was pikestaff plain: Somewhere along the line he suspected police chicanery. Such a radical departure from the accepted avenues of cross-examination—as dangerous as it was unprecedented—would not have been undertaken lightly by someone of Cassels's immense experience had he not entertained the gravest doubts about the inquiry. For his part, Gillan didn't give an inch. He insisted that the experiments had been performed with diligence and honesty. And then he left. Next up was Spilsbury.

His examination-in-chief contained no histrionics, just the usual emphatic statements of fact. For some people in the public gallery, those details were altogether too grueling, and three women had to be assisted from the court. When Spilsbury said that "a crushing blow"[27] had been delivered to the decedent's skull, Curtis-Bennett immediately produced two Indian clubs found outside Thorne's hut and asked if the bruises on the face could have been caused by either implement. Curtis-Bennett was a wily courtroom performer, well aware of the impact that two such murderous-looking items would have on an impressionable jury. Cunningly, he didn't ask Spilsbury *if* these clubs had been used in the assault, only that they *might* have been. Spilsbury, caught off stride, had no alternative but to say yes. Though in fairness to the defense, he stressed that none of the other bruises on the body were consistent with having been caused by the clubs.

All this, though, was mere window dressing; the crux of the prosecution's case came in a single question from Curtis-Bennett to Spilsbury: "Were there any external marks upon this girl to signify that she had been hanged?"

"No, none at all."[28]

Cassels rose to cross-examine. Immediately he foreshadowed the defense theory: that Elsie's heart could have gone on beating for another ten to fifteen minutes after Thorne cut her down, enough time for the circulation of the blood to remove most of the marks of the attempted hanging. Spilsbury listened carefully to Cassels's rather outlandish hypothesis and conceded that there was an authenticated case of the heart of a man continuing to beat after he had been executed by guillotining. It had gone on working for more than an hour, he declared. Then he added, "That's a remarkable case."

Cassels said acidly, "You'll forgive me for saying so, but perhaps this may be also."[29]

Spilsbury wasn't used to being so roughly handled. No one in British legal history had spent more hours in the witness box than the honorary Home Office pathologist. He knew how the game was played, what questions to expect, what ploys the defense might adopt, but this was something new: a blatant attempt to ridicule his testimony. Whatever inner turmoil he may have felt remained buried beneath his customary unflappable demeanor.

Having earlier been drawn into the reluctant admission that one of the Indian clubs *might* have inflicted the bruises, Spilsbury was now forced into the uncomfortable position of having to defend that statement. When Cassels deliberately dropped the club onto the wooden courtroom floor, it made a thunderous noise, and Spilsbury struggled to work up a plausible scenario whereby Elsie could have been struck about the head with this club without either the skin being broken or the skull being fractured. Cassels continued to make headway. He extracted concessions from Spilsbury that all the bruises sustained were as consistent with a fall as they were with an attack. Nor, the witness admitted, did he find any defense wounds on the hands and arms, as was common in victims of violent assault.

The tension rose as Cassels fought to press home his advantage. "On

January 17, when you performed your post-mortem, did you examine microscopically any part of the neck?"

"No."

"Why not?"

"Because it was quite unnecessary. I made a thorough examination of the neck and found no mark."

"Because externally you found no mark, you did not examine further?"

"Oh yes," said Spilsbury, "very much further."

"But did you examine *microscopically*?"

"No. I deeply probed the tissues."

"By the naked eye?"

"Yes."[30]

At this point, Cassels turned to the second autopsy, and the slides that Brontë had made from the neck sections. "Did not microscopic examination definitely show extravasation of blood, consistent only with pressure?"[31]

Spilsbury replied that there was no extravasation to be seen because by the time Brontë made his slides, the tissues were so water-damaged that all traces of blood had been destroyed! Cassels had crossed swords with Spilsbury enough times to realize that such implacability rendered further questioning pointless, and he wisely retreated.

When it came time to open the defense, Cassels observed, "It is indeed remarkable that perhaps upon a microscope slide may depend the great issue in this investigation."[32] As predictions go, it was notably prescient.

Elsie Cameron's death, Cassels said, had resulted from shock caused by suicidal hanging. He then painted a word portrait of Elsie Cameron, the hopeless neurotic: someone who had threatened to throw herself out of a train, someone who imagined people were laughing at her, someone who was frequently too terrified to even cross a street. By the time Cassels finished, it was all too easy to imagine this broken leaf taking her own life. He then called Norman Thorne.

In taking the witness stand, Thorne unraveled much of the good that his counsel had done. Gone was the mud-caked farmhand seen in so many press photographs; in its place was a sleekly dressed young man with crisp shirt cuffs and carefully brushed hair. There was nothing terribly damning about what he said, but his matter-of-fact manner—oddly unemotional and laced with inappropriate smiles—jarred on the nerves. He started with two major strikes against him. First, he was a self-confessed liar; second, juries instinctively shrink from any defendant prepared to segment a human body in the interests of self-preservation. Even his self-confessed anguish after burying the body—"I flung myself on the bed and I cried like a baby"[33]—could not dislodge the view that here was a skilled performer playing the highest stakes poker possible.

Under cross-examination much of his self-confidence drained away. Curtis-Bennett was peerless when it came to phrasing questions designed to damn the responder, whichever form the answer took. Casually he asked Thorne if, when he went out at 9:30 P.M., Elsie still believed they would be married.

"Yes."

"Then why should she commit suicide?"

Thorne, plainly rattled, could only bluster. "Why? She left no message behind, and I don't think it safe for me to say."[34]

Nor could he adequately account for another anomaly: why he had burned some of Elsie's clothes—significantly those she wore at the time of her death—yet buried others? Similarly with her damaged watch, spectacles, and a locket and chain; he professed to have no idea how they all came to be broken. As for the bruises that littered Elsie Cameron's body, these were attributed to his own clumsiness as he cut down the body and it banged into the furniture.

A telling passage came right at the end of his testimony, when Mr. Justice Finlay asked if, after cutting Elsie down, Thorne had made any attempt to resuscitate her?

"No. I thought she was dead."

"Did you ever think of going to fetch a doctor?"

"Not until after I got up from the table . . . about an hour later."

"You have heard, I suppose, that people who are apparently dead are sometimes revived?"

"Yes, I have heard of such things."

"But you never thought of getting a doctor?"

"No."[35]

Like most defendants on the capital charge, Thorne's witness box performance had done little to advance his survival prospects. Maybe the battery of defense forensic experts could work the oracle?

Brontë Launches Attack

Leading the charge was Brontë, who began by listing his qualifications in minute and excruciating detail. Earlier Spilsbury, by contrast, had said nothing: he hadn't needed to. His record spoke for itself.

Brontë declared that the sections he'd taken from the two marks on the neck showed an extravasation of blood. They were not natural creases but grooves. "I consider that Sir Bernard made one mistake in not examining the marks microscopically as I did." Then he added, "A rope could certainly produce that effect, tight round the neck. It could be produced in the process of hanging."[36]

In his opinion, the cause of death was shock following an unsuccessful or interrupted attempt at self-strangulation. It was not unknown, he said, for people intending to die by one means actually dying by another. Borrowing a page from the Spilsbury canon, he offered to bring to court the records of several hundred cases to support his opinion, an offer that the judge was noticeably quick to reject. Brontë's volubility began to grate, as did his wearisome digressions. Eventually Mr. Justice Finlay had to remind the witness to confine his statements to things in his experience.

When Curtis-Bennett queried Brontë about Spilsbury's claim that at the second autopsy, he [Brontë] had agreed that the marks on the neck could be the creases normally found on most women of Elsie Cameron's age, the witness snapped peevishly, "Your suggestion has no foundation, Sir Henry."[37] Brontë's effrontery was breathtaking. Earlier in the trial, contemporaneous notes made by Dr. Gibson on Brontë's behalf had been introduced, and these clearly recorded the marks as "grooves . . . equally creases."[38]

Far more restrained, and infinitely more impressive so far as the defense was concerned, was Dr. Hugh Miller Galt, formerly a professor at the University of Glasgow and a medico-legal examiner for the Crown in Scotland. He agreed with Brontë that the sections taken from the neck could be indicators of suicidal hanging, and he took issue with Spilsbury's guarded opinion that the Indian club might have caused the injuries without breaking the skin. Taking the club from Cassels, he said, "I can guarantee to either Sir Henry Curtis-Bennett or yourself that it would not only make a bruise on either of your heads but would smash the skull with one blow."[39]

Galt was followed by Dr. David Nabarro, director of the pathological department of London's Great Ormond Street Hospital. He, too, declared that Brontë's slides were not incompatible with marks caused by suicidal hanging.

The trial was descending into a quagmire of contradictory expert testimony. Desperate to clarify the situation, the judge ordered all the medical witnesses to meet over the weekend adjournment to try to iron out their differences over the slides.

It was a forlorn hope. On Monday morning Spilsbury was the first witness to be recalled. He told Cassels that nothing had changed: "We all adhered to our original views. We had a frank and free discussion and that's the result."

"What you're suggesting is that the other doctors may have been mistaken, or I think you go further and say *have* [italics added] been mistaken."

"Have been mistaken,"[40] Spilsbury confirmed. In his opinion, the so-called injured blood vessels were actually the degenerative remains of sebaceous glands and hair roots.

It was significant that in rebuttal, Cassels recalled Dr. Galt rather than the excitable Brontë. Galt disputed Spilsbury's claims regarding the hair roots and remained insistent that Brontë's slides showed evidence of extravasation. However, with impeccable fairness, he agreed that Spilsbury's slides showed no such extravasation. To account for this he offered a simple explanation. "All the blood vessels were not lacerated; there were only a few. It's quite possible, in fifty sections made from the same part, that only a small portion would show, and it so happened, in my belief, that Sir Bernard got a section without any."[41]

In closing arguments, Cassels hammered home the fact that three pathologists for the defense and the one for the Crown had failed to agree about what the slides showed, and he sympathized with the jury in their predicament: "You are asked to decide on a section of the neck so small that it can scarcely be seen by the human eye."[42] But it was what he said next that raised eyebrows and pulse rates in tandem. "Did you expect in this case, when you had heard the great Sir Bernard Spilsbury in the witness-box, that there could be any opinion to be given against it? What a tragedy of human justice it would be if the life of a man is to depend on the accuracy or fallibility of one individual."[43]

This was unparalleled, audacious even. Never before had anyone attempted, in such strident terms, to undermine Spilsbury's role as the ultimate arbiter of forensic medicine. "We can all admire attainment," continued Cassels, "take our hats off to ability, acknowledge the high position that a man has won in his sphere, but it's a long way to go if you have to say that because that man says one thing there can be no room for error."[44]

If Cassels was prepared to tackle Spilsbury head-on, then the judge was not. In summing up for the jury, Mr. Justice Finlay made no secret of where his own preferences lay. "Sir Bernard Spilsbury would be the first to disclaim infallibility in matters of this sort, but his opinion is undoubtedly the very best opinion that can be obtained, and you will, of course, consider what he says with the very utmost care." Of Spilsbury's opponent, he merely sniffed, "There is the evidence of Dr. Brontë. He is a pathologist . . ."[45]

At 5:13 P.M. on Monday, March 16, the jury retired. Thorne, down in the cells, seemed confident of acquittal. A prison guard described his demeanor during this hiatus: "Thorne was full of life, full of conversation and explained to me the superiority of the Buff Orpington hen over the Plymouth Rock."[46]

Such confidence proved misplaced. After less than half an hour's deliberation, the jury convicted Thorne of murder. It didn't matter that the defense had drafted in a team of medico-legal experts, of widely varying experience and motives, all of whom disagreed with the prosecution's star witness. So far as the jury was concerned, Sir Bernard Spilsbury *was* the voice of English medical jurisprudence. To deny him would have been tantamount to heresy. The Thorne verdict was a bitter disappointment for Brontë. Nothing, it seemed, other than an utter courtroom demolition of Spilsbury's evidence could shake his impregnable position.

Others felt similarly. As the campaign to save Thorne's life gathered pace, so did the anti-Spilsbury backlash. Outraged letters appeared in the press questioning his pontifical status in the English courtroom. Sir Arthur Conan Doyle, creator of fiction's greatest detective, Sherlock Holmes, and himself a Crowborough resident, was only the most famous of several notables who expressed concern about the medical evidence in Thorne's trial, arguing that for a man to forfeit his life on the back of such contradictory testimony was grotesque in the extreme.

The furor raged right up to the day of Thorne's appeal. For the most part appeals are token affairs, but in this case a most unusual application was made—that the medical evidence should be referred to the arbitration of a special medical commissioner appointed by the court, under Section 9 of the Criminal Appeal Act (1907). This decreed that there was certain evidence so complex, so technical, so beyond the comprehension of the ordinary layperson that its worth could only be gauged by an expert assessor.

In the event the appeal court did not agree. Nor did it side with defense claims that the judge had repeatedly exhibited bias toward Spilsbury's evidence in his summing-up. Thorne's appeal failed. Only now did the prisoner display emotion, crying out, "It isn't fair! I didn't do it,"[47] as he was dragged from the court, off to the same condemned cell at Wandsworth Prison that Patrick Mahon had occupied just seven months earlier. On April 22, trussed, hooded, and noosed, Thorne plummeted through the same trapdoor. This time the execution was uneventful.*

Thorne's trial undoubtedly delivered a wake-up call to Spilsbury. For the first time serious questions had been asked of his role within the English crime-fighting apparatus. In the fifteen years that had elapsed since the Crippen trial, the public had come to expect that science—and for that read "Spilsbury"—could solve any crime. Their belief in him and his belief in himself had created a legal monolith. While there is no evidence to suggest that the public ever lost its faith in Spilsbury, henceforth his testimony did display a newfound circumspection—which was just as well, for the next few years would be the most controversial of Spilsbury's long career.

1   *Times*, June 2, 1924, 11.
2   *Ibid.*, March 17, 1925, 6.
3   *Ibid.*, March 14, 1925, 7.
4   *Public Records Office*, HO 144/5193.
5   *Times*, March 12, 1925, 6.
6   Gordon Honeycombe, *The Murders of the Black Museum: 1870–1970* (London: Arrow, 1984), 290.
7   *Times*, February 12, 1925, 5.
8   Iain Adamson, *A Man of Quality* (London: Muller, 1964), 90.
9   *Times*, March 12, 1925, 6.
10 Edgar Lustgarten, *Verdicts in Dispute* (London: Wingate, 1949), 92–93.
11 *Ibid.*, 93.
12 *Ibid.*
13 *Ibid.*, 93–94.
14 *Ibid.*, 94.
15 *Public Records Office*, HO 144/5193.
16 Lustgarten, *Verdicts in Dispute*, 94.
17 Honeycombe, *The Murders of the Black Museum: 1870–1970*, 293.
18 Adamson, *A Man of Quality*, 91.

* Rumors that Thorne had confessed at the last minute were neither confirmed nor denied by the Home Office. This deliberate government silence was calculated to spare the condemned's family members the heartbreak of possibly discovering that the son or husband in whom they resolutely believed had lied to them as well as the court.

19 Leslie Randall, *The Famous Cases of Sir Bernard Spilsbury* (London: Ivor Nicholson & Watson, 1936), 168.

20 Adamson, *A Man of Quality*, 92–93.

21 Randall, *The Famous Cases of Sir Bernard Spilsbury*, 156.

22 Michael Baden and Judith Adler Hennessee, *Unnatural Death* (New York: Ballantine, 1989), 103.

23 *Times*, January 27, 1925, 8.

24 Randall, *The Famous Cases of Sir Bernard Spilsbury*, 174.

25 *Ibid.*, 95.

26 Edgar Lustgarten, *The Murder and the Trial* (London: Word Distributors, 1962), 97.

27 *Times*, March 13, 1925, 6.

28 *Ibid.*, 4.

29 Adamson, *A Man of Quality*, 94.

30 Lustgarten, *Verdicts in Dispute*, 115–16.

31 *Ibid.*, 116.

32 Adamson, *A Man of Quality*, 96.

33 *Times*, March 14, 1925, 7.

34 *Ibid.*

35 Lustgarten, *Verdicts in Dispute*, 123–24.

36 Adamson, *A Man of Quality*, 96.

37 *Times*, March 16, 1925, 8.

38 *Ibid.*

39 Adamson, *A Man of Quality*, 97.

40 *Ibid.*, 98.

41 *Ibid.*, 99.

42 *Ibid.*, 100.

43 *Times*, March 17, 1925, 6.

44 *Ibid.*

45 Adamson, *A Man of Quality*, 100.

46 *Ibid.*

47 Honeycombe, *The Murders of the Black Museum: 1870–1970*, 298.

CHAPTER SEVEN

Under Siege

In *Hamlet* the king complains that "when sorrow comes it comes not single spies but in battalions," and in 1927 the often painful truth of that aphorism was laid tellingly at Spilsbury's door. On January 20, his great friend and fellow forensic pioneer John Webster suffered a massive heart attack and died at the early age of forty-nine. Self-effacing to the point of near invisibility—certainly so far as the general public was concerned—Webster held the rank of H.O. senior analyst for eight years. During his career he stood shoulder to shoulder with Spilsbury in many of the great cases—Seddon, Armstrong, and Vacquier—and often it was Webster's analytical brilliance, especially where poison was suspected, that clinched the conviction. Spilsbury had complete faith in the quietly spoken analyst, a trust that was echoed by Willcox, who eulogized Webster as "one of the most loyal and charming colleagues. His death will be a great loss to toxicological science."[1]

Scarcely had Spilsbury recovered from this shock than he suffered another blow with the unexpected death of his personal assistant, Hilda Bainbridge. Ever since that brilliant spring morning in 1924

Bernard Spilsbury pictured in his laboratory at St. Mary's Hospital.

Hawley Harvey Crippen and Ethel LeNeve face committal proceedings at Bow Street Magistrates' Court.

The "Brides in the Bath" killer, George Joseph Smith, and his three victims (from left to right, Bessie Mundy, Alice Burnham, Margaret Lofty).

Photograph from author's personal collection

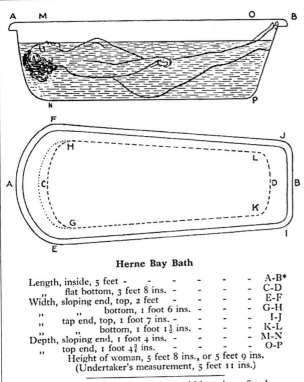

Diagram used in evidence against Smith, depicting the tub in which Bessie Mundy drowned.

Herne Bay Bath

Length, inside, 5 feet -	- - - -	A-B*
„ flat bottom, 3 feet 8 ins. -	- - -	C-D
Width, sloping end, top, 2 feet	- - -	E-F
„ „ bottom, 1 foot 6 ins. -	- -	G-H
„ tap end, top, 1 foot 7 ins. -	- -	I-J
„ „ bottom, 1 foot 1½ ins. -	- -	K-L
Depth, sloping end, 1 foot 4 ins. -	- -	M-N
„ top end, 1 foot 4¾ ins. -	- -	O-P
Height of woman, 5 feet 8 ins., or 5 feet 9 ins.		
(Undertaker's measurement, 5 feet 11 ins.)		

* B is the spot where the taps would have been fitted.

Soho cellar. The barrel in which Voisin hid his victim's head and hands can be seen at the rear.

The kitchen where Emilienne Gerard met her death. The saws that Spilsbury believed were used to dissect the body are hanging on the rear wall.

Herbert Rowse Armstrong leaving court just after being sentenced to death.

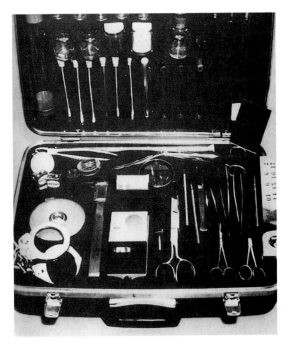

Patrick Mahon, handsome
and deadly.

The murder bag, designed by Spilsbury
after the Mahon case.

Mahon being taken back to the Crumbles bungalow.

Norman Thorne standing on the spot where Elsie Cameron's
body was later discovered.

Inside Thorne's hut.

Sidney Fox, the matricide
with a lazy eye.

The burnt-out car that Alfred Rouse thought would fool the world.

Tony Mancini, the killer who got
away with murder.

Mancini's victim Violette Kaye
(shown in her vaudeville days).

Frederick Nodder, pictured alongside a "Missing" poster
for Mona Tinsley.

Gordon Cummins, the
"Wartime Ripper," who slaughtered
four women in five days.

Evelyn Oatley, one of
Cummins's victims.

when she had marched into Mahon's hellhole on the Crumbles, Hilda had been Spilsbury's loyal factotum, especially on those demanding occasions when duties took him out of London. Many in the press suspected that this enforced closeness led to something deeper, for the strains on Spilsbury's marriage had been there right from the beginning. Certainly, during the Thorne trial, Spilsbury seemed particularly keen to avoid the news photographers as he and Hilda left Lewes Crown Court side by side, holding up a protective hand to shield his face as the prying flashbulbs popped. One thing is certain: following Hilda's death, Spilsbury never looked for a replacement. For the rest of his career, he reverted to that old familiar method of working, just one man and a scalpel, memorizing every single detail for later transcription onto one of his little white cards.

If anything, the criticism leveled at Spilsbury over the Thorne trial only hardened this sense of insularity. He was particularly stung by accusations of self-ordained celestial certainty, for, as the records make clear, instances abound of Spilsbury admitting to gaps in his professional knowledge. One particularly tragic case in November 1927, in which a Tonbridge woman, Margaret Delvigne, admitted administering arsenic to her terminally ill mother in order to ease her suffering and hasten her end, highlighted not only Spilsbury's integrity but also a problem that haunts physicians to the present day: Unless poisoning is suspected, it is damnably difficult to detect. When Spilsbury autopsied Felicia Waite's body he found it riddled with cancer, and he frankly acknowledged that had he known nothing of the suspected arsenic, he would "without hesitation" have said "that she had died from cancer of the liver."[2] Although death would have ensued in a matter of days, he felt it had been accelerated by the presence of arsenic, under half a grain. When psychiatric evaluations made it plain that Margaret Delvigne's mind had been unhinged by her harrowing experiences while serving as a nurse in Belgium during the Great War, she was declared insane and committed to an asylum.

Still, the grumbles about Spilsbury's perceived omnipotence rumbled on, most notably from Brontë. In March 1928, the two men clashed again, this time at the trial of Albert Symmons, charged with murder. The defendant, who seemed to have been teetering on the brink of a nervous breakdown for some weeks prior to the incident, claimed his wife, Eleanor, had asked him for his penknife, then used it to stab herself in the neck. According to Spilsbury, it was "practically impossible"[3] for the knife wound to have been self-inflicted. Brontë didn't see it that way at all, arguing strenuously that suicidal stabbing was possible. As was now customary, the jury chose to believe Spilsbury, and Symmons was sentenced to death. Concerns about his mental state led to him being reprieved.

Not all the criticism directed at Spilsbury came from within the medical profession. A rare example of judicial censure occurred in the summer of 1929, in a trial that marked one of the very few occasions when Spilsbury testified on behalf of the defense.

On May 14, a motorcyclist named Arthur Graham was making his way home after dark in Burnham, Slough, when he was struck by a car and died in hospital three days later. The car driver was subsequently charged with manslaughter. What propelled this story from the local pages into national headlines was the name of the driver: Richard Joshua Reynolds, the twenty-three-year-old playboy heir to the R. J. Reynolds tobacco empire.

Reynolds had been driving along the Bath Road when oncoming headlights had dazzled him, causing him to swerve to the left. At the time he felt a slight bump and lurched into a hedge. Believing that the car had sustained no significant damage, he had then driven on. Only later, when arrested in Chiswick after an erratic car chase—and minus a headlamp left at the crash scene—did he realize that he had hit someone. Or so he said.

Under strong police questioning, Reynolds denied emphatically that he was drunk, although he did admit to having consumed five Pimm's No. 1—roughly the equivalent of eight single whiskies—between 2:30 P.M. and 8:30 P.M., all on an empty stomach. According to the police surgeon, among the many signs of drunkenness exhibited by the swaying Reynolds were his extraordinarily dilated pupils. Once all the evidence had been collated, the tobacco baron wound up facing a charge of manslaughter.

At this point, out came Reynolds's checkbook. An undisclosed sum—rumored to be in the thousands—was paid to the widow, and once it became clear that such munificence was not going to deflect the authorities from their determination to prosecute, that same checkbook was lavished on hiring the very best expert witnesses available. Top of the list was Sir Bernard Spilsbury. He agreed to review the circumstances of the crash and present his opinion. Willcox, too, was placed on Reynolds's payroll, as were Sir James Purves-Stewart, senior physician to Westminster Hospital, and Dr. Bernard Dyer, a consulting chemist and public analyst. On July 1, two weeks after the incident, Purves-Stewart and Willcox examined the defendant, and both concluded that Reynolds's eyes were "easily dilated by emotion."[4] Even more bizarrely, they said that nothing in Reynolds's conduct at the time of the examination indicated a history of insobriety.

Spilsbury's testimony was at least unmarred by such pseudomedical gobbledygook. Judging from the six broken ribs and the pattern of injuries sustained by the dead man, he deduced that Graham had dismounted from his motorcycle and was crouching over the rear wheel, obscuring the light, when he was struck from behind by the car and crushed against the motorcycle carrier, mangling his pancreas and killing him.

So far so good. Then the defense tried to pull a fast one: it asked Spilsbury whether someone driving the car would have been likely to have heard the impact with the motorcycle. This was too much for the judge. Sir Travers Humphreys might have been a newcomer to the bench—he'd been elevated only the previous year—but he wasn't about to let anyone sandbag the judicial system in his court. He intervened, saying, "It is highly undesirable that an acknowledged expert in medicine, as Sir Bernard is, should attempt to become an expert in matters of which he has no more experience than anybody else, including members of the jury. Sir Bernard said that on that point he was only speaking as a member of the public. His evidence as a member of the public is no more valuable than that of a shoeblack, and I think his evidence should be confined to medical matters, with which he speaks with acknowledged authority . . . I cannot allow anyone, however eminent in the realm of science, to come and say what might happen in a motor car unless he was sitting in it himself."[5]

This was sound common sense. Clearly the defense overstepped its brief in asking Spilsbury for such an opinion, but its misplaced zeal does highlight the enormous weight that was placed on his testimony. All advocates realized the value of having the great man on their side, and it often required considerable vigilance from the bench to prevent abuses of this position. In the event, Reynolds was convicted of manslaughter. Because this was 1929, and drunken driving had yet to achieve its current pariah status in society, he received just five months' imprisonment. (At the end of his prison term an attempt was made to deport Reynolds, but he left the U.K. voluntarily.)

Again there had been an erosion, however small, in the mantle of infallibility in which the press and the courts had cloaked Spilsbury. But any satisfaction that Brontë derived from Spilsbury's discomfiture in Reynolds's trial was more than offset by his own recent shortcomings. His bungling had become a matter of public record in the so-called Croydon Poisonings that took place between April 1928 and March 1929, when three members of the same family succumbed in mysterious circumstances. Had Brontë exhibited more care when examining the first of these victims, Edmund Duff, then two other lives might have been spared. Natural causes, said Brontë, at the original autopsy. Not so, said Spilsbury, when Duff's body was exhumed twelve months later. On that day he stood over the body in the mortuary when Brontë sauntered in, smoking a pipe. Spilsbury fixed him with a basilisk stare. "Good morning," he said. "I have no objection to your being present, but you must stop smoking and I wish to have no remarks from you."[6] Furious at being rebuked like some naughty schoolchild, Brontë sulked in a corner, bottling up his anger until it became plain to everyone present that Edmund Duff's body was stuffed full of arsenic. This was more than Brontë's fragile ego could stand. Without saying a word, he turned and stalked from the mortuary. (It subsequently became clear that on the day when Brontë had performed the original autopsy, he had a second cadaver to examine. Somehow he had mixed up the bodily organs and sent the wrong ones for toxicological analysis. Within a year of Duff's death, his sister-in-law, Vera Sidney, and her mother, Violet Sidney, were also poisoned. Although no one was ever charged with these crimes, Spilsbury and most of those connected with the investigation felt that Grace Duff, Edmund's wife, was the culprit. She died in 1973.)

Public humiliations such as these only hardened Brontë's antipathy toward Spilsbury. He was like an annoying bluebottle, buzzing around at every turn. At times he gave the impression of being more concerned with toppling his archrival than in providing an objective scientific opinion. And at the end of 1929 came his best chance yet, in the most contentious case of Spilsbury's career. It concerned the death of an elderly lady in Margate, Kent. She had been found in a smoke-filled hotel room, ostensibly the victim of a tragic accident. Her thirty-year-old son, who stood bawling like a baby as doctors tended vainly to his stricken mother, gave every impression of inconsolable grief, though it's a fair bet to say that his eye rarely strayed from the time. For on the night of October 23, 1929, nothing was more important to Sidney Harry Fox than the striking of the clock.

The Favorite Son

He was born in 1899, and for most of his brief and sorry existence, Sidney Fox was one of those tiresome malcontents prepared to go to any length and suffer any hardship rather than endure the inconvenience of honest employment. Swindling, forgery, blackmail, common theft—it all came naturally to him, and none of it made one iota of difference to his financial standing, which constantly oscillated between shaky and bankrupt. The family came from Norfolk, where his dressmaker mother, Rosaline, had married a railroad porter named William Fox, by whom she had three sons. Sidney, her fourth and last child, was the product of an affair with yet another railroad employee, and everything suggests that he was her favorite son.

At age twelve he was caught misappropriating funds from a charity collection and birched. The beating did nothing to curb his larcenous tendencies. Four years later, whilst working as a houseboy for Sir John and Constance Leslie at their home in Manchester Square, London—other servants dubbed him "little Lord Fauntleroy" because of his affected manner—he first stole some jewelry, then bilked an elderly housekeeper out of her meager life savings. This second abuse of trust was too much even for the Leslies, whose saintlike patience gave way, and he was fired.

Somehow he managed to secure a position at a bank of all places. Here, he honed his forging skills until one dubious transaction too many brought him to the attention of the police. They presented him with a stark choice: prosecution or join the military. He chose the latter, enlisting as a cadet in the Royal Flying Corps. Drawing on his time with the Leslies, which had given him an insight into the workings of the British class system, he now began to affect an upper-crust accent when he spoke. This served him well on one occasion in Brighton, when he duped an elderly lady into believing that he was a grandson of Lady Leslie and promptly swindled her out of a sizable sum. Again he was caught. It was around this time that Fox widened his repertoire to include homosexual blackmail. Posing as a member of the Royal Automobile Club, he used that institution as a poste restante, only to have his mail opened by an indignant management. One letter addressed to him as "The Hon. S. H. Fox" was found to be so compromising that its author, an army brigadier general, was immediately cashiered.

At the end of a three months' prison sentence Fox returned to the army and the Great War. On his demobilization in 1919, armed with a pension of eight shillings per week ($2), he drifted into London's theatrical circles, where his unconventional sex life attracted little comment. Two more prison sentences followed in quick succession.

Despite all his failings, he continued to be the apple of his mother's rheumy eye. On July 14, 1922, she penned a tearful letter to the home secretary, pleading for a remission of her son's latest jail term. The request was not granted. During those infrequent periods when Fox avoided the law's clutches, she doted on him. Always they pooled their resources. Fox's wartime pension, supplemented by Rosaline's modest widow's allowance, gave them a combined income of eighteen shillings per week, a pittance when one considers the luxurious lifestyle they pursued. Nobody would portray Rosaline as a role-model parent. Indeed, by the mid-1920s she was actively assisting Fox in his swindles. Mostly these consisted of defrauding resort hotels on England's south coast. Fox and his mother would arrive without any luggage—it was always "being sent on"—stay a couple nights, abscond without paying the bill, and then repeat the exercise a few miles farther down the road.

Fox was nothing if not flexible. Although proudly and defiantly gay, he wasn't above a heterosexual dalliance, so long as the dangled carrot was sufficiently enticing. The most flagrant example of this malleability came in 1927 when Rosaline moved in with a middle-aged, well-to-do Australian married woman named Charlotte Morse, who lived in St. Helen's Towers, Southsea. At Rosaline's urging, Fox temporarily shelved his natural proclivities and set about seducing the estranged Mrs. Morse. With a husband many thousands of miles away in the Far East captaining a merchant ship, Charlotte was ripe for company. Fox played her like a violin. Romantic nights, first in Southsea and then at the Strand Palace Hotel in London, set Charlotte in a spin. Passion soon elbowed common sense out the door. When Fox suggested that she alter her will in his favor, she jumped at the idea. And she was similarly enthusiastic when he proposed taking out a £6,000 insurance policy on her life, payable to himself. Indeed, her suspicions only became aroused when she awoke one night to find her bedroom filled with gas.

Considering that the gas tap was behind a chest of drawers and impossible to turn on accidentally, Charlotte had good reason to suspect that her young paramour's intentions were some way short of honorable.

She kicked him out immediately. Before leaving, Fox helped himself to some of her jewelry, only to be arrested straightaway. Mrs. Morse—sadder, wiser, but mercifully still alive—revoked her will and caught the first available ship back to the land of her birth, leaving the British police to deal with her erstwhile lover. In March 1928 Fox was given fifteen months for theft.

With her son once again behind bars, Rosaline, penniless and destitute, was thrown into the Portsmouth workhouse.* This glowering Victorian shell, with its mentally deranged inmates and air of grinding desperation, would be her home for the next year; little wonder, then, that her health went into free fall. The problem was Parkinson's disease; and as her nervous system crumbled under its corrosive effects, she was moved to the adjoining infirmary. On his release in March 1929, Sidney supervised Rosaline's discharge and the following month decided it was high time his sixty-three-year-old mother made her will. As Rosaline Fox owned little except the threadbare clothes she stood up in, this smacked of unnecessary extravagance, but she bowed to her son's insistence and made him the sole legatee. (Two of her other sons were dead; Reggie, a munitions worker, was blown to bits in an explosion at Woolwich Arsenal in 1915, followed two years later by James, the eldest, who was killed on the western front. Fox's only surviving brother, William, a respectable hospital orderly who lived in Cosham, had very little contact with either of his dissolute relatives.) Nine days later, on April 30, Fox took out the first of what would eventually be several accidental death policies on his mother's life. Since Rosaline Fox had never before carried a penny of life insurance, it would have been interesting to hear the arguments advanced by her son to explain his newfound concern.

Back in harness again, the couple resumed their peripatetic existence. The summer of 1929 provided a diversion when Fox took his

---

* Although officially abolished April 1, 1930, in a modified form these nightmarish relics from a bygone age survived into the 1940s.

mother to France to visit the grave of her son, James, who had died in the trenches. Following this, it was back to England and the usual round of unpaid bills, worthless checks, irate hotel managers, and lies, lies, lies.

On October 16, 1929, they sashayed into the foyer of the Hotel Metropole on Paradise Street in Margate. A bulky, imposing pile that claimed to be "Nearer to the Sea than any other Hotel on the Coast,"7 the Metropole was used to receiving customers of all kinds, but the receptionist had rarely clapped eyes on such an odd couple. Fox—young, glib, and dangerously plausible—did most of the talking, while his mother, with her large white moon face, shuffling gait, and trembling hands stayed on the sidelines, beaming vacantly. Hotel staff noticed that Rosaline was wearing two stockinette dresses, one over the other, an oddity they attributed to the unseasonably cold weather. In emotional terms, Fox explained how they had just returned from a pilgrimage to France, where they'd paid homage at the graves of his three brothers who'd fallen in the war, and that their luggage had been misdirected to the new home his mother had purchased in Lyndhurst, Hampshire. Unfortunately, Mama wasn't well enough to travel at the moment, hence the need for hotel accommodation. Their request for two rooms was met.

Everyone at the Metropole agreed that mother and son seemed devoted to each other, a genuinely nice couple. So much so that all thoughts of their bill, which mounted daily, were set aside. Most days Fox left the hotel alone, ostensibly on business.

On Sunday, October 20, Fox went, ashen faced, to the hotel manager with news that his mother had taken a bad turn. Joseph Harding found Rosaline lying fully dressed on the bed and, after administering some drops of sal volatile, sent out for medical assistance. When Dr. Cecil Austen arrived at lunchtime he could find very little wrong with Mrs. Fox, other than her inherent ailments, and merely prescribed a mild tonic. Following this incident, Harding helpfully suggested that Mrs. Fox change rooms in order that she might enjoy the benefit of a gas fire. Rosaline duly moved into Room 66. Harding went further; why not, he said to Fox, take the adjoining, somewhat smaller room, number 67? That way, if there were any recurrence of the illness, he could use the communicating door rather than the corridor. Fox agreed.

With mother and son ensconced side by side, life at the Metropole fell back into its unhurried pace. Until 11:30 on the night of October 23. That was when Fox, wearing only a shirt, appeared on the hotel landing, bellowing, "Where's the 'boots'? I believe there's a fire. Where's the 'boots'? There's a fire."[8]

Samuel Hopkins, a salesman enjoying a nightcap in the bar, heard the commotion and ran to help. He followed Fox upstairs and into Room 67. Choking smoke prevented them from even crossing the threshold. Standing in the corridor, almost as an afterthought, Fox then pointed to Room 66 and cried, "My mother's in there. Open it."[9]

Hopkins flung open the door, releasing clouds of thick black smoke that drove him back. Showing immense bravery and initiative, he fell to his hands and knees and crawled into the room, gasping for air beneath the layer of suffocating smoke. He fumbled his way to the bed, where he found Rosaline prostrate, legs hanging over the side. Sliding his hands under her arms, he lifted her off the bed, onto the floor, then dragged her into the corridor. Only then did he notice that Mrs. Fox was clad in just a small singlet.

While all these heroics were occurring, Fox hovered in the background, like some hysterical butterfly, wringing his hands and blubbering, "My Mummy, my Mummy."[10]

In a belated attempt at preserving Mrs. Fox's modesty, Hopkins grabbed his own raincoat and threw it over her seminaked body before hauling her farther along the corridor. Then he collapsed (he recovered fully later). All efforts to resuscitate Mrs. Fox were futile. She was clearly dead. Other guests fought their way into Room 66 and managed to extract the source of the blaze, a smoldering armchair.

When Dr. Austen arrived it was around midnight, and Mrs. Fox's body was already laid out in the hotel vestibule. He estimated that she had been dead for around half an hour. He saw no external marks of injury or signs of burning, and concluded that Mrs. Fox had fallen asleep, then awoke to find the room full of smoke, a shock so great that she collapsed across the bed and died from heart failure. A second physician, Dr. Robert Nichol, nodded agreement when Austen announced his intention to certify the death as due to shock and suffocation. Neither man saw any reason for an autopsy.

Fox took the news of his mother's death badly. He doubled up like he'd been punched in the belly, and had to be given an injection of morphine to calm his raving. In between sobs, he regained enough composure to inquire about a sum of £24 that had been in his mother's handbag; the residue, so he claimed, of a check he had cashed the previous day at Lloyds Bank in Threadneedle Street, London. A search of Room 66 did recover the handbag, burnt on one side, but with its inner compartment intact. There were no notes or traces of burnt notes inside.

When police inspector William Palmer entered the Metropole he saw the heartbroken son kneeling by his mother's body. Fox explained that he'd been asleep until 11:30 P.M., when a rattling window had awoken him. Still half asleep, he suddenly noticed a smell of smoke, ostensibly coming from his mother's room. When he'd tried to open the adjoining door, he had been beaten back by the dense smoke. He then ran downstairs to raise the alarm.

Palmer's inspection of Room 66 showed a bed quite untouched by fire and displaying no signs of a struggle. One slight peculiarity was the pillow; it lay not on the bed but on a cabinet at the head of the bed. As this could have easily been dislodged in the attempted rescue of Mrs. Fox, Palmer dismissed it from his mind. On a chest of drawers near the bed he saw a small medicine bottle almost full of gasoline. Instinctively Palmer sniffed the air. There was no odor of gasoline or any other accelerant, so far as he could tell (he later learned that on the previous Sunday Fox had been seen using the gasoline to clean a suit). Moving to the bathroom, Palmer found the victim's false teeth, both upper and lower plates, in the basin. The hotel staff confirmed that Mrs. Fox had a somewhat relaxed attitude toward her dentures; a few days earlier a maid had found them lying in the middle of the carpet. Everything that Palmer saw in Room 66 bore the hallmarks of an appalling accident. Nothing more.

Downstairs, Fox was inconsolable. Among those who attempted to comfort him was the hotel manager's wife. As Mrs. Harding stroked Fox's thick hair the unmistakable smell of smoke attached itself to her hands. She frowned. According to Fox, he had not entered Room 66; so how had smoke impregnated his hair? Later that night, after Fox had been billeted in a new room, she shared her doubts with her husband. It was the first indication that all might not be well with the death of Rosaline Fox.

Court Decides "Misadventure"

The inquest was held the next day, and Fox testified that the last time he saw his mother alive she had been reading newspapers in front of the gas fire. That was some time after 9:30 P.M. He had then gone downstairs for a drink. From what the hotel chambermaids had to say, it looked as if Rosaline's befuddled negligence had contributed to her demise. They all agreed that the elderly lady was unthinkingly careless with her discarded clothes, leaving them strewn all over the place. Judging from the trail of charred underwear, it appeared as if, on retiring, she had undressed, leaving the clothes where they fell, and that somehow they had caught light from the gas fire. Once the horsehair-stuffed chair ignited, asphyxiating black smoke would have filled the room in minutes. It was the kind of ghastly but commonplace accident that coroners' courts deal with almost daily, so it came as no surprise when a verdict of "death by misadventure" was recorded. After the inquest Fox returned to the Metropole, where Harding added his commiserations. Fox brushed off the sympathy with an ill grace, more concerned about the missing £24, peevishly reluctant to accept Harding's word that the money had not been found.

True to type, Fox left the Metropole without paying his bill. The hotel declined to press for payment, especially with Fox hinting darkly that some light-fingered staff member must have stolen the money. That day the grieving son accompanied his mother's remains on the journey north to her home county of Norfolk.

So far as the police were concerned it was "case closed," and they made plain their disinterest by dumping Mrs. Fox's charred clothing and other personal effects on the corporation landfill. The press, though, had not abandoned the story, and when the proprietor of the Royal Pavilion Hotel at Folkestone, some twenty-five miles along the Kent coast, read of the tragedy, he reached for the phone. Harding listened grimly to the Royal Pavilion's account of how the Foxes had stayed there recently and vanished without paying their bill. Angrily, he called the police.

In the meantime, the funeral arrangements for Rosaline Fox went ahead. On October 29 she was buried in the churchyard at Great Fransham. That same day Fox traveled to the city where he had been born, Norwich, to lodge a claim on one of his mother's life policies. So repelled was the agent by Fox's grasping indifference toward the bereavement that he wired his head office: "Extremely muddy water in this business."[11]

Few business institutions are more attuned to human avarice and deceit than insurance companies, and the head office wasted no time in passing their concerns to Scotland Yard. The case file landed on the desk of Chief Inspector Walter Hambrook. Thirteen years previously, he had been the officer who'd arrested Fox for forgery. He knew Fox as a small-time hustler. Had he now graduated to the biggest league of all? Discreet police inquiries pieced together Fox's actions in the days prior to the fire, and what they revealed set alarm bells ringing.

Two days after arriving at the Metropole, Fox had journeyed to nearby Ramsgate to arrange a £1,000 insurance policy on his mother in the event of accidental death. He produced a proposal form purporting to have been signed by Rosaline Fox. Then, on Tuesday, October 22— just one day before the tragedy—he had caught the train to London, where he called on the Cornhill Insurance Company and requested an extension to a £2,000 accidental death policy that his mother held with them. As this was the third time that Fox had extended the policy's term without any incident, the request was granted. Instead of expiring at noon on October 23, the coverage now lasted until midnight that same day.

All this financial maneuvering wiped out Fox's already skimpy coffers. With no money for his return fare to Margate, he phoned a London guesthouse proprietor whom he knew and pleaded for a loan. Unimpressed by Fox's absence of collateral, the woman told him to clear off. Somehow Fox managed to scrape together the money for his return fare. As he had previously resorted to male prostitution when funds were low, this is much the likeliest source of his train fare to Margate.

He arrived back late that evening at the Metropole. Rosaline, still up despite the late hour, was delighted to see him. The next morning Fox told the staff that they would be leaving on the Thursday for Lyndhurst as his mother was feeling much better. He added, "We have had—mother and I have had—a sham fight, which shows she is well."[12]

This was an extraordinary statement. The notion of Fox, a healthy young man in the prime of life, and his partially paralyzed mother engaged in even the most innocuous roughhousing beggars belief, and one can only surmise that he was laying the groundwork to account for any bruising that might be found on his mother's body. Nothing else seems to make sense.

After dinner that same evening, Mrs. Fox retired to her room. Fox asked the front desk to prepare his bill as they would be leaving the next day. He then bought half a bottle of port and an evening paper, and took them up to his mother. He was last seen going to his own room at 10:40 P.M.

All fell quiet at the Hotel Metropole—until 11:30 P.M.

In all the smoke and the chaos and the heartbreaking tragedy, one unequivocal fact emerged: as several witnesses could attest, by 11:40

P.M. Rosaline Fox was dead, just twenty minutes before the insurance deadline expired. Those twenty minutes meant that Fox would now pocket £3,000.

It was an almost ludicrously suspicious set of circumstances. If Fox had hung an illuminated sign around his neck that flashed, "I'M GONNA KILL MOM FOR CASH!" he could scarcely have attracted more attention. All his life he'd been a bungler who'd propped up his half-witted schemes with pointless and unnecessary lies. Even now, when playing for the highest stakes imaginable, he couldn't help gilding the lily. And this time it was fatal. When Hambrook contacted Lloyds Bank, he learned that they had not cashed a £25 check for Fox on October 22, or any other day for that matter.

Fox spent his last night of liberty in his home county of Norfolk. On November 2 he was arrested on charges of having obtained credit whilst still an undischarged bankrupt and was driven back to Margate. This was just a holding charge, to give Hambrook more breathing space to conduct his enquiries. One of the people he interviewed was William Fox, the prisoner's sole surviving brother. He studied the insurance proposal form that showed his mother's signature and had no hesitation in declaring it a forgery. The writing was far too firm, he said, for his mother's shaky hand. The rest of the document looked to have been filled in by Sidney. On receipt of this news, the H.O. ordered an exhumation.

Spilsbury was dispatched to Norfolk. As he traveled deep into the flatlands of East Anglia, he carried with him Hambrook's suspicion that Rosaline Fox had been poisoned and that the fire had been set to mask this fact; but no one knew better than Spilsbury the dangers of presumption, especially in matters of murder. He would let the autopsy tell him how Rosaline Fox died. Shortly before 10 A.M. on Saturday, November 9, work began on raising her coffin. Six plainclothes police officers carried the casket on a hand bier to the old schoolhouse that adjoined the graveyard. As always whenever Spilsbury supervised an exhumation, there were hordes of spectators on hand, all eager for some glimpse of the activity. Inside the schoolhouse, the coffin lid was unscrewed and the village sexton, Arthur Cross, identified the body as that of Rosaline Fox.

Carbon Monoxide Poisoning

With the formalities concluded, the room was cleared, and Spilsbury began his examination. The coffin had been sealed with putty, making it virtually airtight, a precaution that was reflected in the relatively minor putrefactive changes to the corpse. Like Dr. Austen, Spilsbury found no obvious external marks of injury, no burning or signs of violence. Now it was a question of deciding whether Mrs. Fox had died from smoke inhalation.

Carbon monoxide is horribly efficient and insidious. It kills by combining with hemoglobin in the blood, thereby preventing the blood from transporting oxygen to the body tissues and nerve cells. The symptoms of carbon monoxide poisoning depend on the level of saturation in the blood. Twenty to 30 percent will produce headache, dizziness, and shortness of breath, particularly during exertion. From 30 to 50 percent, may induce nausea and heart palpitations. Above 50 percent the body loses coordination; some people collapse, others may lose control of their bladder and bowel. Once the saturation level reaches 60 percent, the body is in serious danger. Although Spilsbury's records had noted a fatality with the carbon monoxide level as low as 45 percent,[*] experience told him that most lethal readings were in the 60 to 70 percent range.

People who die from carbon monoxide poisoning invariably have a pink tinge to their skin. Not Rosaline Fox. Apart from a bluish color in the lips and fingernails, her body displayed the normal putrefactive

---

[*] Subsequent research has shown that in the very aged and infirm, the lethal level of carbon monoxide can dip into the 30–40 percent range.

hue. It was the same story when Spilsbury opened up the corpse. Human organs exposed to carbon monoxide tend to turn cherry red. Here, they were normal in color. Nor was there any frothy fluid in the upper air passages, often an indicator of gas poisoning. The blood, too, showed no abnormal bright-red coloration. Most tellingly of all, the air passages and the lungs were clear and free from soot. By common consent, Mrs. Fox had been in the smoke-filled room for several minutes before being dragged clear. Had she been breathing at this time, her lungs would have told the tale. Spilsbury concluded that either she was dead before the fire began, or she died almost simultaneously with its outbreak.

So if carbon monoxide didn't kill Rosaline Fox, what did? Spilsbury went looking. The heart showed the usual senile changes found in someone of the victim's age, and some signs of arterial disease; neither, in Spilsbury's opinion, enough to cause sudden cardiac failure. Fatty degeneration of the liver owed more to alcohol abuse than to illness and would not have been life threatening. All the vital organs were removed and placed in sealed glass jars for onward shipment to Dr. Gerald Roche Lynch, assistant analyst at the Home Office since 1920, and who had assumed the senior post on the death of Webster. If there had been any carbon monoxide in Rosaline Fox's system—which Spilsbury doubted—it should remain detectable in the samples for up to six months.

Spilsbury now dissected the victim's neck. At the back of the larynx he found a mark. To his eye it looked like a recent bruise, about the size of a half crown,* caused, he thought, by some handling of the larynx, possibly a human thumb as it exerted pressure in manual strangulation. He also located a pinhead-sized hemorrhage in the epiglottis and what appeared to be a bruise on the thyroid gland. Exploring further, he found another bruise, this time a quarter of an inch in diameter, at the tip of the tongue, most likely the result of Rosaline Fox biting her

---

* Approximately the same size as a U.S. silver dollar.

tongue as she was being throttled. Since Spilsbury doubted that Mrs. Fox could have caused the bruise with toothless gums, he suspected that the act of strangulation had dislodged her dental plates, which Fox then dumped in the sink. Despite the fact that bones and cartilages in the larynx were intact and uninjured—rare in cases of throttling, especially with elderly victims—Spilsbury concluded that the cause of death was asphyxia due to manual strangulation.

On the same day that Spilsbury was busy in Norfolk, the first, belated full-scale examination of Room 66 was undertaken, supervised by Harry Hammond, chief of the Margate Fire Brigade and a member of the Institute of Fire Engineers. A veteran arson investigator with twenty-nine years' experience, Hammond began with the armchair. Most of the fire damage was to its underneath, which had burned thoroughly. The sides and top showed only superficial scorching. Obviously the flame had been very localized, or else the upper part of the chair would have sustained more damage.

The carpet showed no signs of fire damage except for a roughly circular section some three feet from the gas fire. This corresponded to where the armchair had stood on the fatal night, and where firefighters had found a quantity of charred newspapers. (This tallied with Fox's statement that his mother had been reading some papers.) Rereading the official notes, Hammond saw that a quantity of scorched underclothing had been found in front of the gas fire. Since everything pointed to the seat of the blaze being directly beneath the armchair, this led him to initially suspect that a spark had jumped from the fire, ignited these garments, thereby creating a blazing bridge that spread to the newspapers under the chair.

Even as this scenario took shape in his mind, Hammond couldn't drag his eyes away from a small wicker chair that stood by the window. Despite being several feet distant from both the gas fire and the armchair, it, too, was charred. Not just slightly, but enough for its top rail to burn right through. Everyone who had entered Room 66 on the night of the fire was asked about this chair, and all recalled it being by the window when they first saw it. Since Hammond could find no physical reason to explain how this chair came to be burnt, only one conclusion was possible: someone had moved the chair before the alarm was raised.

More curiosities appeared when Hammond inspected the gas fire. It appeared to be in fine working condition, and he could do nothing to make it throw out any sparks. Even when the protective fender became too hot to hold comfortably, it still wouldn't reach a temperature high enough to ignite anything. Having harvested all that Room 66 had to offer, Hammond collected some samples and retreated to his workshop.

The carpet was a good quality closely woven Wilton with a felt underlay, highly resistant to fire. When Hammond applied burning paper, horsehair stuffing from the armchair, and a section of the underclothing to the carpet, all he achieved was minimal scorching. But it was a dramatically different picture when he soaked the underwear in gasoline; this caused the carpet to burn right through. Even here there was a qualifier: the carpet only burned if it was surrounded by air. When laid flat on the ground, it merely smoldered. Similarly with the horsehair stuffing; when packed tightly into a chair, it would not burn; once loosened and exposed to oxygen, it ignited easily. Visual comparison tests with the section of charred carpet convinced Hammond that the fire had been incandescent, meaning that the materials had smoldered more than flamed, and that the fire had lasted for no longer than thirty minutes.

The cane chair continued to pose problems. Even if someone had draped underwear over its top rail, and that clothing had then caught light, burnt through the rail, and dropped on to the carpet, it still would not have generated sufficient heat to cause a fire. When Hammond wrapped up his tests, everything he'd found pointed to the fire being set deliberately.

Two days later the police returned to the landfill and scavenged for the charred clothing and Rosaline Fox's other personal belongings. They found everything except her false teeth. (One of the chambermaids had apparently given them to a friend.) Much the most significant discovery was that one of the newspapers Fox recalled his mother reading was in French, a language with which she was unfamiliar.

While all this was going on, Fox was in and out of the local magistrates' court almost daily, on a holding charge of obtaining credit at the Hotel Metropole by false pretenses. The delaying tactics were designed to give Roche Lynch time to complete his tests.

By December 18, all the results were in. None of the organs or any other sample showed traces of poison or noxious substances. Since the tests that he employed for carbon monoxide poisoning were sensitive to any amount over 20 percent—way below the lethal level—smoke inhalation could be categorically ruled out as the cause of death. The stomach contents were consistent with Mrs. Fox having drunk rather more than a quarter bottle of port about 1½ hours before death, as Fox had claimed. When Roche Lynch examined bedding taken from Room 66, he found a patch of urine. Often, when someone is being strangled, their bladder or bowel will void, and although this tended to support Spilsbury's opinion as to cause of death, strangulation was by no means the only possible cause of this fouling.

The fact that three more weeks passed before Fox was charged with murder highlights the Crown's uncertainty. Despite a barrage of circumstantial evidence, there was an unsettling dearth of physical proof to support Spilsbury's conviction that Mrs. Fox had been strangled, and only after considerable agonizing, over Christmas, did the director of public prosecutions give the go-ahead. On January 9 Fox was charged with that rarest of crimes in the judicial calendar: matricide.

Immediately Fox's defense team began casting around for forensic experts of their own. Brontë—rapidly becoming a witness for all seasons, especially if it afforded the opportunity to tackle Spilsbury in open court—agreed to testify on Fox's behalf. Mindful of the repeated maulings that Brontë had suffered when going toe-to-toe with Spilsbury in the past, Fox's lawyers sought to strengthen their hand. The expert witness they approached was a New Zealand–born pathologist whose outstanding skills had graced two continents and almost twenty years. This wasn't some hothead with a chip on his shoulder, fixated on settling old scores; this was one of the true giants of twentieth-century medical jurisprudence.

The Supreme Rival

Professor Sydney Smith had only held the chair of forensic medicine at Edinburgh University for two years when he was requested to review the evidence in the Fox case. The brief tenure gave no indication of his vast international experience. Rising to prominence in Scotland, in 1917 he'd become the principal medico-legal expert to the Egyptian Ministry of Justice, and the decade he spent in that country, a political hothouse where assassinations were commonplace, had left him with an encyclopedic grasp of homicide in all its forms, especially shootings. More academically inclined than Spilsbury, and certainly more interested in passing on his knowledge to future generations of students, in 1925 he crystallized all this experience in his *Forensic Medicine and Toxicology*, a textbook that quickly became a classic of its kind.

Since returning to Scotland, a country that operates under an entirely separate legal system from that of its neighbor to the south, Smith had occupied a similar status to that enjoyed by Spilsbury in England and Wales. For the most part he testified on behalf of the prosecution. However, he was not similarly constrained south of the border. Curiously enough, the same applied to Spilsbury in reverse. His Home Office responsibilities ended at Hadrian's Wall, and in 1927 this had permitted him to testify on behalf of the defense at the trial of an eighteen-year-old Edinburgh student, Donald Merrett, charged with shooting his mother.

According to Spilsbury and his colleague, ballistics expert Robert Churchill, there was nothing about the death of Bertha Merrett to gainsay defense claims of suicide. The prosecution's star witness was Professor Harvey Littlejohn, Smith's former mentor at Edinburgh

University. Smith, who happened to be in Scotland at the time of the trial, consulted with Littlejohn, and both were convinced that Spilsbury and Churchill had gotten it wrong. But Scottish jurors read the newspapers every bit as assiduously as their English counterparts, and Spilsbury's enormous reputation had preceded him. Against all expectations the jury found the murder case "not proven," that peculiarly Scottish verdict that languishes somewhere in the legal half world between guilt and innocence, although they did convict Merrett of forging his mother's name on checks, and he was sentenced to one year's imprisonment.*

Now, almost three years later, Spilsbury was again giving evidence in a suspected matricide, this time in his customary role as prosecution expert witness. Having studied Spilsbury's report, Smith agreed to testify on behalf of the defense.

The trial was scheduled to begin on Wednesday, March 12, 1930. The preceding Saturday, Smith, accompanied by Brontë, visited Spilsbury's laboratory to see the specimens and samples. Some indication of the Crown's unease can be gauged from the fact that they drafted in Dr. Henry Weir, pathologist to the National Hospital for Diseases of the Heart, to support Spilsbury's position. This would turn out to be a dubious benefit.

Spilsbury, ever courteous, spread out the whole of his exhibits. Chief among these was the larynx, which had been preserved in formalin. Its condition was central to Spilsbury's theory that Mrs. Fox had been strangled. His report had mentioned the half-crown sized bruise. Smith was baffled as to how such a large bruise could have been inflicted without damage to the tissues of the larynx or the neck. He examined the specimen from every angle, while Spilsbury looked on stoically. At long last Smith looked up and shook his head. "I can't see any sign of a bruise, Spilsbury."

---

* In 1954, Merrett, by now calling himself Ronald Chesney, murdered his wife and mother-in-law in London, then fled to Germany, where he shot himself.

"Nor can I," said Brontë.

"No," agreed Spilsbury. "You can't see it now. But it was there when I exhumed the body."

Smith was nonplused. "Where's the bruise gone, then?"

"It became obscure," said Spilsbury, "before I put the larynx in formalin. That is why I did not take a section."[13]

A bruise is caused by the breaking of small vessels, which allows blood to be forced into the tissues, where it clots. This blood remains in the tissues and cannot be removed by postmortem changes. A bruise the size of a half crown would require the extravasation of a considerable amount of blood.

"I don't see how a bruise of that size could have just disappeared," Smith said.

"It became obscure," Spilsbury repeated. "It was there. I saw it myself."

"Spilsbury, I don't doubt that you saw something," Smith said. "But I put it to you that it might not have been a bruise. It could have been a patch of discoloration from postmortem staining or putrefaction."

Brontë chose this moment to drive home the dagger. "We all know how difficult it is to diagnose a bruise with the naked eye after partial putrefaction has occurred,"[14] he cooed, an unmistakable reference to their earlier clash in the Norman Thorne case on this very point.

Spilsbury listened attentively and was very polite but refused to argue the point. The examination moved on.

Smith studied the other signs of alleged injury. The hemorrhage in the epiglottis was there—a pinhead-sized spot, such as might commonly be found in cases of death from natural causes. He also saw the bruise on the side of the tongue, a possible side effect of strangulation, maybe, but just as easily the result of an old lady biting her tongue with badly fitting dentures. Finally, there was the alleged bruise on the thyroid gland, and this led to another difference of opinion. It consisted of a few stray red blood corpuscles, such as might be found in a section of any ordinary thyroid.

"I cannot accept that as a bruise," Smith said, shaking his head, and

Brontë agreed with him. Even Weir admitted that he could see nothing that resembled a bruise. Smith felt that Spilsbury appeared to give ground, and as he and Brontë left the laboratory, he mentioned that, on this point at least, he thought Spilsbury would admit to a possible error. Brontë shook his head. "Not Spilsbury," he said. "You wait till we're in court."[15]

Not for the first time, Brontë got it wrong.

Murder for Money

Once again Lewes provided the setting for the biggest murder case of the year, and when the trial opened on March 13, 1930, the prosecution didn't mince its words: strip out the element of matricide, they argued, and this was a straightforward case of murder for money. Most of the early exchanges were occupied with the circumstantial evidence, with particular emphasis on those insurance policies. And damning stuff it was too. The Crown made great play of the fact that in the 176 days from May 1 to October 23, 1929, Fox and his mother had a joint known income of rather less than £23. Of this sum, Fox shelled out almost half on insurance premiums to cover his mother's life. He might have cheated his way from hotel to hotel in southern England, leaving a trail of unpaid bills in his wake, but he always found enough money to keep the policies in force. In the final days of his mother's life, Fox used his last two shillings to extend the coverage—critically—until midnight on October 23.

When Spilsbury entered the witness box he did so in the knowledge that, for the first time in his career, he had a genuine battle on his hands. He first outlined his reasons for believing that Mrs. Fox was dead before the fire broke out, then, to explain his theory of how Mrs. Fox died, he produced a porcelain model of the human mouth and neck. After explaining where he had looked for soot in the passages, he continued. "At the back of the larynx," he said, pointing to the spot, "I found a large, recent bruise about the size of half a crown. It was then that I had the first indication of the conclusions to which I finally came, that death was due to strangulation."[16]

Spilsbury repeated his beliefs about the bruise on the tongue and the very small hemorrhage on the epiglottis. Then he addressed the thyroid gland. "I found a small dark area just on the surface which I thought might be a bruise," he said. "I made microscopical preparations of it which in my view confirmed the presence of a little bruising. I showed the preparations to Dr. Weir, Professor Smith, and Dr. Brontë, who, however, did not take the same view, and for that reason I prefer that the bruise shall not be considered as a possible injury caused at that time."[17] By Spilsbury's standards, this was a climb down of monumental proportions, unprecedented in his career. Unfortunately for the defense, it would be the only one.

Under cross-examination he refused to yield on the subject of the larynx. When J. D. Cassels, KC, suggested that the discoloration might have been a mark of putrefaction, Spilsbury insisted, "It was a bruise and nothing else. There are no two opinions about it."[18] Cassels wisely let the matter go. Once Spilsbury dug in his heels, no force on earth could move him, and the more implacable he became, the more likely was the jury to believe him.

Smith watched these exchanges with genuine admiration. He might take issue with some of Spilsbury's findings, but there was immense respect for his skill in the witness box. Watching the maestro at work, Smith came to realize why Spilsbury exerted such a hold over the jury: he always sounded so damned certain!

Cassels then turned to the hyoid bone, a tiny horseshoe-shaped bone at the back of the throat, almost invariably broken in acts of strangulation. In Mrs. Fox it was intact. Some idea of the bone's fragility can be gauged from the fact that Spilsbury himself broke it when inspecting it in the presence of Smith and Brontë. Nor was the cricoid cartilage—also in the neck—broken, often another indication of strangulation. Cassels asked, "In your experience of strangulation cases have you ever known a case with fewer signs than this?"

"No, I have not,"[19] Spilsbury admitted frankly.

Dr. Henry Weir, who followed Spilsbury, proved to be a mixed blessing for the Crown. Although he had not seen the half-crown bruise himself, he was prepared to accept Spilsbury's statement. However, he did not share Spilsbury's view that death was caused by asphyxia; instead he agreed with defense claims that it was due to heart failure. In his opinion, "There was sufficient disease in the heart to account for death from natural causes."[20]

This posed a serious problem for the prosecution: their entire case hinged upon Spilsbury's opinion that Mrs. Fox had been strangled. Now, their final witness had undermined that view.

Fortunately for the Crown, the next person to take the stand was Fox himself. He performed disastrously. His phony upper-class accent fooled no one, and there was a genuine sense of revulsion at the smiling self-possession he oozed when describing the death of his mother. All his life he'd lived off his wits. They'd provided him a paltry existence in the past; now they let him down entirely as the attorney general, Sir William Jowitt, KC, coaxed him into a vivid and damning description of how he had opened the communicating door between his mother's bedroom and his own, only to be driven back by the dense black smoke. He had shut the door, run out of his room, and downstairs to summon help.

"If I'd stayed in three or four minutes I should have been suffocated," said Fox.

"So that you must have been greatly apprehensive for your mother?"

"I was."

Jowitt lowered his voice to an accusing whisper. "Fox, you closed that door."

"It's quite possible that I did."

"Can you explain to me why it was that you closed the door instead of flinging it wide open?"

"My explanation of that now is that the smoke should not spread into the hotel."[21]

An audible gasp swept the courtroom. Fox's heartless egocentricity had been stripped bare for all the world to see.

When it came to the defense expert witnesses, Jowitt was less subtle. He made no secret of his contempt for Brontë when the latter took the stand. "Sometimes, you know," Jowitt said, "specialists with the best will in the world may take a preconceived view in a case and make things unconsciously fit with it?"

"I do not think that applies to specialists in the line I specialize in,"[22] Brontë retaliated.

Jowitt baited Brontë further, referring to Dr. Weir and declaring that his willingness to contradict Spilsbury "shows he is a man of courage and conviction." Brontë turned puce. "If you are insinuating that I'm not, then I disagree with you."[23]

"I make no insinuation about you at all, sir."

"If you do I resent that suggestion." Not for the first time in his career, Brontë's temper had hit the flash point. Jowitt fanned the flames. "Do you mean that Sir Bernard did not see what he said he saw?"

"Far be it from me to make that suggestion,"[24] hissed Brontë, turning angrily to the judge and complaining, "The Attorney General is trying to make me belittle Sir Bernard Spilsbury, and I will not do it."[25] In the next breath Brontë went on to make the perfectly valid point that, in the Thorne trial, Spilsbury had declared that putrefactive changes tend to magnify any bruise and make it easier to detect. Here, he seemed to be backtracking.

Under the adversarial system of justice, trials are essentially battles of salesmanship. Each side sets out its stall, and, unless the evidence is overwhelming, the better salesman generally wins. This certainly applied to Spilsbury. All coolness and patrician authority, he had rarely been inconvenienced by the irascible Brontë; Sydney Smith, on the other hand, was an entirely different proposition. Just as calm as Spilsbury, if marginally less experienced, he also understood the importance of presentation. Where he suffered was in recognizability. He might have featured in headline cases in Scotland, but these rarely made the front pages in southern England. To a jury made up of middle-class tradespeople from Kent, he was an unknown quantity. And he was up against another handicap: this was his first experience of giving evidence for the defense, and nothing had prepared him for the aggressiveness of a Crown cross-examination.

Jowitt took the cudgel to this perceived interloper. No digressions were permitted, just hard, unrelenting questions and answers. Once, when Smith attempted to elaborate for the jury's benefit, Jowitt cut him off crudely: "Please answer my question. It may be difficult for a gentleman who gives lectures to answer questions, but I want you to answer mine."[26] The hectoring tone only worsened when he dealt with the subject of the larynx bruise. "Sir Bernard says there can be no two opinions about it."

"It is very obvious there can be," said Smith.

"You are bound to accept the evidence of the man who saw the bruise?"

"I do not think so."

"How can you say there was not a bruise there?"

"Because if there was a bruise there it should be there now. It should be there for ever."[27]

Smith's logic was impeccable. Bruises don't disappear after death; indeed, as Brontë had pointed out, if anything they tend to become clearer with putrefaction. Spilsbury had been caught out in a mistake, plain and simple. A dignified retraction might have done wonders for his standing in the medico-legal community, but Spilsbury was on the horns of dilemma. Any admission of error now, and Fox would undoubtedly walk free. As it was, Spilsbury's intransigence on the "vanishing bruise" threw Fox a lifeline that he probably didn't deserve, as the battle between expert witnesses totally dominated center stage, relegating the defendant to the wings.

Jowitt tore into Smith, waving a copy of *Taylor's Medical Jurisprudence*, which Smith had edited, and quoting a passage that clearly stated that the absence of external signs was no proof that suffocation had not occurred. Although Smith struggled to maintain his composure as Jowitt bored in, he refused to be deflected from his belief that there was no evidence to say Rosaline Fox had been strangled, as the prosecution alleged.

This was a theme that Cassels developed in his final speech to the jury. "You may build round a case of this kind a mountain of motive and surround it with suspicion, but if you don't prove that the person whose death you're investigating was murdered your mountain of motive and your suspicion are without value."[28] Even the insurance evidence, superficially so damning, was not without contradictions. At various times during the summer Mrs. Fox was actually insured for £4,000 rather than the £3,000 at the time of her death. Why not kill her then, said Cassels, when she was worth more money?

It was a question that the jury took very little time to answer. On March 21, after a little over an hour's deliberation, they found Fox guilty of murder. As sentence of death was passed, he whispered, "My Lord, I did not murder my mother. I am innocent."[29] He was then led from public view.

No Appeal

Ever since the inception of the Court of Criminal Appeal in 1907, every condemned murderer had appealed his or her conviction. Fox broke that tradition. Considering the highly disputatious nature of the expert-witness evidence against him—the frailty of Spilsbury's testimony was there for all to see—this decision has to be regarded as curious, to say the least. Maybe, for once in his life, Fox was stricken by remorse. Or maybe he was overwhelmed by a sense of futility. We shall never know. Another historical curiosity attended Fox's brief tenure in the condemned cell, as he became the only person in British history lying under sentence of death to be cited in a divorce action. His liaison with Mrs. Morse had provoked her husband, Captain George Morse, to sue for divorce on grounds of her adultery. The decree was granted on April 7, 1930. The following morning, after having spent the traditional "three clear Sundays" in the condemned cell, Fox was hanged at Maidstone Prison.

So once again a jury had accepted the word of Spilsbury over that of another, this time equally distinguished pathologist. To the end of his life—he died in 1969, having been knighted for his services to forensic science—Smith persisted in his belief that Rosaline Fox died from shock, not strangulation as the prosecution alleged. In his autobiography, Smith makes no apologies for Fox—"he was bad enough for any crime"[30]—only that he felt the prosecution, and that included Spilsbury, failed to prove its case. Few impartial observers would disagree with him.

Given such dubious circumstances, common sense dictates that Fox intended doing *something* to hasten his mother's end. After all, merely setting fire to the room in hopes of suffocating her would provide no guarantee of success, particularly when up against such a tight deadline. Perhaps he intended to gas her, only to lose his nerve as memories of the incident with Charlotte Morse flooded back. Or maybe his mind was set on strangulation, only to find nature lending a hand as he wrapped his fingers around her throat. If so, this would not have aided Fox one jot, as all the insurance policies covered only accidental death. Hence the need for a blaze.

On the eve of the trial, Jowitt and his junior counsel, Sir Henry Curtis-Bennett, KC, sat in their hotel and theorized how the murder might have occurred. One method seemed more likely than any other. Together with Lady Jowitt, they went upstairs to the bedroom of Jowitt's secretary. Lady Jowitt lay down on the bed, and Curtis-Bennett and Jowitt took it in turns to approach the bed, pretend to seize her by the throat with the left hand, snatch away her pillow with the right hand, then use it to muffle any possible cry of terror. Once Fox thought his mother was dead, they reasoned, he placed the pillow on the bedside cupboard before lighting the fire that was to be the apparent cause of death. Significantly, though, this experiment left clear traces of lipstick on the pillow, and as Cassels pointed out, when this particular theory was advanced in court, there were no marks of any kind on the pillow. Had Rosaline Fox been suffocated in this fashion, all the experts agreed that some staining would be expected.

Certainly the Crown sensed it was on thin ice, hence the delay in charging Fox with murder. But they also knew that they held the great ace in the hole: Sir Bernard Spilsbury. Whatever he saw on the larynx left him convinced that Mrs. Fox had been strangled, and the great persuader could always be relied upon in a crisis. Smith maintained that without Spilsbury's evidence, no jury would have dared convict Fox. Cassels, too, shared this view. Three times in the space of six years he'd defended prisoners at Lewes Assizes on the capital charge, and each time he'd seen his client dispatched to the gallows on Spilsbury's say-so. No matter how often Cassels might warn the jury of blindly accepting Spilsbury's word—"no one can say that an individual, what-ever his position and skill, is never likely to be mistaken"[31]—it was pointless. The jury didn't know Smith or Brontë; they knew Spilsbury, and they trusted him wholeheartedly. It was as simple—or as compli-cated—as that.

In a curious twist of fate, the following year Spilsbury and Smith found themselves testifying shoulder to shoulder when a Glaswegian bookmaker's clerk, Peter Queen, was charged with strangling his live-in lover, Chrissie Gall. As this was a Scottish case, Spilsbury exercised his right to give evidence for the defense, and he sided with Smith's view that sufficient evidence existed to suggest that the alcoholic vic-tim had committed suicide. Queen's trial began in Glasgow on January 5, 1932, and it remains one of the great ironies of British legal history that on the only occasion when Spilsbury and Smith were in broad agreement about a particular case, the jury believed neither of them. Queen was sentenced to death, though later reprieved.

A matter of weeks after the end of the Queen trial, Robert Brontë finally succumbed, at age fifty-two, to the heart trouble that had plagued his latter years and left him a virtual invalid. Although barely tolerated by the police and mercilessly lampooned by academia, the mercurial Irishman does deserve some recognition for being the first medico-legal practitioner to highlight the dangers of unquestioning reliance on the testimony of any single expert witness. Where he fell down was in methodology and temperament. Unlike Spilsbury, whose beautifully prepared laboratory samples were all self-generated, Brontë farmed out his specimens, a habit prone to backfire when advocates probed too deeply. And always there was his volcanic temper. Prosecutors soon learned how volatile Brontë could be when testifying and took joy in needling him to the point of explosion. The Fox case was a typical example; Brontë erupted on the stand, and with it went his credibility. That trial marked the last time that he crossed swords with his old rival; and in all those battles, not once did he emerge the victor.

Certainly the latter half of the 1920s had been a troubling period for Spilsbury. For the first time in his life he'd come under serious attack in court, with the criticism reaching its peak in the trial of Sidney Fox. But as a new decade dawned, one fact remained unalterable and inviolate: his stranglehold on the jury. Nothing bar an earthquake, or so it seemed, could shift that.

1 *Times*, January 24, 1927, 7.
2 *Ibid.*, November 23, 1927, 13.
3 *Ibid.*, March 31, 1928, 11.
4 *Ibid.*, July 31, 1929, 16.
5 *Ibid.*, August 1, 1929, 11.
6 Richard Whittington-Egan, *The Riddle of Birdhurst Rise* (London: Penguin, 1988), 242.
7 *Public Records Office*, MEPO 3/862.
8 Iain Adamson, *A Man of Quality* (London: Muller, 1964), 106.
9 *Times*, February 1, 1930, 9.
10 James Hodge, *Famous Trials III* (London: Penguin, 1950), 64.
11 *Ibid.*, 78.
12 *Times*, March 13, 1930, 11.
13 Sir Sydney Smith, *Mostly Murder* (London: Grafton, 1984), 195.
14 *Ibid.*, 195–96.
15 *Ibid.*, 197.
16 *Ibid.*, 199.
17 *Ibid.*
18 Adamson, *A Man of Quality*, 110.
19 *Times*, March 19, 1930, 11.
20 Smith, *Mostly Murder*, 201.
21 Hodge, *Famous Trials III*, 83.

22 *Daily Express*, March 21, 1930, 13.
23 *Ibid.*
24 *Times*, March 21, 1930, 5.
25 *Daily Express*, March 21, 1930, 13.
26 Smith, *Mostly Murder*, 203.
27 *Ibid.*, 204.
28 Adamson, *A Man of Quality*, 110.
29 *Daily Express*, March 22, 1930, 2.
30 Smith, *Mostly Murder*, 206.
31 Adamson, *A Man of Quality*, 111.

CHAPTER EIGHT

A Slightly Imperfect Murder

It is a curious fact that people who deliberately set out to commit murder often draw on the crimes of others for inspiration. Norman Thorne was a prime example of this phenomenon. The carefully clipped newspaper cuttings of the Mahon case recovered from Thorne's shack were a clear pointer to someone who'd studied the blunders that doomed the Crumbles killer and resolved not to repeat them. Armstrong, too, had been notably fascinated by the exploits of his fellow solicitor, Harold Greenwood, devouring every word of press coverage he could lay his hands on. As Thorne and Armstrong discovered to their cost, no two murders are exactly alike, and the banana skin always lies in wait. But willful killers rarely suffer from a shortage of vanity, and in the fall of 1930 yet another plotter was putting the final touches to his own "perfect murder" scheme, ready to test his ego and courage against the vagaries of fate. For inspiration, he turned to events that had taken place earlier that year, at the height of summer.

When the half-naked body of Agnes Kesson was found lying alongside Horton Lane, Epsom, at six o'clock on the morning of June 5, 1930, it looked to be just another tragic case of rape-murder, one quickly solved and almost as quickly forgotten except by those most closely affected. Scotland Yard swung smoothly into action. The crime scene was processed efficiently, and Spilsbury rushed back from Manchester, where he had been testifying at the inquest of a drug-overdose victim to perform the autopsy. He found a deep impression that encircled the lower part of Agnes Kesson's neck in a horizontal direction, and three small bruises on the adjoining skin. On the left side and at the rear of the neck, the single depression diverged into two distinct grooves where the killer had crossed the ligature and then yanked in opposite directions. Bruises covered the arms and legs, there were two contusions on the forehead, and nine more on the upper back. The small of the back showed an ugly discoloration that measured $2 \times 1\frac{1}{2}$ inches. More bruising covered the rear of the head, and the tongue was deeply indented by teeth. Although death was due to strangulation— most likely from a rope, to judge from the pattern marks—Spilsbury had no doubt that Agnes had been beaten ferociously before death and that she had fought like a wildcat for her life. Despite the disarrayed clothing, there had been no sexual assault. Death, he reckoned, had occurred an hour or so either side of midnight.

The bleak desolation of the murder scene at dawn made it almost impossible to believe that just fifteen hours earlier this very spot had staged the biggest event in the British horse-racing calendar, the Derby. Close to a quarter of a million fans had surged across Epsom's rolling acres to either rejoice or tear up worthless tickets as jockey Harry Wragg booted home the 18–1 outsider Blenheim; and at first it was assumed that Agnes had been one of the excited racegoers, but as the day wore on, detectives learned that she waitressed at a tea shop in nearby Burgh Heath. The owner, Fred Deats, sighed resignedly when told the news. Agnes had worked at the tea shop since Christmas, and in that time the twenty-year-old from Falkirk had been a real handful, Deats explained, very hotheaded and untrustworthy. Only a couple of days before, he'd stormed into the local police station, bellowing that she'd been stealing money. After listening more or less patiently to the details, the desk sergeant had refused to issue a warrant and sent him packing. Despite his problems with the quarrelsome Scottish lass, Deats swore that he had nothing to do with her death.

Investigators turned instead to a young man who lived above the tea shop. Grudgingly, Bob Harper admitted having regular sex with Agnes, though this had become less frequent lately owing to her ungovernable temper. In their latest quarrel—one day before her disappearance—she had kicked him several times, and he'd been heard to threaten that if she didn't stop he would choke her. When asked to account for his whereabouts at around midnight on the night in question, Harper claimed that he and the café owner's son, Robert Deats, had gone looking for Agnes after she'd not returned to the café as expected. As alibis go, it sounded weak.

Suspicions about these two young men lingered, and at the subsequent inquest, Spilsbury was asked if the injuries inflicted upon Agnes were consistent with there having been two attackers. Whilst conceding the possibility, he was quick to point out that the evidence might equally point to a single assailant. In short, there was nothing to say definitely, either way.

As always, Spilsbury was burning the candle at both ends. Whilst hard at work on this case, he was commuting daily to the Imperial Conference of Police Chiefs in London, where police officers from around the globe had gathered to exchange ideas in criminal investigation. They listened intently as Spilsbury, aided by Roche Lynch and Robert Churchill, the ballistics expert, explained the latest developments in forensic science.

But nothing could knock the death of Agnes Kesson off the front pages. Public prurience reached boiling point with the sizzling revelation that the dead girl had shared her sexual favors with more than one habitué of the tea shop. The tabloids ran with the story all summer, but as the juicy tidbits dried up, curiosity waned, and after an inquest recorded a verdict of murder by persons unknown, the case slipped into the "unsolved" category, where it remained.

Of the millions of newspaper readers who had followed every sensational twist and turn in this saga, none did so more avidly than a north

London salesman with his own checkered sexual history. As he put it later, "It was the Agnes Kesson case in Epsom in June which first set me thinking," and what he read in the papers convinced him that, provided one was meticulous in planning a murder, "It was possible to beat the police."[1]

A Suspicious Blaze

For almost four centuries the peoples of Britain have organized parties and set off fireworks to commemorate the failed 1605 plot to blow up the Houses of Parliament. Each November 5—Bonfire Night—effigies of Guy Fawkes, one of the principal plotters who was captured in the basement of the House and later executed, are burned on fires that light up the autumnal sky. In times gone by, Bonfire Night also marked an important date in the local dance calendar, especially in more rural areas, and it was from just such a dance, in the early hours of November 6, 1930, that two young cousins, Alfred Thomas Brown and William Bailey, found themselves homeward bound. The hour was late, about 1:50 A.M., but the night was fine for walking, with plenty of bright moonlight to illuminate their three-mile trek home to Hardingstone, a small village just south of Northampton. As they wheeled left into Hardingstone Lane on the last leg of their journey, they saw, about four hundred yards ahead, a large, bright glow, obviously a fire of some description. Nothing unusual in that, they thought. Then something quite extraordinary happened: from a hedge-lined ditch on the south side of the road there emerged a man, out-of-breath, hatless, wearing a light mackintosh and carrying a small attaché case. For a frozen moment he seemed startled by their presence, then he just darted past without a word.

Bailey, squinting ahead into the darkness, said, "What is the blaze?"[2] From fifteen yards or so down the road, the stranger shouted back, "It looks as if somebody has had a bonfire,"[3] then hurried on. Bailey and Brown hastened toward the fire, snatching curious looks back at the stranger, for as Brown later observed laconically, "When you go home at that time in the morning you do not usually see well-dressed men getting out of the ditch."[4] They watched him reach the main Northampton-London road, hesitate as if uncertain which way to go, then head south in the direction of London and disappear from view.

By the time the two cousins reached the fire, they realized it was an inferno, with flames leaping twelve, fifteen feet into the air. Shielding their faces from the intense heat, they peered into the blaze and were just able to discern the ghostly silhouette of a motor car. Deciding that this required some degree of official intervention, they ran into the village, where Bailey awakened his father, who happened to be a police officer, while Brown called out Police Constable H. B. Copping.

Breathless and sweating hard, even in the cold night air, all four men reconvened at the still-blazing car. Copping was puzzled by the way the flames appeared to engulf the entire car with the exception of the hood, which was where most car fires begin. He was still pondering this conundrum when someone pointed excitedly toward the front of the vehicle.

For the next twelve minutes they frantically hurled buckets of water onto the blaze, until finally the flames died down enough to allow them to approach the smoking ruin. Brown's probing flashlight confirmed their worst fears. In the front of the passenger compartment—charred and shriveled to a cinder—lay what once had been a human being. Since the person was obviously beyond medical assistance, Copping gave orders that nothing should be touched while he went off to summon help.

At 3:10 A.M. Inspector James Lawrence arrived from Northampton and took control of the investigation. He noted that the seats had collapsed and the fabric roof had fallen on the victim, whose blackened torso lay sprawled across the passenger's seat, half inclined toward the rear, facedown on the driver's seat. The right arm was burnt off at the elbow. What remained gave the impression of reaching for a gasoline canister that lay on the rear seat. The seams of the canister had erupted from the heat, and its handle was missing. Only when the body was removed could the left arm be seen. The left leg was doubled up underneath the trunk, while the right leg was burnt off below the knee. The stump extended beyond where the passenger side running board had been, to a distance of eight inches from the chassis. The level of corporal destruction was so comprehensive as to make it impossible—certainly for the untrained eye—to tell whether the victim was male or female. One possible clue came via a charred boot heel found near the running board. In shape and size it bore all the hallmarks of ladies' footwear and provided the police with their first hint that the victim was female.

By aiming a police car's headlights onto the tire tracks it was possible to discern the vehicle's direction of travel. It had come from Hardingstone and then halted, about one foot from the grass verge. There were no obvious skid or brake marks. So far as anyone could see, the car had simply stopped and then burst into flame.

As the sky lightened, Lawrence became anxious. Hardingstone Lane lay on a busy bus route, and he didn't want the burnt-out shell blocking the highway. He therefore ordered the car to be moved onto the grass verge, an act of quite monumental stupidity. No notes had been taken of the car's exact position and—vitally—no photographs either, two omissions destined to haunt the Northamptonshire constabulary before this investigation was over. Once again the enormous gulf that existed between provincial police forces and their more experienced counterparts at Scotland Yard, when it came to investigating potentially serious crimes, was brought into sharp relief. And it only got worse. Before long people would be setting off for work, and Lawrence, unnerved by the prospect of commuters gawping at cremated human remains, ordered that the corpse be removed posthaste. Without benefit of photographs, sketches, or even handwritten notes, the remains were bundled up in sacking and carted off to the Crown Inn at Hardingstone, where they were stored in the garage. In the meantime, the car stood unguarded for more than an hour.

During this hiatus the first photographer arrived. Unfortunately—
so far as the investigation was concerned—he worked for a press
agency and began shooting pictures without any supervision. Having a
keen eye for composition and knowing what sold newspapers, he
arranged certain objects to present the best possible picture. When the
police returned they assumed he was an official photographer and allowed him to keep snapping.

The first police photographer didn't turn up until 8:15 A.M., followed at nine o'clock by another. As comparisons of the various sets of
photographs later showed, someone clearly moved the radiator cap,
while the mudguards and other objects, which in the earlier photos lay
on the ground, had since been tossed haphazardly into the car. There
was nothing to say that anything found by the police after 5 A.M. was
in its original position. A more shambolic crime scene would be hard
to imagine.

Daylight brought more discoveries. Fourteen yards in front of the
car lay a mallet with what looked like three hairs adhering to it. But
most attention was still centered on the car itself, a Morris Minor, a
popular vehicle that numbered in the thousands. In the ordinary course
of events, establishing who owned a vehicle so gutted by fire would
have been fiendishly difficult, but for once fortune had smiled on the
investigators. By some miracle, despite the ferocious heat, the license
plate—MU 1468—was still intact. Tracing the car's registered owner
would simply be a matter of checking the vehicle licensing records.

Something else that had survived the inferno was the driver-side
front tire. This was hugely significant. Considering the scale and loca-
tion of the fire damage, and factoring in the wind direction—diago-
nally from the driver-side rear—the fire had apparently begun in the
rear of the car and was then blown forward. Such a blaze, with only the
rear seat cushions for fuel, should have been slow-burning, certainly
slow enough to allow anyone sitting in the front ample time to vacate
the vehicle before the flames reached the gas tank, mounted beneath
the dashboard.

This rudimentary reconstruction, and the paradox it revealed, prompted Lawrence to reread the statements made by Bailey and Brown. Like them, he was intrigued by "the man in the ditch," whom they described as stockily built, and with a small, rounded face.

Later that morning Dr. Eric Shaw, of the Northampton General Hospital, an experienced pathologist, though not someone nationally recognized, began the task of autopsying the remains. At the same time, Lawrence began contacting the hotels and inns of Northampton, to see if any woman had been reported missing.

What became known as "The Body in a Blazing Car" attracted instant national press attention, with late editions of that day's papers full of the first reports. These included a description of the mysterious man in the ditch: aged between thirty and thirty-five, height five feet ten inches to six feet, with a small round face and curly black hair, wearing a light mackintosh, dark trousers, no hat, and carrying an attaché case.

Before the day was out, detectives in north London had traced the vehicle to a thirty-six-year-old commercial traveler named Alfred Arthur Rouse, who lived in Buxted Road, Friern Barnet. When the police knocked at her door, Lily Rouse declared blankly that her husband was not home. She had not seen him since the middle of the preceding night, when he had returned to grab a change of clothes and then left half an hour later. There was nothing unusual in this, she explained; fleeting visits at all hours of the day and night, and long absences from the home were part and parcel of her husband's job as a traveling salesman.

Lily Rouse was driven to Northampton and shown the car, which she identified. Out of deference she was spared the charred corpse. There seemed little point; it was unrecognizable, and everything pointed to the victim being female. When asked to describe her husband, Mrs. Rouse painted a picture of someone remarkably similar to the man in the ditch. But there was a problem. Her recollection, admittedly dulled by sleep and darkness, was that her husband had come home at 2 A.M. that morning. If this was the case, then he could not have been in a Northamptonshire lane—sixty-five miles away—just ten minutes earlier when the blazing car had first been spotted.

At about the same time that Lily Rouse was helping the Northampton police, 150 miles to the southwest, a man was alighting from a bus in the small Welsh mining village of Gelligaer. He was tired, hungry, and frazzled beyond belief. At 8:30 P.M. he trudged up to Primrose Villa and banged loudly. William Jenkins opened the door to his son-in-law and was surprised to see him on foot; normally he drove. The newcomer explained wearily as he trudged indoors, "I have been a long time coming—about eighteen hours. I have had my car stolen while in Northampton."[5]

It was a lie, of course, like almost everything that Alfred Rouse ever uttered, but like Mahon and Fox before him, he was a man fatally attracted to falsehood, even if it gained him nothing and often only doubled his problems.

A Real Charmer

For the previous decade he had traveled the roads and byways of southern England in his job as a company representative. He was a top-notch salesman, no doubt about it, as his annual salary of around £500—more than twice the national average—could attest, and had he been able to rein in his excesses, then who knows what he might have achieved? What undid him was his insatiable sexual appetite. When the police attempted to piece together his background, they often found themselves overwhelmed by its complexity. Everywhere he went, Rouse seduced women and sired offspring. Dozens of mistresses in dozens of towns regularly welcomed him into their beds. It was a harum-scarum existence that would eventually titillate and outrage millions of newspaper readers. But it hadn't always been that way.

Alfred Rouse was born in London on April 6, 1894, and although his upbringing was troubled—he was largely raised by his sister—nothing hinted at the chaos to come. On leaving school, where he excelled on the violin, piano, and mandolin, he worked first in a realtor's office, then found a position with a soft-furnishings store in London's

West End. There he prospered. Dangerous amounts of natural charm allied to a commission-based salary gave him the financial wherewithal to propose marriage to Lily May Watkins, a young woman clerk three years his senior, only for the Great War to intervene. Like millions of others, Rouse was caught up in a tidal wave of patriotic fervor that swept the country, and on August 8, 1914—four days after war was declared—he was standing in line at the recruiting office. A few months later he was posted overseas, but not before marrying Lily on November 29.

The following spring saw him on the western front. It wasn't all trenches, bully beef, blood, and bullets—far from it. Rouse's buttery plausibility worked just as well *sur le continent* as it had at home, and it wasn't long before a local girl fell pregnant to him. Rouse might have been a blackguard, but he was loyal, and for the remainder of his life he continued to support the son in Paris he never knew, sending money regularly. Unfortunately this incident set the template for the rest of his life, and what happened next only seemed to harden his destiny.

In May 1915 he was fighting with his regiment at Givenchy, caught in a fierce bayonet battle, when a shell burst overhead. Everything went black. When Private Rouse regained consciousness, he was back in England, aboard a train conveying him to hospital, where surgeons removed the shrapnel that had punctured the left side of his body. In time the wounds on his thigh healed, but the splinters that had entered the left temporal lobe had profoundly damaged his psyche. Postwar medical reports spoke of someone "unable to wear a hat of any kind . . . memory very defective . . . sleeps badly . . . easily excited . . . talks and laughs immoderately at times."[6]

He was eventually discharged from the services with "capacity reduced three-quarters"[7] and for a short time received a modest disability pension of £2 per week. In 1920 this was rescinded after a follow-up medical examination found that the leg injury had healed. What the doctors didn't spot, or didn't care about, was the psychological damage. That was permanent.

Rouse wasn't one for self-pity. Wartime trauma might have left him with a legacy of headaches and dizziness, but it did nothing to diminish his capacity for hard work, nor did it dull his lightning-quick tongue. He landed a job with W. B. Martin Ltd., a Leicester-based manufacturer of fancy goods, and they found plenty to like in their new star salesman. The bulging client list that Rouse soon accumulated required him to drive several thousands of miles a year, and it was his dependence on generally unreliable cars that turned him into a skilled mechanic, able to perform even complex repair jobs at the side of the road, a talent that he would one day turn to a lethal purpose.

An extrovert personality, a motorcar, and a generous expense account were attributes that set Rouse well apart from the postwar crowd, and he was not slow to take advantage of his status. Impressionable young women from London to Kent to Wales and north to the Midlands, many of whom had never before sat in a car, jumped at the opportunity for a quick spin with the playboy "bachelor." Starry-eyed and breathless, they marveled as the snappily dressed Rouse hurtled skillfully along country lanes, all the while weaving his fictions: the education at Eton and Cambridge, his time as a colonel on the western front, the extensive property portfolio. It was a carefully constructed and oft-repeated script that generally had its denouement in some secluded lay-by.

Helen Campbell was a typical victim. Just fifteen years old when she met Rouse in 1920, she soon fell under his hypnotic spell, blissfully unaware of her paramour's marital state. The following year, on October 21, she gave birth to his child, which died five weeks later. For the next few years she worked as a waitress in her hometown of Chatham, Kent, and throughout this period Rouse shared her bed at every opportunity, forever renewing spurious pledges of imminent matrimony. Even when Helen learned the cruel truth—that the man she loved was already married—she couldn't bring herself to abandon him. On July 22, 1925, she had a second child, a boy, and, as always, Rouse tried to maintain his son. And then his pockets ran dry. Considerable mutual agonizing over how best to remedy what was a devilishly awkward situation produced a novel solution: In the summer of 1930 the boy moved to London to live with Rouse and his wife, who had never had children of their own.

By this time, Lily Rouse had become aware of—if not used to—her husband's serial philandering, and she wearily agreed to the odd arrangement. As summer drifted into fall, and the full extent of his duplicity became ever more obvious—process servers were a regular feature at her door—she threw in the towel and threatened him with divorce. This would prove to be the final nail in Rouse's financial coffin. Besides the mortgage, car payment, and a weekly allowance for his wife, he was already being chased through the courts by a string of ex- and current lovers for arrears of child maintenance orders.

Leading the charge was Nellie Tucker, who lived in Hendon, only a couple of miles from Rouse's home. She'd first met Rouse in 1925 and had swallowed his promise of marriage. The inevitable child came along on May 2, 1928. As Rouse's maintenance payments dwindled from erratic to nonexistent, she was advised to take legal action. Financial hardship clearly didn't affect her devotion to Rouse, and in early 1930 she realized that, once again, she was pregnant by him. This baby was born on October 29, 1930, at the City of London Maternity Hospital. Six days later—on Bonfire Night—Rouse visited his newest child in the hospital. The doting father was a role that Rouse played well and often. But not tonight. The usual silvery flow of words had dried to a trickle. He seemed preoccupied, not his normal cheery self at all. At 7:45 P.M., he kissed Nellie good-bye and left, ready to embark on a flinty and predetermined path from which there was no way back.

As he hurried from the hospital ward, his fingers closed around the telegram in his pocket. More bad news. From south Wales this time, an urgent message begging him to return to yet another "wife" who'd fallen dangerously ill in the latter stages of a pregnancy. Ivy Jenkins had met Rouse while working in London as a probationer nurse and, like almost every other woman who crossed Rouse's path, soon found herself expecting his child. A hurriedly arranged wedding on July 12, 1930—Ivy's twenty-first birthday—relieved and delighted her parents, and as her pregnancy became more pronounced, she returned to the family home in Gelligaer to await the happy event. Every two weeks Rouse would call, with updates on the luxurious townhouse he'd bought for them in Kingston, West London, at a cost of £1,250, sumptuously furnished, of course, and all totally illusory. When the Jenkins family decided that Ivy's elder sister, Phyllis, would accompany the couple back to Kingston and stay with them for the first three months after the birth of their child, Rouse panicked. The erratically constructed house of cards that he'd cobbled together over so many years was collapsing about his ears. By the evening of November 5, Alfred Rouse had reached the end of his emotional and financial tether. Something had to give . . .

And now the climax had been reached in Gelligaer. Rouse, exhausted after his marathon journey from London, was tucking into a welcome supper when a knock came at the door. An excited neighbor, Thomas Reeks, burst in with a copy of the evening paper. It showed a photograph of a burnt-out car in Northamptonshire. Reeks had heard Rouse's story of having his car stolen, and said, "Is this your car, because, if it is, you will see it no more."[8] Rouse briefly scanned the story and shook his head. Just a coincidence, he said, and carried on with his meal.

Suspect Named

The next morning's newspaper wasn't so easy to brush off. It named Rouse as the registered owner of the vehicle. This time he stuffed the paper into his pocket and hurriedly announced his intention of returning to London to clear up the matter. A local man, Hendle Brownhill, agreed to drive him into Cardiff, where he could catch a bus back to London. On the brief journey Rouse again talked of his car being stolen from outside a restaurant in London, and now it appeared to have been burnt by the thieves. When the two men stopped off at the Cooper's Arms Hotel in the village of Ystrad Mynach for some refreshment and Rouse repeated this story, another newspaper was produced, one that contained a startling development: the charred body of a woman had been found in the gutted vehicle. All the color drained from Rouse's face. "Oh, dear, dear." He gasped. "I cannot bear to hear anything about it."[9]

Later that morning Brownhill dropped off Rouse in Cardiff, where he boarded a bus to London. Brownhill watched him leave with a mixture of emotions. Something about the stolen car story didn't ring true. Only after considerable soul searching did Brownhill go in search of a police station.

At 9:20 that night the bus pulled in to Hammersmith, London. An earlier phone call from Cardiff to Scotland Yard meant that Detective Sergeant Robert Skelley was on hand when the vehicle arrived, and before anyone could alight, he walked the length of the bus surveying each person in turn. He paused by a man in a light mackintosh and asked if his name was Rouse. When the man nodded, Skelley showed his warrant card and asked Rouse to accompany him. "Very well," said Rouse. "I am glad it is over. I was going to Scotland Yard. I am responsible. I am very glad it is over. I have had no sleep."[10]

Rouse was taken to Hammersmith Police Station, where he began to talk and talk and talk. Overwhelmed interviewing officers soon had their ranks swelled by members of the Northampton police force. Since the burnt-out car had been found on their "patch," they were keen to establish their authority. Such inter-force rivalry goes some way toward explaining why it was that Sir Bernard Spilsbury, the forensic pathologist best equipped to investigate what was clearly a most unusual incident, was not brought into the case until November 10, fully four days after the body had been found.

Already there had been a botched crime scene; now other indicators of sloppy investigative work emerged. Foremost among these was a revised opinion from Dr. Shaw; closer examination of the incinerated body now convinced him that the victim was a *man*, not a woman. The question was: would Spilsbury agree?

For all the claims of high-handedness leveled against Spilsbury—

usually by people who didn't know him—no one could ever accuse him of criticizing colleagues in public. It just wasn't in his nature. Whenever called in by provincial forces to investigate a crime, as much as possible Spilsbury deferred to the local man, and on this occasion when he examined the remains, which were still housed in the garage of the Crown Inn, he found it easy to appreciate Shaw's dilemma.

In any fire inquiry the questions to be resolved by the investigators are:

1. Did death occur prior to or after the commencement of the fire?
2. Is the cause of death fire related? If so, is the cause of death smoke inhalation, burns, heat shock, or trauma? If not, what is the cause of death?
3. Why was the victim in the fire?
4. Why was the victim unable to escape the fire?

In this case the fire damage had been colossal. Ordinarily, human bodies are quite resistant to fire, but throw an accelerant like gasoline into the mix, and the resulting temperature can reach levels rarely found outside a crematorium.

Here the extreme heat had caused the skull to burst wide open, leaving the brain—all shrunken and burnt—to gape through. Nothing survived of the face or ears. The front of the torso had been incinerated so completely that the heart and lungs were clearly visible. Even so, Spilsbury still managed to find a fragment of what looked like a prostate gland. Further male-related items were found on the body, including part of a trouser fly that was jammed in the fork of the corpse's left thigh where it pressed against the stomach. Even now, four days after the fire, this scrap of fabric gave off telltale fumes, clear evidence that it had been saturated in gasoline. (A more thorough search of the car had also revealed the buckles from a pair of men's suspenders.)

Because the damage to the limbs was so great—both forearms and hands were missing, burnt off by the searing heat, as were the legs below the knees—Spilsbury felt uncomfortable offering any firm opinion as to the height of the victim. Instinct told him that Shaw's estimate of five feet eight inches wasn't too far wide of the mark, but he refused to be categorical.

In order to gauge some idea of the victim's age, Spilsbury paid special attention to the teeth. Besides being the hardest substance in the human body and the most resistant to fire, teeth can, within broad limits, provide a useful indicator of age. In this instance, the degree of dental attrition and neglect suggested someone aged twenty-one to thirty, and most likely from a disadvantaged background. When Spilsbury cut into the lungs and found a black pigmentation such as might be caused by coal dust, he formed the opinion that the man had at some time worked as a miner.

Just one year earlier Spilsbury had autopsied another fire victim, Rosaline Fox, and determined that she had been dead when the fire began. But it was an entirely different story with the "Blazing Car Body." Microscopical examination of mucus from the bronchial tubes revealed a fine black deposit of carbon consistent with the victim having inhaled smoke before death. Visual inspection of the organs—bright pink— confirmed this. The amount of contamination was consistent with someone who had died within thirty seconds of first breathing the smoke. Spilsbury took organ samples for analysis to check if they contained poison or any other severely disabling agent. When it came to the cause of death he agreed with Shaw: shock from the effects of fire. What he needed to know now was whether this was a case of murder or—as Rouse had loudly protested—a ghastly and unpreventable accident.

From the time of his arrest, Rouse had not stopped talking. Over several hours at Hammersmith Police Station, with several amendments and interruptions, he told his story. Because it played such an important role in subsequent proceedings, a truncated version of his statement is presented here:

I do not know what happened exactly. I picked a man up on the Great North Road. He asked me for a lift, and as he seemed a respectable man

I gave him one. I picked him up just this side of St. Albans. He got in and I drove off. After going some distance, I lost my way, and a policeman spoke to me about my lights. I did not know anything about the man. I saw his hand on my case at the back of the car. Later on my engine started to spit, and I thought I was running out of petrol. I wanted to relieve myself, and said to the man, 'There is some petrol in the can; you can empty it into the tank while I am gone,' and I lifted the bonnet [hood] and showed him where to put it in. Before I went he said, 'What about a smoke?' I said, 'I have given you all my cigarettes as it is.' I then went some distance along the road, and had just got my trousers down when I noticed a big flame from behind. I pulled my trousers up quickly and ran towards the flames. I saw the man inside the car. I tried to open the car but could not do so. I then began to tremble violently. I was all of a shake. I ran away as hard as I could along the road where I saw the two men. I felt I was responsible for what had happened. I lost my head . . .[11]

After passing the two men, Rouse had reached the main London-Northampton road where he flagged down a passing truck. He told the driver, Henry Turner, that he had been "waiting for a mate with a Bentley car to take him back to London and he had not turned up,"[12] and Turner agreed to give him a ride. During the journey Turner noticed nothing peculiar or agitated about Rouse, and the two men passed the time discussing cars and their engines. The uneventful nature of the journey can be confirmed by the fact that Turner's codriver, Edwin Pitt, dozed throughout and scarcely paid any attention to the hitchhiker.

After being dropped off at Tally Ho Corner in North Finchley, Rouse made his way home. His wife, deceived by the darkness, timed his arrival at approximately 2 A.M. By his own admission it was closer to 6:20 A.M. when he entered the front door, and about half an hour later when he reemerged into the chilly, gray-streaked morning. A plan had formed in his mind: he would lie low in Wales with Ivy Jenkins and wait until all the fuss died down.

Once on board the bus to Cardiff, he padded out the long journey with fanciful and wholly unnecessary monologues, telling the driver that his car had been stolen on the Great North Road and that he was on his way to Cardiff to see his wife. That night, careworn and exhausted, he finally reached the Jenkinses' house in Gelligaer, only to be thunderstruck that news of the incident had already made the newspapers. It had never occurred to him that a mundane car fire, even if it were fatal, would attract national publicity. After a night's sleep, he said, he resolved to return to London to clarify the situation.

This was the first version that Rouse gave of that night's events, and it was one with which he was to tinker repeatedly. After his initial interview in Hammersmith he was taken to the Angel Lane police station in Northampton. The journey did nothing to stanch Rouse's verbal incontinence, and it was in Northampton that he made the statement that hanged him.

Although there was plenty in Rouse's tale to arouse revulsion—watching a man roast to death and then fleeing the scene without even attempting to fetch a bucket of water are scarcely actions guaranteed to promote sympathy for the onlooker—thus far the police had found nothing to contradict his claim that the fire had been a dreadful accident. There seemed to be no motive for the crime, if indeed crime it was. And then Rouse opened the door. Warming to his audience, the garrulous fancy-goods salesman expanded on his domestic situation:

My wife is really too good for me. I like a woman who will make a fuss of me. I don't think I ever remember my wife sitting on my knee. Otherwise she is a good wife. I know several women, but it is an expensive game. I was on my way to Leicester, to hand in my slip on Thursday morning to get some money from my firm. I was then going to Wales for the weekend. My harem takes me to several places, and I am not at home a great deal, but my wife doesn't ask questions now. I was going to sell my house and furniture. I was then going to make an allowance to my wife. I think I should clear between £100 and £150 from the sale.[13]

Although suppressed by the time of Rouse's trial, the headline coverage given to this statement in the widely reported committal proceedings meant that the damage was irreversible. Newspaper readers across the country had sniggered over details of the philandering salesman, with most reaching the same conclusion as the police: Rouse's "harem" had finally become too much of a financial burden. Drowning in debt, he decided to stage his own disappearance. Far from being a tragic accident, the car fire had been a carefully planned callous murder.

Powerful though that motive might appear, verdicts are won—or should be—on facts, not suspicions, and when the police discovered that Rouse had recently taken out a £1,000 insurance policy, payable on the accidental death of the owner-driver of the vehicle, they decided they had enough to prefer a charge of murder. (Quite how Rouse intended to claim on this policy, given the fact that he was supposed to be dead, was never made clear and perhaps explains why this strand was later swept under the carpet by the prosecution.) Certainly the case against Rouse was by no means ironclad, so that when the trial opened at Northampton Assizes on January 26, 1931, the defense confidently expected to win an acquittal.

For Spilsbury the trial marked something of a watershed: unlike most of his few high-profile murder cases, this time the victim was male. For decades he had been sending lady-killers like Crippen, Smith, Armstrong, and Fox to the gallows; now, in a bizarre twist of fate, he was expected to convince the jury that Rouse had killed an unknown man, for despite a nationwide campaign by police and press alike, the victim's identity remained a mystery.

Experts Wrangle

As was now commonplace in many major trials, much of the testimony was given over to wrangling between the expert witnesses. For the prosecution there was Colonel Cuthbert Buckle, who, as head of a firm of assessors regularly called in by insurance companies to investigate cases of possible arson, had been scrutinizing suspicious fires for a quarter of a century. In the previous four years alone, he had personally inspected fifty-six cases of burnt-out cars. He explained how most car fires occur with the ignition switched on and the engine running, when an electrical fault might make a spark jump and ignite any fuel leakage. As far as he could ascertain the ignition system on the Morris Minor was flawless. More significant still, the car was found parked in second gear, with its ignition off.

The heat had been colossal, at least 1,800°F, hot enough to melt the brass windshield surround, and yet, oddly enough, the engine compartment, which housed the gas tank, was the least damaged part of the vehicle. Buckle resolved this conundrum by tracing the seat of the blaze to somewhere between the dashboard and the rear axle. While a smoldering fire might have begun in this area had, say, a lighted cigarette or match come into contact with the upholstery, the ferocity of this particular blaze ruled out such a source. Also, Buckle found scorch marks *underneath* the rear of the vehicle, again highly unusual since flames burn upwards. He told the court that the only innocent reason to account for these scorch marks would have been a fuel leakage, but he found it impossible to believe that such a flaw—with its insufferable fumes—would have gone unnoticed by anyone inside the car: "You would have an explosive atmosphere."[14]

The fire, Buckle had no doubt, was deliberate, caused by someone tampering with the union joint between the gas tank and the fuel line, just beneath the dashboard. When Buckle inspected this union joint, he found it to be a whole turn loose. Tests on a similar vehicle showed the rate of flow from such a leak to be at one pint every two minutes forty seconds. Asked by Norman Birkett, KC, leading for the Crown, if the union joint could have become loose accidentally, Buckle replied, "I do not think so."[15] Despite repeated attempts to dislodge the fuel line with his foot, he had failed to do so, even with a partially loosened nut. Given the scenario described, Birkett asked Buckle if he would expect to see the passenger lying prone across the driver's seat. "I should have expected to see him on the road trying to put the fire out,"[16] was the pithy reply.

Unsurprisingly, the defense had its own experts who said exactly the opposite. Arthur Isaacs, a motor engineer, was emphatic that, in his experience of car fires, this particular joint was invariably loosened, a phenomenon that he attributed to the contraction and distortion of the metal threads cooling down after the fire.

Birkett rose to cross-examine. "What is the coefficient of the expansion of brass?" he asked almost casually.

Isaacs looked flummoxed and, after Birkett asked the question a second time, was forced to admit that he didn't know. Birkett peered askance over the top of his horn-rimmed spectacles. "But aren't you an engineer? You are not a doctor, nor a crime investigator, nor an amateur detective. Aren't you an engineer? Don't you know what the coefficient of brass is?"

"No."[17]

With that single question Birkett demolished the witness's credibility. Depending on one's point of view it was either inspired advocacy or the sneakiest of low blows. After all, what chance was there that any engineer could give the correct answer—0.0000189—without reference to a table? All the jury saw was a confounded expert, which was, of course, Birkett's intention. And he repeated the trick with the defense's second expert witness. Arthur Cotton, a fire-loss assessor to fifteen different insurance companies, also stated that, following an intense fire, he would expect to find the fuel union nut loosened. But like Isaacs, he floundered over the coefficient question; and like Isaacs, he limped impotently from the stand.

Before all this, the jury had been privileged to see the "incomparable witness" in peak form. The fact that Spilsbury had not seen the body in situ, and was therefore obliged to draw his conclusions from the observations of others, made his testimony uncharacteristically circumspect.

There was little that Spilsbury could add to Shaw's earlier testimony regarding the cause of death. His function was to explain how a person—whom Rouse claimed was filling the gas tank—came to be found sprawled across the passenger seat of a blazing car. Birkett had pinned his strategy on a belief that the man had been bludgeoned into insensibility before the fire began, a theory that drew support from three hairs found adhering to the mallet head. Spilsbury's cautious response to this theory must have irked the prosecution. One hair, he thought, displayed human characteristics under the microscope. "Of the other two, I am very dubious about one as to whether it is human hair at all. The other may be human, and that I think is as far as I can safely go."[18] Spilsbury knew this had been a botched investigation from the outset, and he certainly wasn't prepared to be drawn into any rash statements based on imperfect evidence. He was more confident when discussing the analysis of the various samples. Erratic carbon monoxide levels in the blood led him to believe that death had occurred very shortly after the fire started, or else the blood saturation levels in various parts of the body would have been more uniform.

According to Rouse, the fire had been caused by the man opening the can of gasoline whilst smoking a cigar. Spilsbury didn't think that the position of the body supported that view. "I think it is consistent with the man either pitching forward or being thrown down, face downwards, on to the seats of the car from the near-side door."[19] He explained the effects of fire on the human body; how, when subjected to extreme temperatures, the limbs develop a condition known as heat stiffening, or heat rigor. The effect of this is to shorten and contract the muscles and so cause the limb to bend. The lower leg would be bent to the thigh, and the thigh would then be drawn up to the torso, exactly as it was found in this case.

Birkett wanted to know if such a posture might have been assumed by someone frantically attempting to escape from the vehicle. Could the victim have got across the seat with his left leg doubled up? "Certainly not with the leg in the position in which I found it,"[20] Spilsbury replied.

In Spilsbury's opinion, before the fire began, the passenger-side door had been open and the man had been laid facedown across the seat with both legs extended through the door. As the heat intensified the left leg was drawn up by the method described, until it was bent double. The right leg, obstructed by the weight of the body, remained outside the vehicle, and this is what led to the right foot being entirely burnt off.

So how had the scrap of cloth recovered from the fork of the left leg come to be soaked in gasoline? Spilsbury offered a number of possible solutions. The likeliest accidental cause was if the fuel line somehow ruptured, spraying gasoline throughout the car at seat level before the fire took hold and caused the left leg to double up. Before all this could happen, one would have expected the passenger to vacate the vehicle. Far more probable was that the clothing had been deliberately soaked in gasoline before the fire broke out.

Donald Finnemore, for the defense, wanted to know if the witness had found any signs of violence inflicted on the man before the fire started. Spilsbury replied in the negative and emphasized that the splintering of the skull had been wholly attributable to the fire, not to any physical assault. This was vital for the defense, as it undermined prosecution claims that Rouse had first battered the man unconscious. Finnemore had less success when he asked Spilsbury if the man might have extended his legs through the passenger door in the act of attempting to kick open the door to escape the burning car. Spilsbury was emphatic. "He would have been dead long before that happened."[21]

On reexamination, Birkett concluded by asking Spilsbury, "Assume that a man was trapped in the car and was in the doubled-up posture permitted by a space of 3 ft. 4 ins., face downwards, buttocks up in order to get within that space, that that man dies fairly quickly, and that he remains there dead in this fierce heat until the door falls away. Would that account for the right foot being extruded and the left not?"

"No, it would not, because, as he was dead, he could make no violent movement, and the effect of the intense heat would be to stiffen the contracted limbs in the position in which they already were, and not in any way extend them."[22] The fact that the right leg was extended beyond the running board strongly suggested that the door had been open from the time when the body first assumed that position in the car. Nothing else fitted the facts.

Once again, the strongest witness for the prosecution was the defendant. Rouse—slick, cocky, and garrulous—decided that the witness stand was the perfect forum to air his cleverness. He described his activities that fateful night, picking up the stranger, the quick nap, the unplanned stop, the horrendous fire, and his ungovernable panic when he realized that the man was still inside the burning car. When Birkett suggested that Rouse had thrown the man facedown onto the seats, the defendant actually permitted himself the ghost of a smile. "If I did a thing like that I should not throw him face downwards. I should think where I put him, I imagine."

"You would imagine what?"

"Hardly that I should throw him down like nothing. That is absurd."

"If you rendered him unconscious, would you have a delicacy about his posture?"

"No, but I think if I had been going to do as you suggest, I should do a little more than that. *I think I have a little more brains than that.*"[23] Self-aggrandizement of this magnitude was lunacy. Especially when accompanied by Rouse's nauseating little chuckle.

Earlier, when Buckle had been giving testimony, his gaze kept flickering to Rouse, and he noticed the defendant's amusement almost when he (Buckle) had said that heat might have made the top of the carburetor fall off. This reaction led Buckle to privately wonder if Rouse had actually removed the carburetor top himself. He had passed his suspicion to Birkett, who midway through his cross-examination abruptly produced the carburetor and thrust it into Rouse's hands. For the only time during his testimony, Rouse blanched visibly. He tried to mask his discomfort by a blustering display of technical knowledge that produced exactly the opposite effect. Suddenly he was a man who knew altogether too much about cars and their engines. When Birkett began, "If the cap of that [carburetor] is wrenched off by hand as it could be—" the defendant butted in impatiently, "Yes, it could be. It is not a wrench; I think you simply turn a clip."

Too clever by half, that was the impression gained by all who saw Rouse during his almost daylong ordeal in the witness box. Singularly lacking in all his testimony was any scrap of remorse that a human being had burned to death in his car, even if accidentally. The best that Rouse could muster was, "It is very unfortunate, that is all I can say."[24]

In a trial so replete with conflicting expert-witness testimony, it is surprising that the jury required barely an hour to find Rouse guilty. All they had to guide them was Spilsbury's deductions from the reported position of the body. As in the Thorne case, these deductions were matters of opinion, based on immense experience, but still theoretical, and they were challenged. On January 31, 1931, Rouse was sentenced to death.

Rouse's last public appearance came at his appeal. It was grounded in charges that shoddy crime scene preservation and lurid publicity concerning Rouse's sex life had prejudiced his right to a fair trial, and there was also a heated debate over the fact that Buckle's expertise was not called upon until one month after the fire. None of this impressed the three judges, who threw out the petition. Before Rouse was taken away, he asked to speak to his long-suffering wife. In that brief interlude, Lily Rouse heard the words she dreaded. Rouse finally admitted his guilt, saying that the jury's verdict was just.

On the eve of his execution, a poignant scene unfolded at Bedford Prison. Rouse was in the visitor's area, consoling his distraught wife, when Helen Campbell arrived. Earlier that day she had taken their son to the Home Office in a futile bid to save Rouse's life. Now she wanted to see the man she loved one last time. Hollow-eyed and sobbing, all three clung to each other for the final meeting. To the very end, or so it seemed, Rouse was torn between women.

He was hanged the next morning at 8 A.M. The following day—March 11—the *Daily Sketch* published his full confession. In it, Rouse told how the widely reported and unsolved Agnes Kesson case had inspired him to attempt the perfect murder. His intention was to disappear and start life all over again, without debts, maintenance orders, car payments, and, most of all, too many women hanging round his neck like a millstone. He had met the stranger a few days earlier in a pub, The Swan and Pyramid in Whetstone High Road, in North London. The man had explained that he was unemployed and looking for a ride to East Anglia in search of work. Rouse studied the man closely. In height and build, he was roughly similar to Rouse, and judging from his conversation, he had no family either. So far as Rouse was concerned, he was perfect.

On the night of November 5, Rouse visited Nellie Tucker at the London Maternity Hospital. She noticed that he seemed unusually subdued, as if something were troubling him. At 7:45 he said good-bye to her and their baby. Fifteen minutes later he met the stranger outside The Swan and Pyramid, and the two men headed north. It had been arranged that Rouse should give him a lift as far as Leicester. Rouse, a strict teetotaler, bought a bottle of whisky for his passenger to drink on the journey. The confession continued as follows:

He was the sort of man no one would miss, and I thought he would suit the plan I had in mind.

During the journey the man drank the whisky neat from the bottle and was getting quite fuzzled [sic]. We talked a lot, but he did not tell me who he actually was. I did not care.

I turned into Hardingstone Lane because it was quiet and near a main road, where I could get a lift from a lorry afterwards. I pulled the car up.

The man was half-dozing—the effect of the whisky. I looked at him and then gripped him by the throat with my right hand. I pressed his head against the back of the seat. He slid down, his hat falling off. I saw he had a bald patch on the crown of his head.

He just gurgled. I pressed his throat hard. My grip is very strong . . . The man did not realize what was happening. I pushed his face back. After making a peculiar noise, the man was silent and I thought he was dead or unconscious.

Then I got out of the car, taking my attaché-case, the can of petrol and the mallet with me. I walked about ten yards in front of the car, and opened the can, using the mallet to do so. I threw the mallet away and made a trail of petrol to the car.

Also, I poured petrol over the man and loosened the petrol union joint and took the top off the carburetor. I put the petrol can in the back of the car.

I ran to the beginning of the petrol trail and put a match to it. The flame rushed to the car, which caught fire at once.

Petrol was leaking from the bottom of the car. That was the petrol I had poured over the man and the petrol that was dripping from the union joint and carburetor.

The fire was very quick, and the whole thing was a mass of flames in a few seconds. I ran away.[25]

It was exactly as Buckle and Spilsbury had reasoned. Rouse had chosen Bonfire Night deliberately, feeling that one more blaze on the landscape would go unnoticed, and the first part of his plan worked perfectly. Indeed, had it not been for two young men homeward bound at an unusually late hour, then Rouse may very well have disappeared forever. That chance meeting on an otherwise deserted country lane turned Rouse's scheme upside down, snapped his nerve, and ultimately sent him to the gallows.

The final act in this saga came in a secret ceremony held at dawn on March 21, 1931, when six police officers solemnly carried a coffin into the graveyard at Hardingstone parish church. The coffin was lowered into a grave behind the church. Affixed to the casket was a plate that read: "Man unknown. Died November 6, 1930." Despite considerable sums offered by Fleet Street for information leading to the identity of the unknown man—Rouse said that he had a sporting tattoo on his right forearm, spoke with a southern accent, wore boots that had been given to him by a Metropolitan police officer, and possessed a sports diary—the victim's name remains shrouded in mystery.

Although Spilsbury showed in the Rouse trial that he was back to his imperious best, concerns were now beginning to mount over his impossible workload. A reluctance to delegate tasks and responsibilities meant that at times he spread himself too thinly for his own or society's good. In one Old Bailey trial, the defendant, Henry Andrews, charged with murdering his wife, was acquitted when the judge threw out the case after Spilsbury failed to arrive in time to give evidence. The prosecution had just closed when Spilsbury, sweating and red-faced with embarrassment, came panting into court. He explained that he had been lecturing to a group of police officers, and there had been some confusion over the scheduled time of his testimony. Even though the judge made clear his belief that Spilsbury's absence in no way affected the outcome, he lambasted the witness for his laxity, saying, ". . . a man's life [has] been put in peril. I hope it will never happen again." Suitably contrite, Spilsbury replied, "I am extremely sorry, my Lord."[26]

Clearly such a situation was neither desirable nor healthy, and significantly, it was around this time that younger names began to stamp their mark on the British forensic science landscape. Two in particular, Professors Keith Simpson and Francis Camps, would go on to enjoy glittering, often tempestuous careers of their own, but for now they, like everyone else, were still obliged to toil in Spilsbury's shadow. Deep, dark, and majestic, it still dominated the British courtroom. Few could remember a time when it had been otherwise; fewer still could envision a day when it would ever be dispelled.

---

1 *Daily Sketch*, March 11, 1931, 3.

2 *Times*, January 27, 1931, 7.

3 H. Montgomery Hyde, *Norman Birkett* (London: Reprint Soc, 1964), 298.

4 Dennis Bardens, *Lord Justice Birkett* (London: Hale, 1962), 156.

5 *Times*, December 17, 1930, 9.

6 J. M. Parrish and John R. Crossland, eds., *Fifty Most Amazing Crimes of the Past One Hundred Years* (London: Oldhams Press, 1936), 610.

7 *Ibid.*

8 *Times*, January 29, 1931, 9.

9 *Ibid.*

10 *Ibid.*

11 Statement read at committal proceedings, November 27, 1930.

12 *Times*, November 28, 1930, 11.

13 Statement read at committal proceedings, November 27, 1930.
14 Bardens, *Lord Justice Birkett*, 156.
15 *Ibid.*, 157.
16 *Ibid.*
17 Hyde, *Norman Birkett*, 307–8.
18 *Times*, January 29, 1931, 9.
19 *Ibid.*
20 *Ibid.*
21 D. G. Browne and E. V. Tullett, *Bernard Spilsbury: His Life and Cases* (London: Harrap, 1951), 334.
22 *Times*, January 29, 1931, 9.
23 Parrish and Crossland, *Fifty Most Amazing Crimes of the Past One Hundred Years*, 621–22.
24 *Times*, January 30, 1931, 9.
25 *Daily Sketch*, March 11, 1931, 3.
26 *Times*, May 21, 1931, 11.

CHAPTER NINE

Trunk Calls

At the end of 1931 Spilsbury was asked to investigate what is nowadays a little-remembered case but which at the time provided clear proof that even this most trenchant of self-believers was not immune to the occasional wobble. Maybe he was conscious of the new young breed of pathologists snapping at his heels, maybe he was genuinely baffled, or maybe it was a rare realization that first impressions are not necessarily the best. It concerned a bizarre shooting on a smallholding at Gedney Marsh, in the flatlands of Lincolnshire. James Kitchen was thirty-six years old when, on the morning of December 4, 1931, he began work in his farmyard. Heavy overnight rain had made it muddy and slippery underfoot. Alongside him, propped against a wall, stood a twelve-gauge double-barreled shotgun that he had borrowed three days earlier from a friend, Sidney Arms, who lived in nearby Wisbech.

At about a quarter past eight, Jimmy's sixty-three-year-old father, George Kitchen, was seen running from the yard of Brook House Farm, out into the roadway. When confronted by two passing cyclists, Kitchen abruptly spun on his heels and doubled back the way he had come. From there he ran into an adjacent field where three farmhands were working. "Come on," he shouted to them. "Jimmy's shot!"[1]

Dropping their tools, the workmen dashed after him into the yard and there found James lying on his back about eleven feet from the door of the meal house, bleeding heavily from a gaping wound in his side. Gently they carried him into a barn that stood next to the meal house. Only when his overcoat was unbuttoned was the full extent of his injuries apparent, and it was no surprise when he died within half an hour. In the yard, close to where he fell, the borrowed shotgun lay on its right barrel with the hammers facing the wall, the muzzle some twenty-two inches from the door, and the butt eleven inches from the wall. The right hammer was cocked, and the barrel was loaded with a cartridge. The left barrel had evidently just been discharged.

When George Kitchen, who was almost incoherent with distress, recovered enough to be interviewed, he explained how he'd taken the gun with him that morning when he'd checked the traps on the farm. Upon his return he had set the loaded weapon against the meal house wall, with both barrels cocked, a recklessness he excused on grounds that geese regularly flew overhead and he wanted to be ready at a moment's notice to bag a tasty dinner.

Although George didn't live at Brook House Farm—he was quarrelsome and semi-estranged from the family—he did stop by sometimes to lend a hand and take the occasional meal. These he ate in solitude in one of the outbuildings, never in the main house where he wasn't welcome. On the morning in question, he said, Jimmy had been cleaning a shovel, in the company of a large and very energetic black retriever called Prince, when there was a loud report. "I heard the gun go off and saw him roll over and heard him say 'Oh!' very loudly,"[2] said George. So far as he could make out, the dog had knocked the gun over and it had discharged. Neighbors agreed that the dog was highly excitable; they also said that George had been inconsolable after the tragic incident.

The police were unconvinced. Something about the old man's demeanor struck them as odd, especially when they heard that, two days after the incident, he had been badgering an insurance company to pay out on his son's life. To clarify the situation, they requested Spilsbury's assistance. Alongside him was his close friend Robert Churchill, the ballistics expert. The first thing they noticed was a conspicuous lack of powder burns on the overcoat and body, indicating a shot fired from at least three feet away. When Churchill examined the weapon, he found it in perfect working order, although he agreed with the owner's assessment that the pull on both triggers was exceedingly heavy; even jarring the shotgun failed to make it discharge accidentally.

The autopsy revealed at least one curiosity. Kitchen had obviously been smoking at the time he was shot and, when hit by the bullet, had sucked in his breath so sharply that he swallowed a cigarette, which Spilsbury recovered from the gullet. Kitchen was not a tall man— approximately five feet four inches—and the shotgun blast had entered his left side about six inches below the armpit, in a downward direction at an angle of fifty-five degrees. As the distance of the shot precluded any possibility of a self-inflicted wound, and because the weapon appeared impervious to accidental discharge, Spilsbury took the view— as did Churchill—that some other person's finger had been on the trigger.

When George Kitchen's wife heard that her husband was to be charged with their son's murder, she said stoutly, "I'll stake my life he didn't do it. Him and Jim have been the best of friends."[3] Then she fainted clean away. Since Jimmy's brother, William, had earlier told the police of a deep-seated feud between his brother and father—four years earlier he had seen the rancorous old man chase Jimmy with a gun—clearly someone had their facts skewed.

On April 11, 1932, George Kitchen stood trial for his life at the Old Bailey. The defense made out a convincing case for accidental death, the tragic product of a boisterous dog colliding with a precariously balanced shotgun. A metal tab that dangled from the dog's collar was found to be small enough to fit in behind the trigger, and this, they argued, was what had happened, making the gun discharge. A police constable agreed that the tab did fit, although "it required a little forcing."

"Did you put 98 pounds of weight on it when you forced it through?" asked the defense counsel, Linton Thorp, KC.

"No."

"Well, that is the weight of the dog,"[4] Thorp remarked acidly.

When Spilsbury was called to testify, it soon became evident that he'd been having second thoughts about the incident. As he told the court, "[Everything] turns on the position of the body at the time he received the wound."[5] Had the man been stood upright, the height of the wound was 3 feet 8¾ inches from the ground; had he been stooping, the height would have reduced to about two feet; had he been prone on the ground, the elevated gun would have been fired downward into the unprotected left side.

By providing so many options, Spilsbury clearly unsettled the judge, who said, "It is a ghastly speculation, the whole thing, isn't it?"

"There is nothing exact," admitted Spilsbury.

"It is pure speculation as to how this man died?"

"Put that way, my lord, it is."

Spilsbury had spoken, and that was enough for the judge. Addressing the jury, Mr. Justice Swift said, "Sir Bernard Spilsbury, to whom we all look for assistance in these cases, and who we know will tell us exactly what he believes to be true, has said that nobody can tell what happened. Then how can you possibly say this man is guilty of murder?"[6] After a huddled discussion in the box the jury took the judge's recommendation and acquitted the defendant. Whether Spilsbury's fulsome tribute from the bench was echoed by disgruntled Crown prosecutors is unrecorded, but what this case does demonstrate is that, far from being merely a prosecution mouthpiece, as some have claimed, Spilsbury was his own man, and if that meant occasionally upsetting his employers, then so be it.

Remarkable Chain of Coincidences

Coincidences abound in murder, and May 1927 marked the start of a quite remarkable series of connected events that stretched right into the Second World War. It began when Spilsbury was summoned to the Westminster Coroner's Court mortuary to examine the noxious-smelling contents of a trunk that had been deposited five days earlier at the Charing Cross station left luggage office. The source of the smell was the dismembered body of a young woman, later identified as Minnie Bonati, the estranged wife of an Italian waiter. After a textbook investigation, London businessman John Robinson was charged with the murder and later hanged. One oddity that emerged was the fact that Robinson had obtained his dissecting knife from the same cutlers in Victoria as had been patronized by that other notorious habitué of railway cloakrooms, Patrick Mahon.

The chain of coincidence now leaps forward seven years to June 17, 1934, and another left luggage office, this time at Brighton train station. Eleven days earlier a man wearing a blue suit—that was all anyone could recall about him—had deposited a nondescript trunk measuring $27 \times 17^{1}/_{2} \times 11$ inches; claimed his ticket, G.1945; then left. Almost at once someone noticed a strange smell wafting up from the double-locked trunk. Each day the stench grew more pungent. Finally, unable to bear it any longer, a long-suffering staff member, Joseph Vinnicombe, called the railway police. The lid was levered open to reveal a bloodstained brown paper package, tied with six yards of sash cord and containing the naked torso of a woman, minus the head and limbs, which had been sawn off. The railway police wasted no time in contacting their civilian counterparts.

Brighton, raffish and relaxed, has always been one of the most popular holiday resorts on England's south coast. This was especially true in the interwar years, when the former fishing village that the prince regent—later King George IV—converted into his own personal playground regularly welcomed thousands of visitors. Some were day-trippers from London, some came to admire the fantastical Royal Pavilion, some had other ambitions—with its abundance of anonymous hotels and marvelously uninquisitive reception staff, Brighton was a magnet for the stereotypical "dirty weekenders"—and then there were the holidaymakers who came for the long shingle beach and bracing sea air. Each morning and again at suppertime the train station on the crest of Queen's Road heaved with bewildered tourists rushing this way and that. Whether by accident or design, whoever left the trunk chose his time especially well; June 6 was Derby day, when the station would have been swelled by hundreds of extra passengers, all excited about the trip north to Epsom and the big race.

The local police wasted no time in contacting Scotland Yard, which immediately issued a directive to left luggage offices across the country, asking them to be on the lookout for any suspicious packages. The following day this led to a foul-smelling brown suitcase being opened at King's Cross station in London. Inside lay a pair of legs severed above the knee, done up in brown paper and newspaper, and doused in virgin olive oil. This latter curiosity provided a possible clue. Olive oil had long been used in the Mediterranean region to help stanch the flow of blood from open wounds, and it was hoped that this might hint at the killer's origins. If, as seemed highly likely, the legs belonged to the Brighton torso, it was confidently expected that within days the missing head and arms would materialize, and the human jigsaw would be made complete.

"Spilsbury Speeds to Brighton"[7] ran the *New York Times* headline, an indication of just how far news of this sensational discovery had traveled. He made his preliminary examination, then withdrew to London to continue the autopsy at the Saint Pancras mortuary. From there, he shipped the legs down to Brighton, where they proved to be a perfect match. Spilsbury's notes reveal a woman in her mid- to late twenties, about five feet three inches tall and weighing around 120 pounds, with a trim figure and in robust general health. He could find no evidence of serious disease, nor were there any signs of physical violence. Since the head was missing, he suspected that it held the secret to the cause of death. Judging from the immaculately pedicured size 4½ feet, this was a woman of fastidious habits and some means. The attention to grooming extended to a few strands of detached brown hair that lay loose on the body: these showed signs of having recently undergone a permanent wave. But for Spilsbury, much the most significant factor was that the woman was almost five months pregnant.

Throughout his career he performed hundreds of autopsies on young and not so young women who'd been the victims of botched terminations, and he was messianic in his pursuit of the illegal abortionist, whether they plied their trade in discreet West End surgeries or some filthy back street hovel. In those harsher, more censorious times, the stigma of bearing a child out of wedlock was enough to drive desperate women to take the most appalling risks with their health. Many died within days of their "operation." Septicemia was the most common killer. Spilsbury, unlike many members of the medical profession, had no compunction about testifying against colleagues whom he suspected of dishonoring the Hippocratic oath. There was one particular individual, a sinister former police surgeon named Richard Starkie, who drove Spilsbury incandescent with rage. Their paths first crossed during the Great War when Spilsbury found himself performing autopsies on an alarming number of abortion-related fatalities, all of which led back, by one circuitous route or another, to Dr. Starkie's surgery in Mayfair's fashionable Brooke Street.

This triggered the start of a vendetta that lasted years. In 1921 Spilsbury's testimony helped send Starkie to prison for supplying abortifacient drugs, though the disgraced doctor wriggled out of more serious charges of performing illegal operations. While behind bars, Starkie proved highly popular with the other convicts, who, it was rumored, gave him a slap-up banquet on the eve of his release. Incarceration clearly did nothing to rehabilitate the devious doctor. In 1929 he was again convicted of supplying noxious drugs and sentenced to one year's imprisonment. Following his release, and by now struck off the medical register, in July 1932 he was for the first time convicted of using an instrument to procure an abortion and given eighteen months. Thereafter the Butcher of Brooke Street disappeared from public view.

Although Spilsbury could not detect any evidence of attempted abortion in the Brighton Trunk Murder victim, like most involved in the investigation, he believed that a probably unwanted pregnancy had contributed to the woman's death. He saw no obvious anatomical skill in the dismemberment, which he estimated had taken place a couple of days after death. The sum total of the woman's excellent physical condition, allied to the fact that she could afford expensive cosmetic preening, spoke of someone who had lived a relatively comfortable life in good circumstances, and was therefore someone likely to be missed. An identification looked to be a mere formality.

The press certainly did its best to accelerate the process. *"Brighton Trunk Murder!"* screamed the headlines, and the breathless paragraphs below were packed with spicy detail and speculation. Appeals to the public requesting the names of any women who had gone missing in the past few weeks produced a flood of leads, almost swamping the special murder inquiry headquarters that had been established in a wing of the Royal Pavilion. Every journalistic twist and turn received the hothouse treatment. In the depths of the Depression, there was nothing more diverting or more guaranteed to boost circulation figures than a grisly murder, and Fleet Street was pulling out all the stops.

Rather less than 200 yards from where the body had been discovered at the train station, one particular newspaper reader cowered in his grubby little flat, ashen-faced and quaking with fear. His trembling hand struggled to hold the paper steady. He'd read and reread every single word of press coverage he could lay his hands on, head shaking in stunned disbelief. All his life he'd been a two-bit hoodlum, someone who drifted on the fringes of the underworld, always dreaming of one day becoming a big-shot criminal. Now, when it appeared as if that day were about to dawn—though not in the manner he had envisaged—he had never been so terrified in his life.

Fresh Clues

In the meantime, the trunk itself began offering up clues. Cheaply made from plywood covered with brown canvas, it was obviously new, and was soon traced to a large department store in Brighton. The sales assistants were every bit as vague as their counterparts in the left luggage office: they had no recollection of the purchaser. When microscopical examination of the interior revealed minute traces of saltwater parasites, the search was extended to seamen's missions and other places where seafarers were likely to congregate. Also in the trunk were a facecloth and some cotton wool, but much the most important find was a scrap of brown paper, on which was a single word written in blue pencil, half obliterated by congealed blood. Only the suffix -*ford* was decipherable, preceded by what might be a *d* or an *l*.

A huge team of detectives, armed with a list of more than 700 missing women under the age of thirty, began knocking on doors, not just in Brighton but across the rest of the country as well.* Mostly they targeted places ending in -*ford*. Besides the bigger towns such as Bradford and Salford, inhabitants of out-of-the-way places such as Telford, Milford, and Sandford suddenly found themselves on the investigative map. At the same time clinics and hospitals were canvassed for details of all young women who'd recently attended for prenatal advice or care.

Inevitably most efforts were concentrated in Brighton, and as the days passed with no significant lead, an edgy tension crept into the inquiry. And then, in early July, a new name entered the frame. Violette Kaye, she liked to be known as, a holdover from the days when as one

---

* For a while the inquiries extended to America, as suspicion grew that the remains might be those of Agnes Tufverson, a Detroit attorney who'd gone missing on December 20, 1933, shortly after entering into a bigamous marriage with Yugoslav army captain Ivan Poderjay. Despite Poderjay's protestations of innocence, many suspect he was involved in her disappearance. He was later deported from the U.S. and returned to Belgrade. Miss Tufverson has never been found.

half of Kay and Kay, a music hall duo, she'd earned her living as a vaudeville hoofer. Her real name was Violet Saunders, though no one had called her that for years. Like so many variety performers, she'd been knocked sideways by the runaway popularity of talking pictures. As doomed music halls nailed up the shutters, making stage work almost impossible to come by, Violette, with no other talents to hand or any alternative source of income—there was a husband around somewhere, but he hadn't shown his face for years—sank into prostitution. The coppers in Brighton knew her well. She was a regular catch whenever they conducted one of their periodic netting exercises along the promenade. A night in the cells, a fine in the morning, back at work after sundown, that was Violette's routine. Except that she hadn't been seen since early May. Worried friends who'd called at Violette's basement flat at 44 Park Crescent, a row of small, terraced houses in the shadow of the train station, were told that she had moved out suddenly without leaving a forwarding address.

The first to be alarmed was her sister-in-law, Olive Watts, who had intended to visit Brighton and stay with Violette. On Friday, May 11, one week before her anticipated departure, she had received a telegram that read: "Going abroad. Good Job. Sail Sunday. Will write—Vi." Olive's disappointment at having her vacation plans scuppered was allayed by a genuine sense of relief that Violette had finally landed some more stage work. Since then, she'd heard nothing.

Eventually enough people commented on Violette's disappearance for the police to take an interest. Those coppers who knew Violette also knew her pimp; they just weren't sure of his real name. The twenty-six-year-old slimly built man with the razor-slash scar on his upper lip had at various times called himself Hyman Gold, Jack Notyre, Luigi Pirelli, and Antoni Luigi—the last two aliases a testament to his Italian appearance—but his real name was Cecil Lois England. To add to the confusion, most police officers in Brighton knew him as Tony Mancini, and that is the name by which history remembers him.

Born to a perfectly respectable couple in 1908, Mancini went wrong from an early age. At first his minor brushes with the law were excused on grounds of teenage exuberance, but in March 1933 official patience ran out, and he was given six months for breaking into a house and stealing clothes. On his release he secured a waiter's job at a restaurant in London's Leicester Square, and it was here, in October 1933, that he met Violette Kaye. She was sixteen years his senior and already an experienced prostitute. Mancini, ruthless and pragmatic, sensed that here was his passport to easy street. He moved into her Bayswater Road flat, and then, after they relocated to Brighton, they shared a succession of low-rent addresses until March 1934 saw them take over the lease at 44 Park Crescent. Whenever Violette brought home a client, Mancini would retreat to another room, wait until the groaning had subsided, reemerge to snatch the money, then hightail it to some local nightspot. While Violette freshened up her lipstick in readiness for the next trick, Mancini was buying rounds of drinks and dancing the night away with a succession of other women. As a lifestyle it was squalid and short-lived. Unfortunately, Violette's fading physical charms cut little ice among the johns who trawled Brighton's esplanade after hours, and trade dwindled almost to nothing. With his goose suddenly off the gold standard, on May 5, Mancini grudgingly took a job as a handyman/waiter at a local eatery called the Skylark Café.

And it was here, on July 14, that he was approached by a police officer and asked to account for Violette's whereabouts. Mancini strolled over to the temporary police headquarters, where he cheerfully explained that Violette had landed a dancing job somewhere abroad—Paris or Germany, he wasn't sure which—and that the contract was for two years. He hadn't seen her since May 10. Once it became apparent that Violette Kaye was aged forty-two at the time of her disappearance—at least twelve years older than the estimated age of the trunk victim—the interviewing inspector thanked Mancini for his time and sent him on his way.

When Mancini emerged from the Royal Pavilion, chances are he did so with one of his trademark smirks; after all, he'd been eliminated from inquiries about the Brighton Trunk Murder. So it makes his actions over the next few hours all the more peculiar. Instead of

returning to the small flat in Kemp Street that he'd rented just a few
days after Violette's disappearance, he headed to a regular hangout,
Sherry's dance hall. With his pencil-trim figure, greased-back black
hair, and sallow complexion, he gave off a certain Mediterranean
charm that plenty of women found attractive, and for some weeks he'd
been supplementing his Skylark wages by acting as a dance hall
lothario. Tonight, though, he seemed distracted. While schmoozing
with Joan Tinn, a teacher at Sherry's, he predicted cryptically that he
"only had four days of happiness left."[8] Just after midnight he and another dance instructor, Robin Robert Taylor, adjourned to a nearby
greasy spoon. Mancini stirred his mug of tea gloomily and muttered
that he needed to get away from Brighton, fast; some unstated trouble
with the police, apparently. He announced his intention of traveling up
to London on the first available train. Taylor agreed to accompany him
to the station. It was still dark as they walked to Mancini's basement
flat. The first thing that hit Taylor when he stepped into the living
room was the emetic stench. Trashy neighbors, Mancini said, raising
an explanatory eyebrow in the direction of the upstairs flat. Hurriedly,
he shaved, washed, threw some clothes into a large expanding suitcase,
then donned a pinstripe suit and felt hat. He counted out all the money
he had in the world—£4—and stuffed it into his pocket. A couple of
hours later Taylor saw the anxious Mancini onto a train; not at the
main Brighton station, which was just around the corner from where
Mancini lived, but one stop north at Preston Park (Mancini had feared
the main station would be under police surveillance). As the 7:28 A.M.
to Victoria slid out of the station, Mancini settled back in his seat and
heaved a sigh of relief. He had fled just in time.

Barely two hours later workmen called to 52 Kemp Street to repair
some brickwork also found their senses rebelling against the basement
stink. It became so bad that thoughts and comments harked back to
the Brighton Trunk Murder and those missing body parts. At midday
the police arrived. When they knocked and gained no answer, they
broke down the door.

In the far corner of the room, by the fireplace, stood a large black trunk bound with thick cord. Gingerly, one of the officers cut the rope and raised the lid. A rush of fumes almost knocked him over. The contents were covered by a black coat and some other garments. When pushed aside they revealed a hideous sight. Immediately the officer snapped shut the lid and summoned his superiors. Later that day the trunk was removed to the Brighton mortuary. The remains were undoubtedly human, but what stunned everyone connected to the investigation, utterly bowled them over, in fact, was the realization that this gruesome discovery had absolutely nothing to do with the first trunk murder—for here was *an entire female body*!

Second Trunk Victim

It seemed too incredible to be true. In searching for one trunk murderer, detectives had apparently succeeded in flushing out another; or—and this was really worrying—they might have stumbled across a serial killer. No crime novelist would dare invent such an outrageous coincidence. Just a few weeks earlier, when the first set of remains had been found, Brighton's white-haired mayor, Miss Margaret Hardy, had mounted her high horse and sternly lectured a group of reporters. "The case belongs to London," she thundered. "Nothing like that ever happened in Brighton."[9] Now, she and her fellow burghers were forced to eat those words in the most humiliatingly public manner possible. For a town so dependent on the tourist trade, the discovery of a second corpse stuffed into a trunk amounted to a PR catastrophe.

Once again Spilsbury found himself traveling down to the south coast. He performed his autopsy that Sunday afternoon. The woman's body, intact and partly clad, was too decomposed to say how long she had been dead. He put her age at forty. On the scalp behind the left ear and at the level of the right ear were what appeared to be bruises caused shortly before death. She had been five feet two inches tall, with bleached hair that showed brown at the roots. A silk scarf was knotted around the neck, but the advanced putrefaction prevented Spilsbury from gauging what part, if any, it had played in the woman's death. There was a metal bracelet on the left wrist and a wedding ring on the left hand. Among the articles of both male and female clothing packed around and underneath the body was a piece of newspaper dated April 2, 1930. In a pathetic attempt to mask his or her misdeeds, the killer had scattered mothballs throughout the trunk.

Spilsbury thought the woman had been killed by a violent blow or blows with a blunt object, possibly a hammer, causing a depressed fracture extending down to the base of the skull, with a short fissured fracture extending up from its upper edge. It appeared to him as though the woman's head had been held down on the ground, then hit repeatedly, or else banged against something.

Back at Kemp Street, blood smears were found in a corner cupboard, along with a hammer. The landlord gave the name of the missing tenant as Tony Mancini, who had rented the flat from May 14. Prior to this, he thought, Mancini had lived at 44 Park Crescent with some woman. There now seemed to be little doubt that the body in what became known as "Brighton Trunk Crime No. 2" was that of Violette Kaye.

A nationwide appeal went out, detailing Mancini's description and known haunts. On July 17, at 1:35 A.M., a man was seen by two passing police officers, struggling with a suitcase along Eltham Road in Southeast London. Stopping their car, they approached the stranger and accused him of being the wanted man. Mancini, utterly exhausted, made no attempt to deny it. As he was being driven into custody, he sighed, "I didn't murder her. I would not cut her hand off. She has been keeping me for months."[10]

His story, when interviewed, had a Thorne-like familiarity. He had returned to 44 Park Crescent on the night of May 10 and found Violette "lying on the bed with a handkerchief tied round her neck, and there was blood all over the sheets and everywhere . . . I hadn't got the courage to go and tell the police what I found . . . there was [sic] always men coming to the house . . . I don't know who killed her; as God is my judge I don't know . . . I am quite innocent except for the fact that I kept the body."[11]

The following day he bought a trunk in which to conceal the corpse. Next on the agenda was a change of residence. On May 14, he and a crony from the Skylark Café, Thomas Capelin, had lugged the trunk up the steep flight of stone steps that led from the basement flat and placed it on a handcart. Once the handcart was full of Mancini's furniture and meager effects, it was wheeled a couple of hundred yards to his new place in Kemp Street. There, for almost two months, he lived, ate, and slept alongside the rotting corpse. When acquaintances and girlfriends called round, he parried questions about the singular smell with a variety of excuses—unhygienic neighbors, sweaty soccer boots, dead rabbits, the landlady's reluctance to open windows in the warm weather, once even claiming that the previous tenant had expired from TB and that attempts to disinfect the room had been ineffectual. When his landlady complained about a brownish fluid that seeped from the trunk, he tutted that some French polish had leaked and that he would see to it. That night he cleaned up the mess and placed sacking under the trunk.

Friends curious about Violette's whereabouts were given roughly the same story that Mancini had told the police; that she had secured a dancing job in Montmartre. Others heard that Violette had set up home in Paris with a wealthy bookmaker. On one point everyone agreed: Mancini seemed mighty relieved by the fact that Violette was no longer around. So relieved, in fact, that the police didn't buy a word of his story. They were convinced he'd murdered his mistress, plain and simple, because she had become a liability.

Word filtered through that on the last day that she was seen alive, Violette, reeling from the effects of drink or drugs, had staggered into the Skylark Café to visit Mancini and, while there, had kicked up such a fuss over the attention he lavished on another employee, Elizabeth Attrill, that she was thrown out. Later that same day she was seen back at Park Crescent by a chauffeur named Thomas Kerslake. He told her that his boss, a bookmaker called Charlie Moores (Violette always referred to him as "Uncle"), would not be able to keep his regular appointment that day as he'd been incarcerated in a mental institution some six days earlier. On hearing the news, Violette had reacted bizarrely, becoming very excited and nervous, whether from booze or dope, he wasn't sure. As Kerslake returned to his car, he saw another man, a stranger, descend the steps to the flat. He also heard two voices, both male, coming from the flat.

Just a few hours later, so the police reckoned, Mancini came home, got into a fight with Violette, battered her to death, and the next day sent the forged telegram to Violette's sister-in-law. Then he set about covering his tracks.

That evening found him skulking around Sherry's dance hall, this time in the company of Elizabeth Attrill. After explaining that Violette had left abruptly for Paris and wouldn't be coming back any time soon, he smooth-talked Elizabeth into moving in with him. As a welcoming present, Mancini gave her clothing that Violette had left "because she could not get them into her case."[12]

During her two weeks at the flat, Elizabeth didn't see any trunk but did find her nose wrinkling over an increasingly malodorous smell that came from one of the cupboards. She also noticed some blood spots on one of Mancini's shirts, blemishes that he attributed to shaving cuts.

When Elizabeth decided that she'd had enough of Mancini's predatory sponging and moved on, her erstwhile minder set about seeking a replacement. His roving and rapacious eye soon settled on another prostitute, Joyce Golding, whom he knew well. He spun the familiar yarn of Violette having left suddenly for Paris, adding, "I hope she is not coming back, as I do not want her to follow me about in the streets shouting names after me."[13] He claimed to have received a letter from her. Joyce, deciding that she didn't need to share her hard-won earnings with some worthless layabout, rejected Mancini's offer to become her pimp.

As the weeks stretched out uneventfully, Mancini's anxiety eased, and he began cruising the dance hall and nightclub circuit once again, bragging and swaggering, always on the lookout for some easy cash.

Then came the bombshell discovery at Brighton railway station.

Mancini had to gulp back his disbelief. *Two bodies stashed in trunks within two hundred yards and two weeks of each other?* It was a coincidence spooky enough to unnerve the strongest constitution. Each day stretched his nerves tighter than piano wire. The snapping point came on July 14 with the interview. Convinced it was now only a matter of time before his own indiscretions were exposed, he decided to make a run for it.

At the time of his arrest, Mancini's luggage was seized and sent to Roche Lynch for analysis. Two shirts showed blood spots, six in all, ranging in size from a quarter of an inch down to one-sixteenth. There were also traces of blood on two pairs of trousers. Acting on Spilsbury's recommendation, Roche Lynch paid particular attention to the hammer head. He didn't find any blood, or anything else for that matter, because it appeared to have been thrust into some kind of flame, which had the effect of destroying any foreign matter present. Roche Lynch had marginally more success when he analyzed samples taken from the victim's organs. They showed minute traces of morphine, though too small to quantify the original dosage.

When Gerald Francis Gurrin, one of the top British handwriting experts, compared Violette's farewell telegram with a handwritten menu from the Skylark Café known to have been compiled by Mancini, he found enough similarities in the block capital writing to be confident that the same person had written both exemplars. This looked to be the final piece in the forensic jigsaw.

Few defendants have faced a blacker set of circumstances than did Tony Mancini when, on December 10, 1934, he stood trial for the murder of Violette Kaye. He had a criminal record; he had lived upon the dead woman's immoral earnings; he had concealed her body, even moving it from one place to another; he had told countless lies to explain her disappearance; he had blood on his clothes; and finally, he had fled when he feared discovery. The case looked open and shut.

Peerless Defender

Fortunately for Mancini, he was defended by Norman Birkett, KC, arguably the greatest British advocate of the twentieth century. No one, not even Edward Marshall Hall, saved more people from the gallows than did this unassuming draper's son who had abandoned the ministry for the law. As evidenced by the Rouse case, Birkett could be a deadly prosecutor, but it was as a defender that he really shone. If Marshall Hall came from the old school of histrionics and thundering passion, then Birkett had both feet firmly entrenched in the modern camp. He dealt in facts and ice-cold logic, always beautifully enunciated with the actor's flair that all successful courtroom lawyers need but always taking care to avoid the flamboyant petulance that occasionally tarnished Marshall Hall's advocacy.

In the Mancini trial it can be argued that Birkett's weighty task was certainly lightened by the caliber of witness that the Crown was obliged to call. Hookers and hustlers don't make for the most credible witnesses—or they certainly didn't in the prim and proper 1930s—and it was noticeable that the conveyor belt of Runyonesque characters wheeled out by the prosecution did betray a witness box uniformity that contained more than a whiff of behind-the-scenes coaching. One after another they trotted out extravagant accounts of how Mancini regularly boasted of abusing Violette. One fellow even claimed to have heard Mancini say, "What's the good of knocking your woman about with your fists? You only hurt yourself. You should hit her with a hammer, the same as I did, and slosh her up."[14]

Too good to be true? Birkett thought so. As fast as the prosecution put 'em up, Birkett knocked 'em down, picking apart their dubious testimony until it lay threadbare and valueless. But these were the easy victories. He knew this case would be won and lost in the test tube, and when it came to tackling expert witnesses head-on, nobody has ever surpassed Norman Birkett.

First in the firing line was Roche Lynch. Birkett wanted clarification of the minuscule morphine levels found in Violette Kaye's body. Given the advanced decomposition, surely the fact that he'd found any morphine at all meant that more than a medicinal dose had been ingested? Roche Lynch agreed. Therefore, shortly before her death, Violette must have been under the influence of a high dose of morphine? Again, Roche Lynch concurred. He followed this up with a frank admission that had Violette Kaye been an addict, then he doubted whether he would have found any morphine at all. Birkett raised a quizzical eyebrow: "Why . . . ?"

Because, said Roche Lynch, in the case of addicts, morphine is so quickly destroyed by the body as to be almost impossible to detect.

"Can you say with certainty that it would not be found in the decomposed body of an addict?" asked Birkett.

"I am certain that it would not."[15*]

With this acknowledgment, Birkett had made his first, albeit small, dent in the prosecution's forensic case, implanting in the jury's mind the possibility that Violette Kaye might have been intoxicated by drugs at the time of her death. Next, he turned to all those bloodstains. Roche Lynch explained, in rudimentary fashion, the usefulness of the human blood grouping system in the field of crime investigation. "If an alleged murderer has blood on his clothes, and the group of that blood is the same as his victim's and different from his own blood group, he naturally has to make an explanation."[16]

Birkett asked if any of the blood spots on Mancini's clothing matched the blood group of the dead woman. "Owing to the decomposed state of the body," said Roche Lynch, "we were unable to discover the blood group of the dead woman."[17] A second small victory, but there was more to come; contamination of the shirt also made it impossible for Roche Lynch to group these bloodspots, as well. Birkett,

---

* Modern advances in gas chromatography mean that this is no longer necessarily the case.

having armed himself with a microscope, peered through it at a shirt and trousers both stained with blood. "You say these marks indicate that the blood was splashed upon it?"

"Yes."

"Do you know when this shirt was bought?"

"I do not."

"Or when the trousers were?"

"No."

"If I were to establish that these trousers were not in the accused's possession during the woman's life, it would be clear, do you think, that the blood could not be hers?"[18]

The sudden gale of laughter that swept the court only emphasized Roche Lynch's discomfiture. From somewhere—or so it appeared—Birkett was about to pull a legal rabbit out of the hat. He'd done it often enough before. Suddenly doubts crept into the Crown camp. Was their case against Mancini really the mortal lock they had imagined?

For the time being, Birkett kept his cards close to his chest. Instead, he now sprang another surprise. Because the press accounts of Mancini's alleged mob connections had made him out to be some kind of cockney Al Capone, Birkett demanded that his client's full criminal record be exposed to public view. The task of reading it out fell to Chief Inspector Robert Donaldson of Scotland Yard, the officer in charge of inquiries into both Brighton Trunk Crimes. He told the court that, prior to his six-month prison sentence, Mancini had two other minor convictions; once for theft and once for loitering with intent to commit a felony.

"Then there has been no conviction for the crime of violence?"

"No, sir,"[19] said Donaldson.

Ordinarily lawyers do everything in their power to suppress any mention of their client's past, dreading its impact on the jury. In taking this radical step Birkett not only cleared the air and dispelled an awful lot of overblown nonsense that had been written about Mancini, but also laid the groundwork for what he knew would be the pivotal moment in this case.

"Call Sir Bernard Spilsbury."

The prosecution was in the hands of J. D. Cassels, KC, in a rare departure from his customary role as a defense counsel. For someone who'd been on the wrong end of so many verdicts when opposed by Spilsbury, he must have drawn comfort in the fact that, for once, he and the H.O. pathologist were lined up in the same camp.

By this stage of his career Spilsbury was the most experienced witness alive and scarcely needed any coaxing from Cassels as, holding a human skull aloft, he pointed to the injuries that the dead woman had received. The depressed fracture, he said, had been produced by a violent blow with some blunt object, not sharp enough to cut through the skin. When shown the hammer found in Mancini's flat, he acknowledged that either end of the hammerhead could have caused the wound. Unconsciousness would have been virtually instantaneous; death would have followed in a few minutes.

Eyes widened when Spilsbury dramatically produced a piece of bone from the dead woman's skull. Over strident objections from Birkett, Spilsbury was permitted to say how he had found it, lying against the dead woman's brain. Beneath the fracture there was an artery, and there must have been a considerable rush of blood as soon as the fracture was inflicted.

Cassels was eager for clarification on one point. "You know that a minute trace of morphine was found in the body. Did this woman die from morphine poisoning?"

"No."[20]

"Could you observe any signs on the body of any struggle on her part?"

"There was no evidence of it."[21]

Birkett rose slowly to his feet. Outside of court, he and Spilsbury were good friends; inside the legal arena, it was gladiatorial combat, with the great defender out to destroy the incomparable witness. First, he needed to chip away at the pedestal that the British public—rather than Spilsbury himself—had erected beneath the witness. "Your views," Birkett asked politely, "are rightly described as theories, are they not?"

Birkett was a master of the loaded question, and Spilsbury wisely hesitated before replying; after all, most testimony given by expert witnesses contains, at the very least, some element of speculation. "I am not quite sure that is right," he said at last, "when my opinion is based on experience."

"They are the results of your experience but are mere theories without question?"

Spilsbury—as honest as the day was long—conceded graciously. "They are, in the sense that they are not facts."[22]

Round one had gone to Birkett, and he quickly pressed home his advantage. "How long have you been in possession of the small piece of bone which has been produced here for the first time on the third day of the trial?"

"Since my first examination," replied Spilsbury.

"Your first examination—July 15?"

"Yes."

"Five months ago?"

"Yes."

"Did it not seem to you that the defense might have been informed that that small piece of bone was in your possession?'"

"I am afraid it did not occur to me."[23]

This was a rare admission of fallibility from Spilsbury, and Birkett was determined to extract maximum value from the lapse. "You appreciate that there was no doctor for the defense present at the postmortem?"

"No, I don't think there was."[24]

For Cassels, looking on, this must have resurrected painful memories. Almost ten years earlier, in this selfsame court, he had defended Norman Thorne and had protested futilely against the admission of Crown evidence of procedures conducted without the defense being told or represented.

Birkett then unleashed one of the cleverest strings of questions ever posed to an expert witness, each perfectly phrased to produce the desired answer. "You will concede . . . that there are many other possible theories available for the death of this woman?"

"Yes."[25]

"Take morphine. Dr. Roche Lynch has said that he could not be sure whether a fatal dose had not been taken. Assume it *was* a fatal dose. Does not that account for death?"

"Why, certainly, if nothing else were done."

"A person can get severe injuries on the head, be unconscious, and recover?"

"Yes."

"A person can get injuries akin to the injuries here, and recover?"

"Akin, yes."[26]

Spilsbury's caution was well-placed. He may well have sensed what was coming next. The steps leading down to the basement flat at 44 Park Crescent were noticeably steep and worn, and at the top of the steps was a raised stone brace. Birkett referred to this now: "Do you agree that a person slightly drunk, or under the influence of drugs, might trip [over this brace], might lose consciousness and then recover and do all sorts of things—difficult things—before death supervenes?"[27] After Spilsbury again conceded the possibility, Birkett suddenly referred to a windowsill that jutted out at the foot of the steps. "I am suggesting to you quite plainly that if someone fell from the top step [and struck this window ledge] it could produce such a depressed fracture."

"I think it is impossible."

"Are you really telling members of this jury that if someone fell down the flight and came upon the stone ledge he would not get a depressed fracture?"

"He would not get this fracture,"[28] Spilsbury insisted; a fall of the kind described by Birkett would leave bruising over other parts of the body. He had found none.

Birkett's hypothesis, that Violette Kaye had fallen, recovered sufficiently to walk into the flat, undress, and only then collapse on the bed, received a disdainful reception from Spilsbury. "If she had survived any extent of time she would not have died from shock; she would have died from hemorrhage of the brain," he said. Somehow Birkett managed to turn even this setback to his advantage, exclaiming, "This is the very first time that has been suggested in the whole history of the case!"[29]

With this flourish, Birkett sat down, having almost effortlessly steered the witness into a string of concessions. It was masterful advocacy. In another revolutionary move, he now decided against pitting defense expert witnesses against Spilsbury. What was the point? Any *mano a mano* contest involving Spilsbury could only have one outcome. The sheer weight of his name was sufficient to crush most opposition. Instead, Birkett had relied on his own peerless talents, certain he could pick enough holes in Spilsbury's testimony to raise doubt in the jury's mind.

Now it all depended on Tony Mancini.

Masterful Performance

Unlike most defendants on the capital charge, his witness box performance was superb. He pushed all the right buttons, ostentatiously fingering a rosary as he took the oath; sounding regretful as he recalled the numerous men who came calling on Violette at all hours of the day and night; always insistent that he kept news of Violette's death from the police because "a man who has been convicted never gets a fair and square deal from the police."[30] Craftily he offered his own current peril as proof of this claim.

All his denials were resolute; he'd had nothing to do with the death of Violette Kaye; had never seen the hammer found at the flat; had never bought drugs for the dead woman, though he had seen her often taking sips from a mysterious bottle, the contents of which mystified him. He hotly refuted accusations made by earlier witnesses that he had often boasted of beating Violette, and in this assertion he was supported by Spilsbury's admission that he saw no sign of bruising on the body. When asked to describe his feelings for Violette, Mancini lowered his voice to barely a whisper. "Strange as it is, I used to love her. We were always on the most affectionate terms. There were no quarrels."

"Did that cover the whole time?" asked Birkett.

"Yes, every second she was alive."[31]

When Mancini left the witness box the mood in court had shifted. At the earlier committal proceedings, Brighton holidaymakers clad in bathing suits had temporarily abandoned the beach to jeer and hiss the defendant as he was hurried in and out of court. Now, through twenty-four-karat advocacy and ice-cool self-possession in the witness box, he left many wondering whether he was the innocent victim of pretrial publicity.

With perfect timing, Birkett administered the coup de grâce. He called Walter Blaker, a tailor with premises in Kemp Street, to the stand. What Blaker had to say was devastating. He identified the allegedly bloodstained trousers as having been made in his workshop, and that Mancini had not taken delivery of the trousers until June 2, fully *three weeks after* they were supposed to have been splashed by Violette Kaye's blood. Such a statement—if true—not only made a liar out of Elizabeth Attrill, who said that the trousers were in Mancini's possession just days after the death of Violette Kaye, but also had potentially calamitous consequences for the rest of the prosecution. If the jury accepted Blaker's testimony, all the Crown's blood evidence would fly out the window; and once the cracks had opened in that particular forensic edifice, then nothing, not even Spilsbury's testimony, was safe.

In his closing address Birkett launched a blistering attack on the Crown's expert witnesses. "I am not attacking the good faith of either Sir Bernard Spilsbury or Dr. Roche Lynch. Men have names and reputations, degrees, distinctions; but high and low, famous and obscure, known and unknown, men are all human and fallible. We have the firm fact clearly proved that those garments upon which the greatest stress was laid about blood being deposited from a distance, were neither worn by the prisoner nor in his possession until after the death of this woman. The case for the Crown is simply riddled with doubt."[32] At the climax of his peroration, Birkett implored the jury to demonstrate that "people are not tried by newspapers, nor tried by rumor, but tried by juries called to do justice . . . I ask you for, I appeal to you for, and I claim from you, a verdict of Not Guilty." He paused for a moment as if about to sit down, then exhorted the jury to "Stand firm!"[33]

On December 14, the all-male jury considered their verdict for two and a quarter hours before returning to court. In that time they mulled over the evidence of prostitutes and police, pimps and pathologists. When they announced their verdict—not guilty—gasps swept the court. Some women in the public gallery even broke down in tears.

Spilsbury had been on the losing side before in a major murder trial—most notably the Elvira Barney case in 1932—but on that occasion his evidence had been peripheral to the ballistics testimony that dominated proceedings. Here, he and Roche Lynch had been given a stinging and very public slap in the face. For a quarter of a century the word of Sir Bernard Spilsbury had been accepted as canonical truth in English courtrooms; and in some ways the trial of Tony Mancini marked the end of an era. Birkett had demonstrated how inspired and persistent advocacy—shades of the O. J. Simpson trial six decades later—could undermine even the most formidable looking medico-legal case. One tiny seed of doubt, properly tended and cultivated, was all it took.

Mancini himself seemed totally nonplused by the verdict. Afterwards, in a room adjoining the court, he was retrieving his belongings when Birkett came in. Mancini stared at his benefactor as if in a daze, mumbling over and over again: "Not guilty, Mr. Birkett? Not guilty, Mr. Birkett?"

Gently, Birkett nodded. "Now go home and look after your mother," he said, "she has stood by you and been a brick."[34]

Talking later to a family member, Birkett confessed it was a victory that "strangely enough has given me very little pleasure." Birkett knew only too well how fortunate his client—"a despicable and worthless creature"[35]—had been.

In all the excitement about Mancini's acquittal, public concern about "Trunk Crime No. 1" had been unceremoniously shoved onto the back burner. For those officers linked to the investigation, it was a frustrating time. Despite a huge investment in manpower, and enquiries that ranged as far afield as France and Germany, no one ever came close to positively identifying the dismembered woman or the man in the blue suit who had deposited the trunk at Brighton train station. The mystery remains unsolved to this day.

As for Mancini, the streetwise hustler, the trial provided an unexpected bonus. Cashing in on his new won notoriety, he joined a traveling fair as "The Infamous Brighton Trunk Murder Man," with an act that involved him "cutting off" an assistant's head with a trick guillotine. What Spilsbury thought of these shenanigans is not recorded. However, the bizarre chain of coincidences attached to this case continued. Seven years later, Spilsbury was again the leading prosecution witness when another Antonio "Tony" Mancini—his real name—was convicted and later executed for a gangland murder.

Well before this, the original Mancini had faded into obscurity, and there he remained until 1976, when as a sick man in his late sixties, he briefly hit the headlines once again when he walked into the offices of a Sunday newspaper and offered to sell them his confession. Headlined "I've Got Away with Murder," the story purported to tell the truth about Violette Kaye's death. Shrouded in the protective cloak of double jeopardy, Mancini told how Violette had brooded for days over his friendship with Elizabeth Attrill, convinced the two were having an affair. Her sulkiness had spilled over in the basement flat when the argument erupted into violence. Suddenly she flew at him with the hammer. They had grappled for a moment, enough for him to wrest the hammer from her grasp. When she demanded that he return the hammer, he had flung it unthinkingly. "It caught her on the left temple."[36] Maddened with rage, he then grabbed her head and banged it repeatedly on the grate fender. "I honestly didn't mean to kill her—I had just lost control of myself in the heat of the moment."[37] When the red mist finally cleared, he realized, too late, the enormity of what he had done. Violette Kaye lay dead on the floor. The survival instinct now took over. "When I gave my evidence," he said, "I had carefully rehearsed my lines like an actor . . . I had practiced how I should hold my hands and when I should let the tears run down my cheeks."[38] As we've seen, it was an Oscar-worthy performance that culminated in an eventual and totally unexpected acquittal.

A lifelong liar, Mancini couldn't help mythologizing, and every journalist who came to call thereafter received a slightly differing version of events. But in essence, he corroborated almost every detail that Spilsbury had given in his testimony all those years before.

On that bitterly disappointing day in December 1934 when Spilsbury exited the court in Lewes, he could at least console himself with one small grain of comfort. One of his pet projects was near to completion. In recent years the medico-legal literature from abroad, but especially France and the U.S., had been packed with exciting news of the latest forensic advances. As Spilsbury read these articles, his frustration mounted. For years he had been infuriated by the fragmented research procedures and incompetent lab technicians of his homeland, and had made the need for a more integrated approach to forensic science a constant theme in his speeches to various academic bodies.

In 1935 all of his pleadings finally came to fruition. On April 10, he was on hand for the inauguration of the Scotland Yard police laboratory at Hendon in North London. At long last all the medico-legal disciplines could be housed under one roof. This meant that test results came through more quickly, there was greater interaction between the scientists, ideas and theories were exchanged not shelved, and the criminally disposed found it that little bit harder to avoid the consequences of their actions. This latter inconvenience was further enhanced when Scotland Yard developed a portable scientific laboratory that could visit any crime scene at a few minutes' notice, an innovation that led to dramatic improvements in evidence processing.

All these developments allowed Spilsbury to expand his already hectic academic curriculum. Although he was still accumulating notes for the medico-legal textbook that he'd been promising to write since the Great War, in June 1937 he now accepted an invitation to share his knowledge with the students at St. Thomas's Hospital Medical School in Lambeth, being appointed lecturer in forensic medicine.

At this period of his life, with his name a daily occurrence in the newspapers, Spilsbury was one of the most famous men alive. So famous, in fact, that when the celebrated drama critic James Agate was asked which eleven persons, going back to Adam, he would include on his "perfect dinner list," alongside the great figures from history, such as Cheops (builder of the Great Pyramid), Hannibal, and Queen Elizabeth I, was recorded the name of Sir Bernard Spilsbury.

---

1 *Times*, January 27, 1932, 6.

2 *Ibid.*, February 19, 1932, 9.

3 *Ibid.*, April 13, 1932, 9.

4 *Ibid.*

5 *Ibid.*

6 *Ibid.*

7 *New York Times*, June 20, 1934, 3.

8 *Times*, December 12, 1934, 4.

9 *New York Times*, June 20, 1934, 3.

10 Edgar Lustgarten, *The Murder and the Trial* (London: World Distributors, 1962), 284.

11 Dennis Bardens, *Lord Justice Birkett* (London: Hale, 1962), 216.

12 *Ibid.*, 215.

13 *Ibid.*

14 *Ibid.*, 220.

15 *Ibid.*, 221.

16 H. Montgomery Hyde, *Norman Birkett* (London: Reprint Soc, 1964), 404.

17 *Ibid.*

18 Lustgarten, *The Murder and the Trial*, 297.

19 *Ibid.*, 302.

20 *Times*, December 13, 1934, 4.

21 Hyde, *Norman Birkett*, 407.

22 Lustgarten, *The Murder and the Trial*, 303.

23 *Ibid.*

24 *Ibid.*

25 *Times*, December 13, 1934, 4.

26 Bardens, *Lord Justice Birkett*, 223–24.

27 *Ibid.*, 224.

28 *Times*, December 13, 1934, 4.

29 *Ibid.*
30 Hyde, *Norman Birkett*, 412.
31 *Ibid.*, 411.
32 *Ibid.*, 415.
33 Lustgarten, *The Murder and the Trial*, 314.
34 Hyde, *Norman Birkett*, 418.
35 *Ibid.*
36 *News of the World*, November 28, 1976, 1.
37 *Ibid.*
38 *Ibid.*

CHAPTER TEN

The Dark Decade

As the 1930s began to unfold, Spilsbury's case notes took on a decidedly darker, more sinister edge. At firsthand he witnessed an emerging and sickening trend that endures to the present day: the abduction and murder of children, particularly young girls. One of his earliest such incidents came in the summer of 1931, when eleven-year-old Ivy Godden went missing at Ruckinge, Kent. Forty-eight hours later, on July 5, her body was found, trussed with rope and wrapped in sacking, buried in a wood about six hundred yards from her home. Although she had been beaten savagely about the head, Spilsbury detected no evidence of sexual interference. In a little over two months, a neighbor, Arthur Salvage, aged twenty-three, was arrested, charged, convicted of murder, and sentenced to death. As he did not appeal, the date of his execution was fixed for October 6. However, four days before his intended date with the hangman, Salvage was examined by a panel of psychiatrists, declared insane, and sent to Broadmoor for life.

A couple of months later, in the Notting Hill district of London, Vera Page, a lively eleven-year-old, also went missing from her home. Two days passed before her violated and strangled body was found amongst some shrubbery close to where she lived. Spilsbury's autopsy card recorded unusually advanced decomposition for the time of year, from which he deduced that Vera had been murdered shortly after her disappearance, then kept somewhere warm before her body was dumped where it was found. Although suspicion briefly alighted upon a married man known to the Page family, insufficient evidence existed to bring a charge, and the case drifted into the unsolved file.

Similar frustration attended the murder of little Pamela Coventry in 1939. Again, she disappeared in broad daylight, and again Spilsbury was called in after her naked body was discovered in an Essex ditch. What singled out this autopsy from the thousands that had gone before was the fact that Spilsbury—the great loner—was assisted by the young and ferociously ambitious pathologist, Dr. Francis Camps. For the old master, it was the starkest reminder yet that his hegemony was no longer absolute. In the event, Camps would prove to be a loyal ally who at one time even contemplated writing a biography of Spilsbury, but for now the older man was on his guard as the two medical examiners went about their work. What they found was horrible; ugly manual strangulation and the cruelest assault imaginable. Circumstantial evidence led to a local man named Leonard Richardson standing trial for her murder, though the case against him was notably thin. Eventually the jury lost patience with the prosecution and passed a note to the judge, who then discharged the prisoner. As with Vera Page, the murder of Pamela Coventry remains unsolved.

Sandwiched in between these two latter tragedies was yet another sensational case of child abduction/murder that made international headlines. This case was unique for the remarkable reason that by the time of Spilsbury's involvement, the name of the little girl's killer was already known and loathed from one end of the country to the other.

A Child Goes Missing

It was just after four o'clock on the afternoon of January 5, 1937, when Mona Tinsley, aged ten, left the Guildhall Street Methodist School in the Nottinghamshire market town of Newark and hurried homeward. Small for her age, she had good reason to be thankful for her jumpsuit, brown tweed coat, and stout Wellington boots as she burrowed into the winter gloom. The evening was fine but cold, and ordinarily it was a twenty-minute walk to her home in Thoresby Avenue. Tonight, though, something went terribly wrong. Somewhere along that journey of rather less than one mile, Mona Tinsley vanished. Five o'clock. Six o'clock. Seven o'clock. All came and went. And still no sign of Mona. Astonishingly, she was almost three hours overdue before her parents raised the alarm. And even then it was a tepid affair that pointedly excluded their immediate neighbors along Thoresby Avenue, an oversight that would have haunting repercussions. It wasn't until 9:45 P.M. that Wilfred Tinsley called in to the local police station to report his daughter missing.

All through the long winter night, teams of officers scoured the rabbit warren of streets and alleyways that lay between Mona's school and her home. Daybreak brought a bleak gray light and unearthly silence. Still no news. As the morning wore on, searchers spread out into the adjoining countryside, even though the breakthrough that they craved had been right under their noses all the time. Although eleven-year-old William Plackett lived next door to the Tinsleys at 13 Thoresby Avenue, it wasn't until midmorning that investigators learned that the lad had seen Mona the previous afternoon between four thirty and five by Newark bus station, talking to a mustachioed, round-shouldered man. It turned out that William Plackett wasn't the only person along Thoresby Avenue with a story to tell. Annie Hird, at number 15, spoke of having seen a man hanging around outside Mona's school at about the time the pupils left for home. She'd recognized him as someone who'd once been a lodger at the Tinsleys' house. Frederick Hudson, she thought his name was.

When this news was relayed to the Tinsleys, they admitted that Hudson had stayed with them in October 1935, although Lillian Tinsley, Mona's mother, dismissed any suggestion of his involvement, saying, "Oh, it couldn't be him."[1] She explained that Hudson had come to them on the strong recommendation of her sister, Edie Grimes, who lived in Sheffield. Hudson, a motor mechanic who sometimes drove a truck for a living, had stayed with the Tinsleys for just three weeks, and during that time he'd become very friendly with the seven children, all of whom called him Uncle Fred. The only reason he'd left was because he had trouble paying the rent.

From Newark to Sheffield is a distance of forty-five miles, and it was noon by the time detectives reached the house of Edie Grimes and her husband. They ran headlong into a wall of silence. The couple flatly denied knowing anyone called Hudson. Gradually, as tensions relaxed and the questioning became more informal, Edie let her guard drop, and the name Nodder slipped out. Investigatorial ears perked up. Further questioning—much keener now—established that Frederick Hudson and Frederick Nodder were one and the same person. Having grudgingly admitted this fact, Edie Grimes now dug in her heels again and insisted that she had not seen Nodder for several months, nor did she know his current address.

Such belligerent reticence prompted suspicions that some other misdemeanor was being concealed. Sure enough, at Sheffield police station, detectives learned that a "bastardy warrant" existed against Nodder for nonpayment of £18 maintenance to a young woman who had given birth to his illegitimate child. The scandal had ruined Nodder's marriage—he also had two grown-up children—and he'd left the marital home, since which time he'd stayed one step ahead of the process servers by putting up at assorted lodging houses. Convinced that Edie Grimes was being deviously economical with the truth, detectives began questioning her neighbors. Within minutes they dug up a promising lead; just recently a strange truck had been seen parked outside the Grimeses' house, with the name Retford painted on the side.

Retford was a small town midway between Newark and Sheffield, and inquiries at local garages and pubs soon revealed that a vehicle similar to that seen outside the Grimeses' house was driven by someone called Nodder, who lived in Hayton, a village just over three miles away. Nodder's address was a house called Peacehaven in Smeath Road, and at 7 P.M. on January 6—scarcely twenty-one hours after Mona Tinsley had been reported missing—Harry Barnes, chief constable of the Newark Police Force, knocked at the door. Receiving no reply, he and two fellow officers braced themselves for a long and possibly frustrating wait.

At 11 P.M. a man, whose description matched that of Frederick Nodder, loomed up out of the dark. Seeing Barnes, he stopped and asked if there was some problem. Barnes replied by thrusting the maintenance warrant into Nodder's face and growling, "I do not suppose you have £18 for this, have you?"[2] When Nodder shook his head, Barnes suggested they go indoors. The man he found himself studying was in his midforties, medium build, with a heavy mustache; beery breath; and pale, watery eyes, and wearing a blue overcoat and brown cap. The inside of Nodder's house matched the occupant: seedy and unkempt. After glancing quickly about, Barnes revealed the true nature of his call, the disappearance of Mona Tinsley. Nodder listened to what Barnes had to say and shrugged. "I know nothing about it."[3] He claimed to have not seen Mona for fifteen months, and although he admitted being in Newark the previous day, he said he had been on a mission to find work for himself and his truck. With the unpaid maintenance warrant as authority, Barnes took Nodder into custody, and the next day he was placed on an identity parade.

Annie Hird had no difficulty identifying Nodder as the person she'd seen lingering outside Guildhall Street Methodist School, and Plackett similarly picked him out as the man at the bus station with Mona Tinsley. Another witness, a bus driver, deepened Nodder's problems when he identified him as the man who, accompanied by a young girl, had alighted from his bus at Retford at about six o'clock on the evening of Mona's disappearance. The eyewitness evidence continued to mount. Two drinking companions of Nodder's—he was a chronic alcoholic who'd lost countless jobs because of intemperance—recalled seeing him with a young girl in Retford at approximately 6:45 P.M. that same night, though neither could definitely identify her as Mona Tinsley.

Five people had therefore seen Nodder in the company of a young girl, more than enough reason for Barnes to hold Nodder in custody whilst the search for Mona widened. After forty-eight hours in the cells—with no sign of a break in the case—Nodder suddenly asked to speak to a detective sergeant. "If you will get Mrs. Grimes over from Sheffield I will make a statement which will lead to the recovery of Mona Tinsley alive and well."[4]

A car sped to Edie Grimes's house, and in the early hours of January 9, she was bustled into Newark police station. Nodder didn't waste any time. "These chaps know all about us," he told Edie, a reference to their four-year-long affair, before asking, "Have you seen Mona? Is Mona at your house?" When Mrs. Grimes replied in the negative, Nodder said, "Then I'm responsible."[5] He tagged this enigmatic remark by announcing that he wished to make a statement.

He admitted that on the Tuesday evening, in Newark, Mona had seen him by the school and had cried out excitedly, "Hullo, Uncle Fred!" During a bubbly conversation that lasted several minutes, Mona bemoaned the fact that she hadn't seen her Aunt Edie's new eight-month-old baby. When Nodder mentioned that he would be seeing both the next day, Mona clamored to go with him. "Foolishly, I agreed, repenting my action as soon as I started off,"[6] he said. (Earlier, he had told the police that Edie Grimes was in the habit of clandestinely visiting Peacehaven at least once a week.) Mona had, according to Nodder, spent the night at his house, sleeping in the only bed while he used the couch downstairs.

Wednesday morning brought a nasty surprise: a letter from Edie Grimes, saying she would be unable to come over that day. As was his custom with all billets-doux from Edie, Nodder destroyed the letter immediately. With his plans turned upside down, only now did the gravity of his situation strike home. However unsettling this inner turmoil may have been, it didn't prevent him from deciding—in early January—that the garden was in need of some titivation. Grabbing a spade he began to turn over the muddy soil; at the same time he exchanged pleasantries with his next-door neighbor. At midday another woman, who did cleaning work two doors down, happened to glance across and see a young girl in a light blue outfit framed in the back doorway, watching Nodder at work.

This sighting was hugely significant. Had Mona's neighbors been apprised of her disappearance immediately on the Tuesday evening, eyewitness evidence might well have led the police to Nodder's house that same night, at which time Mona was undoubtedly alive, if not necessarily unharmed. Even more infuriating, so far as the police were concerned, at the very moment that Mona was seen in Nodder's back doorway, Edie Grimes was angrily denying all knowledge of her lover's whereabouts.

Nodder continued his tale. After giving Mona a meal and then fetching some provisions from the nearby village of Clarborough, he revised his plan of action: he would deliver Mona to her Aunt Edie in Sheffield, in hopes that she would contact the distraught family, explain that Mona had been with her all along, and somehow get him off the hook. At 6:45 P.M. he and Mona boarded the bus from Retford to Worksop. During this eight-mile journey he gave Mona a handwritten sheet of directions to Edie Grimes's house in Sheffield. He dared not make the trip himself because of the warrant out for his arrest. At Worksop, he saw her onto the Sheffield bus and watched it leave. It was, he said, the last time he saw Mona.

Unsurprisingly, the police didn't believe a word of Nodder's story. The notion of whisking a ten-year-old girl away from her parents without permission, keeping her overnight, and then packing her off alone on a winter's night on a nineteen-mile bus journey to a major city where no one was expecting her arrival, and armed only with the vaguest directions, stretched the bounds of credibility to breaking point. Nor could anybody be found who had seen either Mona or Nodder on any bus journey between Retford and Sheffield on the night in question. And then there was that mysterious phone call . . .

He Said, She Said

In 1937 very few U.K. residents could afford the luxury of a telephone. One of the few in Hayton to buck this trend was Nodder's neighbor, Mrs. Maggie Simpson. A kindly soul, she frequently accepted calls for other residents along the street, and on the morning of Mona's disappearance, a woman had phoned, asking to speak to Nodder. Mrs. Simpson had run next door and fetched him. The caller turned out to be Edie Grimes. Her version of the conversation had her telling Nodder that she would be unable to keep their assignation on Thursday as arranged. By contrast, Nodder claimed the call dealt exclusively with an upcoming truck purchase, for which Edie Grimes had agreed to lend him money, and that there had been no mention of any aborted visit. If Edie Grimes *was* telling the truth, this call drove a stake right through Nodder's claim that when he met Mona that evening he was still expecting her aunt the following day. Whatever the substance of this conversation—and it was never clarified satisfactorily—it did nothing to alter the undeclared but nonetheless strongly held official view that Mona Tinsley was dead, and that when her body was found, sufficient evidence would exist to charge Nodder with murder. In preparation for this eventuality, he was given a full physical examination for signs of scratch marks or a struggle. It turned out negative. Similarly with his clothes; not a speck of blood or any unusual trace evidence on the overcoat or suit, and his brown shoes were spotless.

In the meantime, Mona's body resolutely defied discovery. Given Nodder's ominous horticultural activity on January 6, his backyard was dug to a depth of twelve feet. Nothing. It was the same story inside his house. Plenty of filth and grime; no useful clues. Hopes that chemical analysis of the bed linen and bedding would reveal traces of semen or blood came to naught. Tucked between some newspapers was a slip of paper covered with childish handwriting that, when compared to Mona's school exercise books, seemed to match, but as Nodder didn't deny her presence in his house, the evidential value of this discovery was nil. Most worrying of all, there was nothing to suggest Mona's current whereabouts.

As the Chesterfield Canal ran within fifty yards of Nodder's house, attention soon centered on this waterway. It was dragged for a distance of five miles, and some sections were drained completely. All to no avail. A search party that grew to more than 800 anxious persons combed coppices, woods, and gravel pits for the missing girl. Broadcasts on national radio and the thousands of posters that were circulated nationwide and reprinted in the press briefly made the face of Mona Tinsley one of the best-known images in the country. And still there was no sign of her. In the end frustration forced the official hand, and when Nodder stood trial on March 9, 1937, at the Warwick Winter Assizes, it was on the lesser charge of abduction.

This did nothing to dilute the venomous level of antagonism that was directed at the accused. Nor was Nodder aided by the choice of trial judge. Sir Rigby Swift, his mind unhinged by the recent death of his wife, was fighting his own battle with terminal illness when the trial began, and throughout the two-day hearing he never once bothered to veil his detestation of the prisoner. He bullied, he sneered, he forestalled the defense at every turn in a performance that owed more to the Bloody Assizes of Judge Jeffreys than it did to a twentieth-century courtroom. His summing-up was breathtaking, merciless in its bias and bile, and so littered with inaccuracies that Crown counsel Norman Birkett, KC—obviously with one anxious eye on the appeal court— was forever bobbing up and down to correct him. Tapping his pencil repeatedly to emphasize every point, Mr. Justice Swift fulminated over Nodder's refusal to testify, snarling that the defendant had denied the court the only full account of that day's tragic happenings. By any standards it was a lamentable performance, though whether it affected the outcome is debatable. Given the pretrial publicity, Nodder would have needed a miracle to gain an acquittal, and he came up short. Sentencing Nodder to seven years' penal servitude, the judge added a bitter rider: "What you did with that little girl, what became of her, only you know. It may be that time will reveal the dreadful secret which you carry in your breast."[7]

When Nodder took his case to the appeal court, even Birkett's frank admission that "there were matters in the summing-up which permitted of legitimate criticism"[8] failed to dent the judicial mind-set, and Nodder was sent back to prison to serve out his sentence. All that remained now was for Nemesis to point her avenging finger.

That came just two months later, on Sunday, June 6, a fine summer's day, perfect for boating on the river. Walter Marshall, a gasworks manager who lived at Bawtry, a village just across the county border in neighboring Yorkshire, was rowing his family and some friends along a stretch of the River Idle when he noticed an unusual object near the bank. Maneuvering closer, he made out what appeared to be a child's body. The trunk floated on the surface of the water, with the legs hanging down, and the head entirely submerged. Immediately the police were summoned. Because the head was trapped in the mud on the river bottom, it took several minutes of careful manipulation with an oar before the body bobbed free. The remains were lifted onto the bank, then taken to an outbuilding at the Ship Inn, in nearby Newington, to await the arrival of Wilfred Tinsley. A single glance at what was left of the features, the dark brown hair, and the distinctive clothes was enough to convince him that his gut-wrenching ordeal was over. He nodded his head grimly—Mona Tinsley had been found. News of the discovery reached as far as America, where one headline read, "Girl's body is found after five-month hunt."[9]

Detectives studied local maps. From Nodder's house to Bolham Shuttle, the nearest point on the River Idle, was 1.9 miles. From Bolham Shuttle to where the body was found was another 14.7 miles. Assuming Nodder *had* placed the body in the Idle at this point—by no means a certainty—then it had taken five months to float almost fifteen miles.

The next day Marshall was back at the river as part of the search team. Four feet down in the water, directly beneath where the body had been found, he now recovered Mona's brown tweed coat from the riverbed silt. Alongside him, Police Constable Ernest Slater also found a solitary Wellington boot.

While the search of the river and its banks continued, Dr. James Mathewson Webster, director of the West Midland Regional Forensic Science Laboratory and an experienced criminal pathologist, examined the body. His presence reflected a recent policy change in the administration of forensic science. At that time in England and Wales—an area roughly the size of Georgia—there were no fewer than 183 separate police forces, all with widely varying medico-legal capabilities. Beginning in 1936 the Home Office attempted to impose some order on this chaos by rolling out a string of forensic science laboratories nationwide, each designed to serve its own geographical region. The prototypic Metropolitan Police Laboratory in Hendon would continue to deal with cases originating in London and the southeast, while the new facilities—called Home Office forensic science laboratories—were sited in Nottingham, Birmingham, Preston, Wakefield, Bristol, and Cardiff. The intent was to shrink the disturbing gulf in medico-legal expertise that existed between London and the provinces, and the death of Mona Tinsley was an early test of the system.

Webster found that, apart from the missing boot and both socks, the body was fully clothed. As a rule, five months' exposure to the elements would cause heavy decomposition, but not in this instance. The waxy looking face provided the first clue, and confirmation came when the body was fully undressed; the body had been converted almost entirely to adipocere. Sometimes called grave wax, adipocere is a foul-smelling, suetlike substance that forms in the fatty parts of the body, such as the cheeks, thighs, and breasts. It is the product of a chemical reaction in which fats react with water and hydrogen in the presence of bacterial enzymes, and can start to form within a month after death, although this depends on the temperature. The colder it is, the slower the onset. One side effect of adipocere, highly useful to the pathologist, is that it helps preserve the internal organs.

This allowed Webster to ascertain that Mona suffered from no organic disease at the time of her death—not that he expected to find any in a ten-year-old—that she had not eaten for some considerable time before her death, and that she had been dead before she was thrown into the river. Had she drowned, the lungs and probably the stomach, as well, would have shown traces of water. In each instance they were dry. As something else had obviously caused Mona's death, Webster turned to a single, even mark, much darker in color than the surrounding skin, that encircled almost the entire neck, apart from a gap at the rear. Such marks, almost invariably, indicate death by strangulation.

When a medical examiner suspects asphyxia, he or she usually goes looking for petechiae. These are tiny hemorrhages, pinpricks of blood caused by burst capillaries, and they happen when the heart is unable to do its job properly. Ordinarily the heart keeps the body supplied with the oxygen and other elements it needs to survive. If something happens to impede that pumping, the blood backs up in the veins and exerts pressure on the capillaries, the smallest of the body's vessels, causing them to erupt and form petechiae. This reaction is most commonly seen in the whites of the eyes.

Here, the eyes were of no evidentiary use at all, having been totally destroyed. However, all was not lost. Petechiae are far from being the only indicator of asphyxiation. In this case there was a distinct row of dental impressions gouged deep into the tongue. When someone is being strangled they will fight like a demon to survive, and one frequent side effect of this struggle is a clamping down of the teeth onto the tongue, leaving the telltale marks that Webster saw here. The body also offered up other clues. The mucous membrane in the windpipe was much redder than normal, again an indicator of asphyxial death, as was the fact that the right chamber of the heart was dilated as compared to the left. All these factors, in concert with the deep groove around the neck, led him to conclude that Mona had been strangled by some kind of ligature being tightened around her neck. Only when dead had she been tossed into the river by her killer.

Although this had been essentially a straightforward autopsy—one well within Webster's compass—because of the controversial circumstances surrounding the case, local pressures began to build for consultation at the highest level. Underlying this agitation was a realization that defense lawyers were becoming far more adept at countering medical evidence on cross-examination. Fearful that Nodder's team might ferret out some flaw, and thereby save their client from the gallows, the Home Office asked Spilsbury to travel north to add his weight to the investigation. On June 27 he presented himself at Webster's laboratory in Birmingham, where he examined sections taken from the body and other microscopical specimens. These came from the groove around the neck, the tongue, the lungs, the heart, the larynx, and the windpipe. He paid particularly close attention to sections excised from the genitals. From the absence of bruising, and by studying photographs of the corpse, he judged, to the surprise of many involved in the case, though not to Webster, who had already reached the same conclusion, that there had been no sexual penetration. This was a crucial finding, one bound to be seized upon by the defense, who would argue that since no obvious molestation of Mona had occurred while she was in Nodder's presence, this only strengthened his protestations of innocence.

Careful as always to avoid treading on any overly sensitive provincial toes, Spilsbury pursued his enquiries in discreet fashion. When he was done he declared himself in complete agreement with Webster; Mona Tinsley had died from ligature strangulation.

At first blush, Spilsbury's presence in the case bore all the symptoms of bureaucratic overkill, but as events unfolded, the director of public prosecutions would have cause to heave a huge sigh of relief that the honorary Home Office pathologist had been called in.

Now that the body had been discovered and the cause of death established beyond a medical doubt, there was nothing to prevent Nodder being charged with murder. What is perhaps surprising is that this didn't happen until July 29. The reasons for the delay were twofold; first, proper observation of the inquest formalities; second, to allow the Tinsley family a decent interval in which to bury their daughter before being subjected to the harrowing ordeal of a murder trial.

In essence the second trial of Frederick Nodder, which began on November 22, 1937, at the Shire Hall, Nottingham, was a carbon copy of the first. There were the same witnesses, who told the same stories, the same lawyers for each side, the same set of damning circumstances against Nodder, the same implausible explanations. The only significant difference was the presence of a body and how that body came to be in the River Idle. At the outset Nodder's counsel argued that the extraordinary circumstances of the case, stoked up by inflammatory press coverage, made it impossible for his client to have a fair trial. Since there could hardly have been a newspaper reader in the country unaware of Nodder's involvement in the abduction of Mona Tinsley, it was a valid point. And one, quite obviously, destined for the rejection pile. The trial judge, Sir Malcolm Macnaghten, merely contented himself with reminding the jury that they were duty bound to try the case only on the evidence placed before them, and that meant paying particular heed to the testimony of the Crown's two expert witnesses.

Webster came first and delivered his evidence with admirable fairness. When asked if the formation of adipocere provided a reliable indicator of how long the body had been in the river, he said that it was "not a process you can tie down to a time."[10] His best guess, and he emphasized that it was nothing more, was approximately five to six months. Death, he said, had been the result of strangulation. He then explained the significance of the hyoid bone in strangulation cases, how it is often fractured in cases of manual strangulation, more especially when the victim is elderly. As bones become more brittle with age, so they become more likely to fracture, and the hyoid is no exception. In Mona Tinsley's case, neither the hyoid nor the adjoining cartilage in the larynx showed any visible signs of distress, phenomena that Webster attributed to her youthfulness. She had been strangled, he said, not manually, but by a thin ligature, a string, cord, or bootlace.

When defense counsel Maurice Healy, KC, cross-examined Webster, he turned immediately to those indentations on Mona's tongue. "Is it a fact that you sometimes do get those indentations after death by drowning?" he asked. Couched in those terms, Webster had to concede the possibility, and Healy continued. "In the same way, is it not just possible that the mark on the neck would have been caused after death?"[11] Again Webster agreed.

Next, Healy speculated on what kind of ligature might have caused the mark to Mona's neck; a hawser, perhaps? Too big, replied Webster. Then how about one of the straps on Mona's jumpsuit? This seemed to catch Webster off guard, and he had to think carefully for a moment before allowing, "If pulled from behind and pulled up."[12]

"If, by chance," Healy asked, "the girl's frock caught on a tree or something of that kind, so that the weight of the body went against it, is that a possible cause of [the mark]?"

"If done immediately after death, and if released from that position before adipocere had formed."[13]

Healy had his opening. "Take the case of any kind of a fall in which the girl's frock got hooked up so as to cause a tightening around the neck, could that possibly have been caused before death?" Backed into the tightest of corners, Webster had no alternative but to say yes, and Healy pressed on. "And if it happened in that way, in those circumstances, would all the other marks that you have described be there as well?"

"Yes, that is quite possible."[14]

At last the defense had tipped its hand. Mona's death was not some willful murder but rather a tragic accident, caused by her falling into the river, snagging her clothes on an overhanging tree branch or some such obstruction, and then being asphyxiated by the weight of her own body. Imaginative and superficially plausible, this defense theory caused more than a ripple of unease on the prosecution bench.

An interested observer of all this verbal sparring was Spilsbury him-self. As was usual in high-profile trials, he had been granted permission to sit in the well of the court from the beginning and listen to all of the evidence as it unfolded. Not only did this enable him to shape the di-rection of Crown questioning on medical matters but, crucially, it also allowed him to prepare for his own witness box tenure. It was an ex-traordinary, wholly unjudicial privilege that delighted prosecutors and reduced many defense lawyers to wig-tearing frustration. Just recently a brave few had taken to insisting that Spilsbury be excluded from court while other testimony was being given and had seen their de-mands met. The only surprise here is that Healy didn't lodge a similar request.

Spilsbury Takes the Stand

So it was that Spilsbury, somewhat in the position of a general who holds the enemy's battle plan in his hand, marched confidently through the hushed court to take his place on the witness stand. He began with his trademark fluency, the low, beautifully modulated voice hypnotic in its effect. He stated that he was in complete agreement with Webster as to the cause of death, then went on to explain the gap in the groove that ran around the victim's neck. "In my view it clearly indicates that the ligature had been held over the head and drawn backward from behind the back so that it was not in contact with the back of the neck itself at all."[15] The ligature had been yanked viciously tight, much tighter than necessary to cause death, and unconsciousness would have occurred within one minute, possibly much sooner. Assuming that the pressure was continuous, death would have ensued no more than five minutes after the attack began.

The indentations on the tongue were just as lucidly explained. Had they been mere pressure marks contracted in the normal course of events, he said, they would have faded away with time. These marks, he had no doubt, "were caused at the time of death . . . by the pressure of a ligature which has left its mark."[16]

Norman Birkett, KC, appearing for the last time as prosecuting counsel in a murder trial, wasted little time in returning to the defense hypothesis of how that mark had been caused. "You have heard [the theory] about the little child's dress being caught upon a branch?" Spilsbury acknowledged that this was so, and Birkett continued. "If you had a girl suspended by something that caused [her] death, what kind of mark would you expect to find upon the body?"[17]

Spilsbury agreed that such a scenario would leave some kind of pressure mark, caused by the upper part of the clothing. But in this case, "from what I could see there was no narrow band along the upper portion of the dress." Any mark made by the jumpsuit straps "would be shallower and broader than the one found in this case."[18]

This was unequivocal enough, but what came next provided a textbook example of just why Spilsbury had been brought into the case. Probably no medical examiner in the world had greater experience of violent or unusual death, and certainly when it came to courtroom charisma and authority, he was, as one colleague memorably put it, "An astral figure in orbit, beyond all challenge."[19] Where Webster faltered, Spilsbury was firm and assured. The twelve-man jury leant forward spellbound as he explained the crucial difference between marks caused by strangulation and marks that result from suspension. It was all a matter of angles. "Where the suspended ligature is not completely surrounding the neck," he said, "it always drags upwards at the side, and therefore would leave an oblique mark not a horizontal one."[20] As Spilsbury spoke, the jurors passed photographs of the body amongst themselves, and as these made horribly plain, the deep mark that almost entirely encircled Mona Tinsley's neck had indeed been horizontal.

Standing in the dock, Nodder must have felt his spine turn to ice. With those few words, Spilsbury had virtually kicked the trapdoor from beneath his feet.

And he wasn't done yet. Next came an explanation of the effect of temperature, time, and ambient conditions on postmortem changes to the human body. In the ordinary course of events, putrefaction is normally evident within forty-eight hours of death; but the sections and specimens taken from Mona Tinsley's body showed only "very slight"[21] signs of decay. Clearly something had happened to retard that process, and the likeliest culprit, in Spilsbury's opinion, was the icy water. He also cited this as the reason for the five-month delay in finding the body. Normally when a body is immersed in water, chemical changes distend the corpse with air, inflating it like a balloon so that it eventually floats to the surface. However, when the killer of Mona Tinsley slid her body beneath the icy January water, he might just as well have slipped it into a refrigerator; the putrefaction process was slowed to a crawl, only to reawaken in late spring as the water warmed up. Once the gases of putrefaction reached a certain level, physics took over, and the body slowly bobbed back into view. Asked if the condition of the organs was consistent with putrefaction having begun *before* the body entered the water, Spilsbury was emphatic. "No, it was not."[22] He had little doubt that Mona had been strangled and then thrown in the river almost immediately.

Healy faced an uphill struggle of vertiginous proportions. Spilsbury's logic was flawless, there was certainly no gainsaying his experience, and nothing in the medical testimony eliminated Nodder as a possible murderer. No matter how obliquely one viewed the evidence, Nodder had the means and opportunity to kill Mona Tinsley. Healy's only hope was to fashion some set of circumstances—no matter how arcane—to account for that damning horizontal mark around Mona's neck. What if, he asked Spilsbury, Mona had slipped on the riverbank, only for her progress to be checked "by some obstacle like a bit of overhanging timber . . . the first effect of that would be to pull the garment back before her weight caused the suspension?"

"Yes, that is quite true."

"In those circumstances then, the first pressure on the neck would be exactly the same as if a cord had been thrown round?"

"Yes, [for] the first moment, but as it continued the mark would extend up the sides of the neck and not round it, if the child's weight
were suspended."

Healy blustered. "Here we are on speculative ground?"

"Yes, I agree, it is a *very* speculative case,"[23] said Spilsbury.

Desperate to wring something—anything—out of the exchange,
Healy began snatching at the frailest straws. "As regards the dates, do
you agree that the body might have been alive as late as the end of
January and might have been dead as early as the beginning of December?"[24]

It was a cunningly worded question, which, of course, permitted
only one answer, and Spilsbury had no hesitation in agreeing. He was
an old hand at the cut and thrust of courtroom testimony, well aware
that as concessions go, this was minuscule and unlikely to have any
bearing on the outcome.

In his first trial Nodder had been pilloried for his refusal to take the
stand. Determined not to repeat the blunder, he entered the witness
box and told his story of abduction, contrition, and bafflement as to the
whereabouts of Mona Tinsley after he placed her on the bus to Sheffield.
Then came the cross-examination. Birkett, wielding his interrogative
scalpel with surgical precision, probed every word that Nodder uttered.
Absurdities piled on top of mind-numbing callousness, piled on top of
more lies and more incongruities all contrived to create a mountain of
circumstantial evidence against the shrunken figure in the witness box.
Nothing better demonstrated the defendant's heartless egocentricity
than his response when asked if he had considered the distress that
Mona's disappearance might have on her parents: "No, it never entered
my head."[25]

Nodder slunk off back to the dock, leaving his counsel with the un-
enviable task of trying to salvage something from the wreckage. In his
final charge to the jury, Healy made the most of obvious weaknesses in
the prosecution. At no point had they attempted to demonstrate *when*
or *where* the murder took place; nor could they prove that Mona had
actually been dead on January 6. Since Mona had been seen alive at

midday that day, and Nodder had been under arrest from eleven o'clock that same night, in order for him to be the killer, he had either to first carry out the crime and then somehow transport Mona's body unseen at least two, possibly more, miles from his house to the River Idle, across muddy fields, past other houses, then stop off at two pubs on the way home, without anyone noticing anything peculiar in his manner and without getting a speck of dirt or trace evidence on his person. Or else—and this was the theory favored by most police officers—he somehow spirited Mona Tinsley alive to the riverbank and murdered her there, again without transfer of trace evidence. Also in the defendant's favor, argued Healy, was the absence of sexual inter- ference on the victim's body. Had Nodder abducted Mona to satisfy some perverted lust, then surely someone of Sir Bernard Spilsbury's eminence would have been able to find evidence of bruising or lacera- tions? Valid points, maybe, but beneath the bluster Healy knew he was fighting a doomed cause.

Like Nodder's first trial, this hearing also lasted two days, and its outcome was never in doubt. There was, however, one bizarre inter- lude. With the jury already locked away considering its verdict, Walter Marshall suddenly made a reappearance. The man who had found Mona's body, and her submerged coat the following day, now suddenly recalled another boat trip he had undertaken—this time in mid-May before Mona's body had been found and on the Ryton, a stream that flowed into the Idle—and rowing past a sack "big enough to contain the body of a child."[26] What had made this bulky sack so memorable was its foul odor. Because this mysterious bundle had been seen several miles from where the body had been found, the defense seized on it as further proof that Mona had been murdered by someone else, not Nodder, and that the killer had then thrown her body into the Ryton, where it drifted into the River Idle. To counter this claim the Crown recalled Webster (Spilsbury had returned to London to testify in an abortion case). Webster told the jury that for a human body to give off the kind of stench such as Marshall described would require considerable putrefaction, and as he and Spilsbury had made plain, the decom-position of Mona Tinsley was minimal, and nor were her clothes im-pregnated with any kind of stench. Whatever the foul-smelling sack contained, he was quite sure it wasn't the body of Mona Tinsley.

Once again the jury resumed their deliberations. Forty minutes later they were back. Guilty. Ironically, the judge in Nodder's first trial who had foretold this day did not live to see it pass. Just one month earlier on October 19, Sir Rigby Swift had died. But in passing sentence of death, Mr. Justice Macnaghten echoed his former colleague's prophecy when he told Nodder that "justice has slowly but surely overtaken you."[27] Nodder responded with a sly chuckle, "I shall go out of this court with a clear conscience, sir."[28] Following the dismissal of his ap-peal, Nodder was executed at Lincoln Prison on December 30.

Although justice seems to have been served, the tragedy of Mona Tinsley's death did raise many troubling questions:

Why, on a bitterly cold January night with a gale blowing, was the disappearance of a ten-year-old girl not acted upon until seven o'clock?

Why were the neighbors so pointedly excluded from the search that night?

What reason did some of the witnesses, especially those closest to the tragedy, have for being so obstructive to the enquiry?

Why was Walter Marshall's evidence about that mysterious sack kept from the court until the jury was already deliberating?

And, most baffling of all, just why did Nodder abduct Mona Tins-ley? The Crown offered no motive for the crime, and according to Spilsbury there were no obvious signs of molestation. But not all forms of sexual abuse are visible—especially after five months' immersion in a muddy river—and most of those who brushed up against Nodder during the course of his two trials were convinced that he had made some perverted use of Mona Tinsley before choking her to death. *"A monster!"*[29] shuddered one prosecution team member, when later recall-ing Nodder in private conversations.

The Declining Years

By 1939 it was clear that the grim nature of Spilsbury's casebook was being reflected and magnified in the wider geopolitical picture. In September the Nazi war machine blitzkrieged Poland, and Europe was once again plunged into darkness. When hostilities began, Spilsbury had just entered his sixties, and the decades of overwork were catching up fast. He was worn out. In May 1940, while thousands of Allied servicemen were being ferried off the killing beaches of Dunkirk, England's premier pathologist was fighting his own private battle in a London hospital. He had collapsed while performing yet another autopsy. The stroke wasn't severe enough to incapacitate, but the Spilsbury who emerged from University College Hospital in June profoundly shocked all who knew him. He seemed to have aged a decade, and there was now a deathly pallor to him, so different to the fresh, high color of his younger years. Nor were the changes merely physical. The stroke had also robbed him of his witness box crispness. Juries might still have been overawed by the illustrious name, but those who knew Spilsbury best and worked alongside him on a daily basis—the police, the judiciary, the coroners—all were struck by the alien hesitancy that now dulled his testimony.

Intensely proud and still mentally acute enough not to be unaware of his mortal changes, Spilsbury fought back valiantly, and as Hitler's bombs rained down in the fall of 1940 and the mortuaries of London started to fill, his caseload remained at an exhausting level. With the capital growing more dangerous by the day, Spilsbury and his wife, Edith, boarded up the family home at Marlborough Hill, and as she had done a generation earlier, Edith retreated to the relative safety of Malvern in the West Midlands. This was no mere family evacuation. This was the final death knell for a marriage that had limped along halfheartedly for years, and never again would Spilsbury and Edith live together. He took lodgings at Verulam Buildings, an old haunt of his in the heart of London's legal district. Even in failing health, he performed more than 300 autopsies that year alone. Then came a crushing blow.

On September 15, 1940, a bomb struck St. Thomas's Hospital. Among those killed was Spilsbury's son, Peter. He was just twenty-five years old and had only qualified as a doctor one month earlier. A straight-backed stoic like Spilsbury would never have admitted to a broken heart, but colleagues always dated his eventual decline more to this tragedy than to his earlier illness.

The personal setbacks kept piling up at Spilsbury's door. On July 8, 1941, his mentor, Sir William Willcox, died suddenly from a stroke at the house on Welbeck Street where the two men had spent so many hours sifting the evidence in so many notorious cases. Following on from the death of A. J. Pepper five years previously, this now left Spilsbury as the sole survivor of the pioneering St. Mary's team that had virtually invented English medical jurisprudence.

In typical fashion he masked any sadness by immersing himself in work; it had always been his most soothing balm. As the struggle against Hitler hardened, Spilsbury found himself drafted into the war effort in unique fashion. Throughout the war, Germany's military intelligence unit, the Abwehr, was relentless in its attempts to insinuate secret agents into the U.K. Most were captured the day they set foot on British soil and given a stark choice: either agree to be "turned" and become a double agent, or else face the hangman. For those who chose the latter option, it generally fell to Spilsbury to perform the final legal requirement in the mortuary rooms at either Wandsworth or Pentonville Prisons; although in the summer of 1941 he was involved in a historical curiosity when he autopsied Josef Jakobs, the last person to be executed at the Tower of London. Unlike all the other spies condemned to death in World War II, Jakobs was not hanged but shot.

At a few minutes past seven o'clock on the morning of August 15, Jakobs was taken to the old .22 rifle range in the Tower's grounds, where the First World War spies had been shot, and placed in a brown Windsor chair (he had injured his right leg before being captured), and a white lint target was pinned on his chest over his heart. The eight-man firing squad then ended his life. Later that day, a post-mortem performed by Spilsbury recorded that one shot had hit Jakobs in the head, the other seven had been around the target area.

Even Britain's chief executioner, Albert Pierrepoint, was kept in the dark about this quirk of history. Writing years later of his wartime activities, he boasted, "I dealt with every man sentenced to death under the Treachery Act."[30] What Pierrepoint didn't know was that Jakobs, unlike his fellow spies, was tried and sentenced by a court-martial and therefore subject to a military sentence.

Earlier that year, in February and again in March, enemy bombers had struck Verulam Buildings, where Spilsbury lived. One attack he could cope with, but the second proved too much and drove him to move in with his two unmarried sisters, Constance and Gertrude, who lived in a residential hotel in Hampstead. Commuting from this hilliest of London suburbs to his laboratory at University College in Gower Street put an ever-increasing strain on his already overworked heart and the crippling arthritis that had reduced him to hobbling along on two walking sticks. Each day Spilsbury struggled in to work, little realizing that he was just about to come face-to-face with the worst serial killer to hit London in half a century.

Murder in the Blackout

The first victim was found on the morning of February 9, 1942, in an air raid shelter in Montague Place, Marylebone. She had been strangled, and the killer had rifled through her handbag, leaving a thumbprint. Nearby lay a small cycle lamp, a commonly carried item during the blackout. Later that day she was identified as Evelyn Hamilton, an unmarried forty-year-old teacher from Essex, en route to take up a new job in the north of England. Everything suggested that she had been the hapless victim of a bungled mugging.

The following evening a thirty-five-year-old prostitute named Evelyn Oatley was found in her Soho flat, lying seminaked across the bed, throat slashed open, her lower body hideously mutilated with either a knife or a can opener that showed some smudgy fingerprints. As a final obscene indignity, the killer had rammed a flashlight into her vagina. Apart from Spilsbury's observation that Evelyn had probably been choked into unconsciousness prior to the ferocious assault, there was nothing to connect the two murders.

Spilsbury knew better than anyone the appalling risks run by women who worked in the world's oldest and most dangerous profession. In the past decade his case notes had recorded a sharp upward spike in the homicide rate among prostitutes. The fact that so many of these murders went unsolved cast no reflection on Spilsbury and owed more to an investigative system that—consciously or not—imposed a pecking order on victims. Some were thought more worthwhile than others. Given the circumstances, had Evelyn Oatley's killer now decided to lie low, in all likelihood he would have never been caught. But that wasn't his way.

Forty-eight hours later Spilsbury was summoned to yet another West End flat. This time the victim's name was Margaret Lowe, forty-three, though her customers called her Pearl. Over the years hundreds of clients had passed through her tiny flat in Gosfield Street, near to the BBC's Broadcasting House; the final one to do so took it upon himself to throttle her with a tightly knotted silk stocking as she lay on her single bed. Then he went to work on her lifeless body with a bread knife, two kitchen knives, a poker, and a candle. In grabbing the candle from its holder, he had left a fingerprint on the glass surface. He had been equally careless in the kitchen, daubing his prints on a half-empty beer bottle. When Spilsbury finished his initial examination he turned to the detective in charge and asked quietly, "Have you seen the others?"[31]

Chief Inspector Edward Greeno shook his head. Spilsbury's expression was grim. "I have."[32] Something in Spilsbury's tone made Greeno edgy. "Are you thinking the same as I am?"[33] he asked. Spilsbury nodded.

Just at that moment a police motorcyclist arrived with a message. Greeno read it quickly. Spilsbury waited until he finished, then spoke: "Not another one?"[34]

This time it was Greeno's turn to nod. Immediately he and Spilsbury went downstairs, got into a police car, and drove the mile or so to Number 187, Sussex Gardens, in Paddington.

Doris Jouannet, thirty-two, was tall, slim, and elegant with blonde hair, and married to a man more than twice her age. By day she managed a small hotel; by night, after her elderly Paris-born husband had vanished into the blackout—he was manager of the Royal Court Hotel in Sloane Square—Doris, calling herself Olga, hit the West End bars and clubs. Here, she was popular with Allied servicemen eager for female company to brighten their furloughs.

It was her husband who'd found her, sprawled across her bed, strangled and mutilated. When Spilsbury arrived she was still warm, a chilling reminder that while he was en route to examine the body of Margaret Lowe, the killer was already out stalking his next victim. It was almost a carbon copy of the previous killing: silk-stocking ligature and the same sickening mutilation. Spilsbury showed Greeno how the killer had held up the woman's breast and almost sliced off a nipple with a razor. "You've got a madman on parade here,"[35] he breathed, lowering himself to more closely inspect the angle of the wound. When he straightened up, he said, "When you catch him I'd like to know if he's left-handed."[36] Although the killer was more careful this time, Scotland Yard fingerprint experts soon determined that the same person was responsible for the three previous murders; unfortunately, his prints were not listed in criminal records.

Four women slaughtered in five days. Even in a city virtually immunized against shock by the horrors of the blitz, carnage of this type and scale was bound to create panic. Not since the days of Jack the Ripper, in 1888, had London been so terrorized by an individual. Women were urged to stay behind locked doors. Most didn't need any second bidding, terrified to go out alone after dark. One who did decide to brave the stygian blackout, Greta Heywood, soon had cause to regret her recklessness. On the evening of February 14, she fell into conversation with a well-spoken, dashing airman in Piccadilly. Shared sandwiches and drinks were okay, but when the stranger attempted to force his attentions on her and she resisted, in a flash his hands went round her throat, shoving her into a darkened doorway just off the Haymarket. Her cries and kicking struggle alerted a passing delivery boy, whose intervention prompted the brutal assailant to flee, leaving behind an RAF gas mask, which bore the name, rank, and serial number—525987—of twenty-eight-year-old aircraftman Gordon Cummins.

Just hours later came news that another woman had had an even closer brush with death that same evening. Catherine Mulcahy, aged twenty-two (she had a string of aliases including Phyllis O'Dwyer and Kathleen King), had picked up Cummins outside a Regent Street restaurant and taken him back to her Paddington flat. After £5 had changed hands, she quickly stripped down to her necklace and boots. The former was retained for decorative allure; the latter because the flat was freezing cold. In the event, the boots saved her life. The coupling was swift and began normally enough, only to quickly degenerate into a terrifying fight for life as the stranger, eyes blazing, suddenly clamped his hands around Catherine's neck and began squeezing with insane fury. Frantically, she fought back, and with her last ounce of strength managed to lash out with her foot. The boot caught the man full on the shin. He gave a howl of pain and pulled back. Then he jumped from the bed, dressed hurriedly, flung another £5 down on the bed, and fled. This time he left his belt.

It required no great detective work to track Cummins to his billet in St. John's Wood, and the RAF cadet was arrested for the two vicious assaults on February 14. By this time he was also the prime suspect in the murders, but there was a problem: army attendance logs recorded Cummins as being in his barracks at the crucial times. On the surface, he had a bulletproof alibi. Then it emerged that some of the more adventurous aircraftmen in the billet were in the habit of shimmying down an unguarded fire escape after lights out. Other servicemen named Cummins as chief beneficiary of this ploy. At a stroke his alibi lay in tatters. Small items of jewelry and other personal effects from each of the victims, found in his possession, were the icing on the investigational cake.

Yorkshire-born Cummins had been a minor troublemaker ever since leaving school. He was lazy and shiftless, found jobs hard to hold, and, like Sidney Fox, had a fondness for affecting an upper-class accent. He had joined the RAF in 1935 and had recently been accepted to train as a pilot. His fellow recruits dubbed him "the duke" or "the count" on account of the airs and graces he adopted. What provoked his sudden maniacal explosion is a mystery. He had been happily married for five and a half years, and his wife bravely stuck by him, fighting to the last to save him from the gallows.

At the police station, Cummins agreed to make a statement. Afterwards, he read it over carefully, and under Greeno's watchful gaze, he signed the document—with his left hand. After he was charged with the dual assaults, his fingerprints were taken as a matter of course. They quite clearly matched those found at the murder crime scenes.

As in World War I, the sheer scale of international turmoil and a shortage of newsprint conspired to push wartime murder coverage onto the inside pages, and the trial of Gordon Cummins was lightly reported—exceptionally so, given the unique circumstances of the case, making it hard to escape the suspicion that some kind of governmental pressure was exerted on the press to hush up the proceedings. With the war going badly, Whitehall wanted RAF heroes, not throttling maniacs. After a false start—there was a mix-up over some evidence— the trial only lasted two days. Following British legal tradition Cummins was charged with one murder only, that of his first victim, Evelyn Hamilton. With utter predictability he was convicted and sentenced to death on April 28, 1942. His only words were, "I am entirely innocent."[37]

Four weeks later, on the morning of June 25, Spilsbury's car threaded an uncertain path—he was never much of a driver—through London's bomb-devastated streets until he reached the studded doors at Wandsworth Prison's main entrance. By the time Spilsbury was admitted through the wicket gate, Cummins was already dangling from the hangman's noose. An hour later, his rapidly cooling body lay on Spilsbury's autopsy table.

Although Cummins was certainly guilty of four murders, he was strongly suspected of complicity in the unsolved deaths of two other women in northwest London in late 1941. The first, Mabel Church, nineteen, was found seminaked and strangled in a bombed-out house just off Regent's Park on October 13. Four days later and a few hundred yards away, Edith Humphries, a middle-aged widow, was battered to death in her two-room flat in Gloucester Crescent.

The case of the so-called "Wartime Ripper" had a profound effect on Spilsbury. Nothing, not even a lifetime of investigating violent death and hideous abuse, had prepared him for such horrific and arbitrary slaughter. In describing the injuries that Cummins inflicted as "quite dreadful,"[38] Spilsbury was indulging the classic British appetite for understatement, whilst the randomness of the carnage sickened him. Remarkable as it may seem to modern eyes, this was Spilsbury's first confrontation with a hard-core serial killer. When George Joseph Smith drowned three women in the bath, there was never any sense that he killed for kicks; he was far too pragmatic for such frivolity. His murders were hardheaded business decisions born out of frustration: he couldn't get his hands on their money by any other means. Now, thirty years on, Spilsbury knew that the criminal world order was changing, and like everyone around him, he was powerless to influence its direction. He had been just a lad when first Jack the Ripper and then Neill Cream launched their homicidal campaigns against the prostitutes of London; now any hopes that these two psychopaths had been a late-Victorian aberration had been well and truly scotched by the madness of Gordon Cummins.

Personal Tragedies

Spilsbury's depression was made blacker still by more grim news much closer to home; his beloved sister, Constance, had died. It was one more ripping away of the social fabric that had underpinned his life. His health took another tumble, he became even more reclusive, and the arthritis that had made the last few years so arduous now tightened its grip. He was caught in a vicious circle. Alarmed by the way in which newcomers like Camps, Simpson, and Donald Teare were picking up the medico-legal plums that would once have been his by right, he refused the medical treatment he needed, driven by a fear that the young pretenders would extract still more fees from his pocket. All his life he had scorned money; now he was scrabbling desperately to make ends meet. To save a few pennies he ate at the restaurant at Euston train station, with few fellow diners aware that they were sharing their meal with the legendary Spilsbury. In the main it was kindly coroners who kept him going. They knew that his reports were as meticulous as ever; they just took longer to arrive nowadays.

Like most people in Britain Spilsbury's spirits rallied with the end of the war in Europe. But the respite was short-lived, as another stroke further dug into his fast-diminishing reserves of good health. Shortly after this, his eldest son, Alan, came to work with him at his Gower Street laboratory in the Department of Pharmacology at University College. It should have been the happiest of reunions, but Alan, never blessed with the strongest of constitutions, suddenly fell ill in November 1945, and within three days was dead from tuberculosis.

Spilsbury reeled from this latest body blow. In five years he'd lost two sons, a sister, a close friend, and a marriage. Little wonder that his health deteriorated so precipitously, and now there was the agony of insomnia to contend with. As his decline gathered pace, it became obvious that the much-awaited medical textbook that he had been threatening to write all his life would remain a pipe dream. He was still the expert of choice for anyone seeking the greatest authority—for instance, when Allied troops emerged trembling from the horrors of Buchenwald concentration camp, it was Spilsbury who was asked to analyze a particularly sinister lampshade that had been recovered. He confirmed it was made from human skin—but the big showcase trials were no longer coming his way.

His final murder case of note involved the shooting death of Alec de Antiquis, a passerby gunned down by three young thugs during a bungled jewel robbery in London's West End on April 29, 1947. When Spilsbury came to autopsy the body, he did so in the presence of longtime friend, the coroner W. Bentley Purchase, and Detective Superintendent Robert Fabian. Both were shocked by Spilsbury's fumbling hesitancy. They writhed in uncomfortable silence as he searched in vain for a bullet exit wound, seemingly baffled by its absence, unable to discern what was glaringly obvious to the onlookers—that the slug was still lodged inside the skull. As the examination progressed, the bullet fell out. Fabian handed it to Spilsbury, attempting to soften the blow by declaring that Spilsbury had found it earlier. Spilsbury's embarrassed half smile said it all. He'd been rumbled. He was an old man in a fast-changing world. Pedophiles, serial killers, gun-toting tearaways; it was all so removed from the buttoned-up Victorian society that had bred him. Then murder, no matter how sensational, had been largely a domestic matter, usually men killing inconvenient wives or girlfriends; in this harsh new world, strangers were killing strangers for money, sex, and thrills.

He had no desire to become an object of pity, there was too much pride in him for that, and there can be little doubt that he planned his end with the same meticulous attention to detail that had hallmarked his career. It had always been his custom to order autopsy forms in batches of five hundred, but in 1947 his last order was for just one hundred. Slowly he worked his way through them. Alone, of course, for that was always his way. When the pile of cards was almost gone, in mid-December, he wrote a letter to his closest friend, Dr. Eric Gardner, a Surrey-based pathologist and former medical officer at Brooklands auto racetrack, who was vacationing in Switzerland. In it, Spilsbury stated his intentions. Then, on the evening of December 17, after a meal at his club, he returned to his laboratory in Gower Street. The time was about seven thirty. At 8:10 P.M. a colleague passing in the corridor outside glanced up and saw from the light above the door that Spilsbury was still working. Then he noticed the smell of gas. When he tried the door and found it locked, he summoned a janitor. Armed with a passkey, they opened the door.

Spilsbury lay slumped across his workbench, gas hissing from the unlighted Bunsen burners. All attempts at resuscitation were fruitless, and he was not admitted to hospital. At 9:10 P.M. Sir Bernard Spilsbury was pronounced dead. He was seventy years old.*

His death, like his life, was headline news. An era had passed, and the press, so long his ally, didn't abandon him now as they published long eulogies detailing his triumphs. Even across the Atlantic the loss was felt. According to the *New York Times*, Britain had lost the "Nemesis of slayers," a man whose "unrivaled knowledge and his genius for deduction made him a household name in criminal jurisprudence."[39]

The inquest, held on December 19 at the draughty Saint Pancras court where Spilsbury, bundled up in an overcoat, had spent so many freezing hours patiently explaining violent or unusual death to the coroner's jury, was chaired by W. Bentley Purchase. Witnesses pieced together the picture of someone painfully aware of his own physical decline but, more than that, someone absolutely terrified by the prospect of spending his final years in a mental fog. For Bentley Purchase, the whole ordeal was distasteful in the extreme. In declaring that he had reached a verdict of suicide "with repugnance," he added sententiously, "the Sir Bernard who did this is not the Sir Bernard who made the reputation he has made."[40] Nothing could have been farther from the mark. Bentley Purchase, better than most, should have

---

* By a strange quirk of fate, Walter Dew, the police officer who arrested Crippen, died the previous day.

known that once Spilsbury had made up his mind, he was immovable. There was nothing in Spilsbury's life more typical than the controlled and deliberate manner of its conclusion. Three days later the body of Sir Bernard Spilsbury made its final journey to the crematorium at Golders Green.

1 Winifred Duke, *The Trials of Frederick Noddler* (Edinburgh: Hodge, 1950), 3.
2 *Ibid.*, 190.
3 *Ibid.*, 55.
4 *Ibid.*, 10.
5 *Ibid.*
6 *Ibid.*, 10–11.
7 *Ibid.*, 106.
8 *Ibid.*, 234–35.
9 *New York Times*, June 7, 1937, 4.
10 Duke, *The Trials of Frederick Nodder*, 155.
11 *Ibid.*, 162.
12 *Ibid.*
13 *Ibid.*
14 *Ibid.*
15 *Ibid.*, 166.
16 *Ibid.*, 167.
17 *Ibid.*, 166–67.
18 *Ibid.*, 167–68.
19 Keith Simpson, *Forty Years of Murder* (London: Harrap, 1978), 27.
20 Duke, *The Trials of Frederick Nodder*, 168.
21 *Ibid.*, 170.
22 *Ibid.*
23 *Ibid.*, 171.
24 *Ibid.*
25 *Daily Express*, November 24, 1937, 2.
26 *Ibid.*, 224.
27 *Ibid.*, 229.
28 *Ibid.*
29 *Ibid.*, 25.
30 Albert Pierrepoint, *Executioner: Pierrepoint* (London: Coronet, 1977), 135.
31 Edward Greeno, *War on the Underworld* (London: Digit, 1959), 101.
32 *Ibid.*
33 *Ibid.*
34 *Ibid.*

35 *Ibid.*

36 *Ibid.*

37 *Daily Mirror*, April 29, 1942, 1.

38 Gordon Honeycombe, *The Murders of the Black Museum: 1870–1970* (London: Arrow, 1984), 374.

39 *New York Times*, December 18, 1947, 10.

40 *Ibid.*, December 21, 1947, 13.

Afterword

The void left by Spilsbury's death proved impossible to fill. Not because there was a shortage of forensic pathologists—far from it, post-war London was positively awash with top-class medical examiners—but because Fleet Street had shifted its focus. When Spilsbury started out, circulation-conscious newspaper editors thought nothing of publishing 10,000 words daily on the latest sensational murder trial. Such in-depth coverage focused national attention on everyone connected with the legal process and made "Spilsbury" a household name. By the time of his death, press priorities had changed. Crime reports now had to struggle for space with the terrifying annihilation prospects offered by the Cold War; there was more news from Hollywood; celebrity switched from the legal arena to the sporting field or the latest bobby-soxer. In that sense Spilsbury's timing was perfect. He ushered in the golden age of crime reporting, was its chief beneficiary, and then ushered it out again.

For many, the greatest regret attached to Spilsbury's life was its lack of academic achievement. There were no great textbooks, few adoring students at his knee, nothing for future generations to mull over and digest. Mostly this vacuum was brought about by pressure of work. Until the formation of the regional Home Office forensic science laboratories, Spilsbury notched up thousands of miles per annum, investigating any murder, suicide, or suspicious death that hinted of anything out of the ordinary. Whereas modern pathologists tend to be gatherers of evidence, which is then analyzed by individual specialists, Spilsbury was the proverbial one-man band. For the most part, he was expected to perform all the work himself, and if that meant crawling round a crime scene on hands and knees, looking for trace evidence, then so be it. Such a backbreaking schedule left little time for the contemplative revision of case notes so necessary for a full and comprehensive textbook. All his life he had gathered data for the great volume, and certainly the world of forensic pathology would have benefited enormously from the insights that he alone was qualified to provide, but when the time came he was exhausted, then cruelly betrayed by the first knockings of dementia. Spilsbury's legacy lay elsewhere. The court was his classroom, the jury his pupils. No one has ever given evidence better, and for almost four decades his was the voice that juries believed. Unlike his predecessors he didn't talk down to jurors, or lecture them as if they were preparing for some examination; instead he banished the jargon and the long words, delivering his opinion in simple, honest-to-goodness English. And they loved him for it. His reward was a string of victories that reinforced his position as the most powerful figure in British justice. When, during the Armstrong trial, Mr. Justice Darling told the jury, "Do you remember Dr. Spilsbury, do you remember how he stood and the way in which he gave his evidence? . . . Did you ever see a witness who more thoroughly satisfied you that he was completely impartial, absolutely fair, absolutely indifferent as to whether his evidence told for the one side or the other?"[1] he was merely echoing a nationally felt sentiment.

Such acclaim and the overpowering influence that accrued inevitably provoked jealousy. For some reason the medico-legal world has always been a spectacularly fertile breeding ground for feuds, a minefield where reputations are eviscerated more thoroughly than a teaching corpse, and for the last twenty years of his life, Spilsbury was under constant and not always muted attack from adversaries. Brontë came first; then the unstintingly hostile Professor Keith Simpson, who never missed a chance to sink his fangs into the H.O.'s honorary pathologist. (In a bizarre flight of imagination, Simpson even took Spilsbury to task over the Rouse case, claiming in print not only that the body was dumped in "the rear compartment"[2] of the car and had been battered to death with a mallet, but that the victim was *female*!)

Spilsbury's invariable response to all this sniping was silence. Significantly, those who worked alongside him—hard-nosed detectives, overawed provincial doctors, and the mortuary attendants to whom he was unfailingly generous—rarely had a bad word to say about him. Dr. Denis Hocking, the county pathologist for Cornwall for half a century, fondly remembered his student days at Horseferry Road mortuary, where he fell under the spell of "the doyen of forensic science, Sir Bernard Spilsbury. He took me under his wing and gave me invaluable advice, and did all he could to encourage me."[3] One point to bear in mind, though, is that Hocking never had to oppose him in court.

For beneath the urbane façade, Spilsbury was tough as nails. And he knew how to look after himself in the legal bear pit. All those early years of unopposed success left him with an immense regard for his own opinion, and that, coupled with his unbreachable reputation, made him a terrifying opponent. Revisionists who point to his didacticism and blinkered self-certainty—two faults he certainly had in spades—are often guilty of turning a blind eye to his other qualities. Foremost among these was integrity. In a career that spanned four decades, no one, not even Brontë, ever impugned Spilsbury's honesty. It was the lifeblood that ran through his every action, his every deed. The Olympian standards he set for himself he applied to others; backsliding was not an option. And his highly developed sense of fair play extended to some unlikely areas. At a time when many outraged males threw up their hands in horror at the prospect of women entering forensic medicine, it was Spilsbury who helped dismantle some of the prejudice by taking the post as lecturer in forensic pathology at the

London School of Medicine for Women. Nervous young female students soon learned to set aside their anxieties in classes delivered by their legendary tutor.

Although he was the finest forensic pathologist of his time and a superb diagnostician, it would be churlish to pretend, as some hagiographers have done, that Spilsbury was immune to error—the Fox case will forever be his albatross—but claims that he was a mere prosecution puppet, the killing arm of British justice, don't stand up to close inspection. Far too many defendants owed their lives to his testimony for this to be the case. James Bogue was a prime example. On August 10, 1930, this London carpenter was arrested after a pub fight had ended with the death of fifty-year-old Jack Hill. Witnesses agreed that Hill had started the brawl and that Bogue had scarcely touched him, but it was Spilsbury who found the burst tumor inside Hill's brain that had really killed him, a condition that could have led to death at any time. Bogue walked from court a free man.

There was similar confusion in 1935 when the mummified remains of eighty-year-old William Ellis were discovered in a London pub cellar. Suspicion soon alighted on barman Cecil Johnson, who admitted finding and concealing the body almost twelve months earlier, and had not Spilsbury stepped in to say that nothing in his autopsy findings contradicted Johnson's story that Ellis had fallen accidentally down the cellar steps, then Johnson might have easily gone to the gallows.

A decade earlier, in November 1924, it had been Frederick Morgan, thirty-two, and his lover, Nellie Cutler, twenty-three, who owed their lives to Spilsbury's intervention. When Nellie's baby daughter, Doris, was found dead in their trailer home, things looked black indeed for the Luton couple. But Spilsbury's autopsy revealed a ruptured spleen and liver, and at their joint trial for murder in January 1925, he testified that such injuries might have been caused inadvertently by a fully grown adult rolling and covering the child with his or her full weight while asleep. As a result, both were acquitted.

The list could go on, revealing a side of Spilsbury that has all too often been airbrushed out of history. But in the end, it is his groundbreaking triumphs that we remember best. When he burst upon the scene, English forensic science was "the sick man of Europe," crippled in the eyes of most jurors. Inside a decade all that changed. By harnessing the latest technological advances and transforming them into the crime-fighting weapons that we nowadays take for granted, Spilsbury took forensic science from the pages of Sherlock Holmes and into the real world. Without his soaring presence, the bruising battle for acceptance of medico-legal evidence in the British courtroom might have dragged on for decades longer. It was a phenomenal achievement.* For the dozens of killers who heard their last hope of survival crushed by the footfall of his testimony, the tall bespectacled figure in the immaculate pinstriped suit who dominated every court he ever stood in must have exuded a Torquemada-like terror. It was their unfortunate lot to find out, in the harshest way possible, that with his peerless gifts of deduction and uncanny ability to re-create and recount crime scenes, Sir Bernard Spilsbury was far more than just the finest pathologist of his age; he was, quite simply, the greatest medical detective the world has seen.

---

1 *Exhumation of a Murder*, 180.
2 *Forensic Medicine*, 127.
3 *Bodies and Crimes*, 26.

---

* Ironically, a century on and following several high-profile cases blighted by contentious expert-witness testimony, the wheel has now turned full circle in the U.K., with courts once again reluctant to proceed solely on the basis of forensic science.

Bibliography

Adamson, Iain. *A Man of Quality*. London: Muller, 1964.

Baden, Michael, and Judith Adler Hennessee. *Unnatural Death*. New York: Ballantine, 1989.

Bardens, Dennis. *Lord Justice Birkett*. London: Hale, 1962.

Bolitho, William. *Murder for Profit*. London: Elk, 1962.

Browne, D. G., and E. V. Tullett. *Bernard Spilsbury: His Life and Cases*. London: Harrap, 1951.

Cullen, Tom. *Crippen: The Mild Murderer*. London: Penguin, 1977.

Cuthbert, C. R. M. *Science and the Detection of Crime*. London: Grey Arrow, 1962.

Dearden, Harold. *Death Under the Microscope*. London: Hutchinson, 1934.

Duke, Winifred. *The Trials of Frederick Nodder*. Edinburgh: Hodge, 1950.

Galton, Francis. *Memoirs of My Life*. London: Methuen, 1908.

Goodman, Jonathan (ed). *The Railway Murders*. London: Sphere, 1986.

Graham, Hamilton M. *Light and Shade at Scotland Yard*. London: Murray, 1947.

Greeno, Edward. *War on the Underworld*. London: Digit, 1959.

Hocking, Denis. *Bodies and Crimes*. London: Arrow, 1994.

Hodge, James. *Famous Trials III*. London: Penguin, 1950.

Honeycombe, Gordon. *The Murders of the Black Museum: 1870–1970*. London: Arrow, 1984.

Hyde, H. Montgomery. *Norman Birkett*. London: Reprint Soc, 1964.

Jackson, Robert. *Francis Camps*. London: Panther, 1984.

Lucas, Norman. *The Sex Killers*. London: Star, 1988.

Lustgarten, Edgar. *The Murder and the Trial*. London: World Distributors, 1962.

———. *Verdicts in Dispute*. London: Wingate, 1949.

Marjoribanks, Edward. *Famous Trials of Marshall Hall*. London: Penguin, 1950.

Morland, Nigel. *Science in Crime Detection*. London: Camelot, 1958.

Odell, Robin. *Exhumation of a Murder*. New York: St. Martin's Press, 1989.

Parrish, J. M., and John R. Crossland, eds. *Fifty Most Amazing Crimes of the Past One Hundred Years*. London: Oldhams Press, 1936.

Pierrepoint, Albert. *Executioner: Pierrepoint*. London: Coronet, 1977.

Randall, Leslie. *The Famous Cases of Sir Bernard Spilsbury*. London: Ivor Nicholson & Watson, 1936.

Rowland, John. *Murder Revisited*. London: Long, 1961.

Simpson, Keith. *Forensic Medicine*. London: Arnold, 1947.

———. *Forty Years of Murder*. London: Harrap, 1978.

Smith, Sir Sydney. *Mostly Murder*. London: Grafton, 1984.

Thorwald, Jürgen. *Dead Men Tell Tales*. London: Pan, 1968.

Tullet, Tom. *Murder Squad*. London: Triad/Granada, 1981.

Watson, Eric R. *The Trial of George Joseph Smith*. Edinburgh: Hodge, 1922.

Whittington-Egan, Richard. *The Riddle of Birdhurst Rise*. London: Penguin, 1988.

Whittington-Egan, Richard, and Molly Whittington-Egan. *The Bedside Book of Murder*. Newton Abbot, England: David & Charles, 1988.

Willcox, Philip H. A. *The Detective-Physician*. London: Heinemann, 1970.

Index

Page numbers followed by an "n" indicate notes.